# THAT'S WHAT FASHION IS

# THAT'S WHAT FASHION IS

### LESSONS AND STORIES FROM MY NONSTOP, MOSTLY GLAMOROUS LIFE IN STYLE

## JOE ZEE

*with*

### ALYSSA GIACOBBE

THOMAS DUNNE BOOKS

ST. MARTIN'S PRESS

NEW YORK

THOMAS DUNNE BOOKS.

An imprint of St. Martin's Press.

THAT'S WHAT FASHION IS. Copyright © 2015 by XYZ Productions. All rights reserved.
Printed in China. For information, address St. Martin's Press,
175 Fifth Avenue, New York, N.Y. 10010.

www.thomasdunnebooks.com

www.stmartins.com

All photographs are courtesy of the author unless otherwise noted in the captions.

In addition:

P. 36: iStockphoto.com/Coldimages

Pp. 109, 112 (phone frame): iStockphoto.com/deepblue4you

Pp. 252–53: iStockphoto.com/Antagain, epantha, ajt

Production Manager: Adriana Coada

Designed by Headcase Design

The Library of Congress Cataloging-in-Publication Data is available upon request.

ISBN 978-1-250-04294-1 (hardcover)

ISBN 978-1-4668-4093-5 (e-book)

St. Martin's Press books may be purchased for educational, business,
or promotional use. For information on bulk purchases, please contact the
Macmillan Corporate and Premium Sales Department at 1-800-221-7945,
extension 5442, or write to specialmarkets@macmillan.com.

First Edition: October 2015

10 9 8 7 6 5 4 3 2 1

## TO ALL MY READERS AND VIEWERS,

because without you guys, none of this
would be possible or worth it

## TO ROB,

for making coming home always the
best part of my busy schedule

We keep moving forward,
opening new doors, and doing new things,
because we're curious and curiosity keeps
leading us down new paths.

—WALT DISNEY

There's only one very good life,
and that's the life you know you want,
and you make it yourself.

—DIANA VREELAND

# THAT'S WHAT FASHION IS

# INTRODUCTION

I WILL NEVER FORGET THE NIGHT I LEARNED THAT OSCAR DE LA RENTA HAD DIED.

There are a few reasons for this. The first, of course, is that Mr. de la Renta was, and always will be, a fashion legend, a man who dressed thousands of VIW (very important women), including all the first ladies of recent history, from Jackie Kennedy to Michelle Obama, to Oscar winners and chart-topping pop stars. He was also a personal inspiration to me, so his death was an even deeper loss. Mr. de la Renta's reputation throughout the fashion world was unwavering; he was always gracious and welcoming, no matter who you were. In essence, a true gentleman. He was classy and classic, and working with him—which I did on a number of occasions, including twice in the Dominican Republic, his home country, and several times back in New York—was always a rich and rewarding experience. From Mr. de la Renta, I learned about how to treat people and what sophistication in style truly meant. (And yes, he was always Mr. de la Renta to me, and not because he insisted on that formality but because I had so much respect for the regal way with which he approached fashion.) But really, despite all my memories of his remarkable character, that night was also another example, for me, of all my worlds coming seamlessly together.

Ready for the red carpet before red carpets existed (circa 1977).

A world where I would again balance everything I love to do.

It was a fairly calm and quiet evening back in October 2014 when I found out about Mr. de la Renta's death in a fairly unconventional way, even for me. A few years earlier, I might have read about it online in my morning news feed. Now I was the one helping to create that morning news feed. Five months prior, I'd left *Elle* magazine and accepted a new position as editor in chief of *Yahoo Style*, where I set about launching a new digital fashion magazine for one of the world's largest tech companies. There, my vision was to marry my favorite conventions from my vast print experience—original photography, shooting covers, and bold, provocative imagery—with the quick practicality of the web: delivering real news, stories that captivate the reader, in real time. That October night, my site, *Yahoo Style*, had been live for close to a month when I got that call. Breaking news for us, up until that point, had consisted mainly of Fashion Week coverage and store openings.

Mr. de la Renta's passing would be a different story.

It was 6 p.m. and I was driving through Los Angeles from Beverly Hills (where I had been doing an interview for an upcoming story) to downtown LA, racing to meet my friend Sophia Amoruso, the founder and CEO of Nasty Gal and an entrepreneurial hero for young girls, for dinner. For those who know anything about the layout of LA and its massive traffic pattern during rush hours, you know that crossing from Beverly Hills to downtown at that time, especially on a freeway, is strictly reserved for those brave souls with patience and stamina. So I was already on edge and fretting about arriving late to dinner when my cell phone rang through my car's Bluetooth. It was Anderson Cooper's office.

"Hello," said the sweet but somewhat frantic producer on the other end of the line. "I'm calling from CNN, and I wondered if you can confirm for us that Oscar de la Renta has died? Do you know if that's true?" Confirm? True? *Died?* I can still hear those words ringing in my ears. I remember thinking, *I have no idea*, and though I knew Mr. de la Renta had been ill on and off, I had believed that he was on the mend.

"Are you serious?" I replied. "No. I haven't heard anything but I've also been driving through LA for the past hour and have not looked at my phone or a news feed. What happened?" She very nicely explained to me the rumors that had been whizzing around their newsroom and she was reaching out to me now to see if I could shed any light on this situation or just confirm his death. But I couldn't—not without real facts. I knew I needed to call my staff back in New York right away. If Mr. de la Renta had indeed passed away, we had to write his tribute, and fast.

I hung up and almost immediately got another call from another CNN producer for Don Lemon who had the time slot after Anderson Cooper's. Finally, I decided I had to pull over and scan my emails, and that's where I saw one from ABC News. It was true: Mr. de la Renta had died, and my heart sank. I knew I was going to be late for dinner but this required my immediate attention. It was now a personal and professional situation for me. I had lost someone I truly admired and respected but I also had to cover it as news in real time. It was all new territory for me.

I dialed one of my editors back home in New York. It was late but it was also an emergency, and in the Internet world, you never stop working. We chatted quickly about what a good man Mr. de la Renta was and how the tribute I wrote should be personal because I just couldn't see honoring him any other way. We decided, in an effort to be fast and to get me to dinner on time, I would dictate to this editor while I drove. Multitasking: the story of my life. And my fashion career has always taught me how to handle it well.

"Just tell me what you remember and love most about him," my editor said. "I'll string it together right now and send it back to you to look at."

Less than an hour later, I would be sitting at dinner at Bestia when that finished story came through on email. I excused myself and ran to the bathroom (so as not to be rude at the table, of course), scrolled through the text quickly, typed a few notes, and off it went. That memorial tribute would be up on my site and live in less than a minute for hundreds of millions of people to see. Back at the table, though, I confessed. I told Sophia, my dinner partner, about all the balls I had been juggling that night on my way to dinner and she, of all people, completely understood. If there is one thing the fashion industry prepares you for, it's creative juggling. Wearing many hats—figuratively and literally—is the very foundation of finding success in my industry, and after more than twenty years of laying that foundation in the fashion world, I'm now prepared for the frontlines of any battle.

Consider me that ultimate style-obsessed, multitasking ninja, nodding and saying yes to everything that crosses my path and always delivering my best on it. I—and Sophia—know that accomplishment well. A feeling we both really love.

After all, she is the #GirlBoss. I am the Slashie.

For my entire professional career, in fact, for pretty much my entire life, I've been the ultimate juggler, the multihypenate, the boy who does too much. The year before I launched *Yahoo Style*, I launched a clothing collection for QVC called Styled by Joe Zee where I would bring a beautifully designed, trend-driven, mix-and-match line to women everywhere. My philosophy was that getting dressed each morning didn't have to be frustrating but should be fun, and chic. And my collection set out to do just that: like I was styling every woman's wardrobe each morning. While I was promoting the line, I did a series of interviews and one particular blogger asked me what it was like to be the ultimate slashie. And *bam!*, that was it. She was right. That single word defined so much of who I was.

We are officially living in the Slash Generation. And thank God, fashion had prepped me.

If you think about it, it makes perfect sense. In our parents' day, you had one job your whole life where you would rise through the ranks and were proud of the success path you carved out for yourself, and if you had two jobs, well, it meant you were in dire straits and wasn't something to brag about. Today, if you aren't doing multiple things, it becomes a hang-your-head-in-shame moment. A recent thirty-year-old millennial employee of mine who only wanted to be hired as a contractor versus becoming a full-time staffer declared that he or she did not want to be perceived as doing only one thing, even though he or she was. A single job was now taboo.

Looking back, I realized I was always this way, even as a kid. An overbooked, overambitious, overzealous overachiever. I'm a person who only feels normal when his head is just short of spinning off into the galaxy, and always have been.

{ ABOVE }

Taking a break from giving fashion advice at this very table to celebrate my birthday (1974).

Here's my proof: In my formative years, I was a school kid/wannabe piano player/after-school disco-dancing student/weekend window shopper/ overall know-it-all.

In my teens, I was an annoying hand-raising, first-row-sitting student/ concert violinist/music arranger/school fashion show producer/yearbook captain/weekend retail guy/part-time busboy/chronic television addict.

In my twenties, I moved to New York and everything got bigger. It was here that I could do even more. I found myself filling the roles of a fashion student/intern/school newspaper editor/part-time club kid/self-taught publisher/party promoter/fashion assistant/DJ.

By the time I got to my thirties, things were settling in. I was firmly ensconced as the fashion director of *W* magazine and I had discovered the joy of freelance styling, from celebrity red carpets to music videos to major ad campaigns all at the same time. Here I was, a wide-eyed Toronto kid, living my American Dream, with more and more possibilities stacked on top of one another. I look back and can say my thirties defined a lot of who I am today: an editor/stylist/marketer/negotiator/celebrity wrangler/wardrobe therapist/networker. In those years, I was just working hard to establish myself in the fashion business.

Now, halfway into my forties, the world is changing, I'm still evolving, with more slashes to add, and I'm proud of that. Here I am, a magazine editor/designer/fashion stylist/TV reality guy/red carpet commentator/school speaker/TV producer/talk show host/blogger/ accidental techie/wannabe backup dancer—and, yes, now an author, too.

I know many of you can relate, maybe not necessarily with my zigzag, nutty schedule, but to the fact that we have so many things we love to do, and frankly, we're at a time now where we can actually do them all. More than ever, I am so impressed with all the young people I meet whenever I am interviewing them or working with them because in so many ways, they remind me of myself. I can see all the amazing possibilities of what that next generation can accomplish, doing incredibly creative multiple things and then sharing it with the world through social media.

If there's only one thing that the fashion world trains you for, it's the Tackle.

For the sake of sounding like a fashion dinosaur living in this Slashie Gen, I can only speak from personal experiences. While my peers in the industry can be reluctant to embrace change—ironic for a business that prides itself on newness every six months—I feel that I have been a person who hasn't always been afraid to take a risk. Jumping in the deep end when I don't even know how to swim, I've learned that my perseverance in tackling what I want to do has become my precious lifesaver, and that's a lesson that feels so prevalent with my younger counterparts. Just look at your average fashion industry twentysomething's social media accounts. No one's just a writer anymore. Or a stylist. Now they're also bloggers, bakers, digital entrepreneurs, florists, or even cat mothers. Multicareers are the new black.

{ BELOW }

I was a poser even back then (1972).

\* \* \*

WE WRAPPED UP DINNER, after discussing Sophia's new brick-and-mortar store and my new job, and said our good-byes in an old warehouse parking lot, with Oscar de la Renta still on my mind. I never did give confirmation to Anderson's show, but that was fine. I got in my car to head back to the city and along the way, I got back to work, calling my editor in New York and having her reread me the Mr. de la Renta memorial tribute story that had been posted during dinner so I could dictate some additional edits.

That's when my phone rang again. It was Becky, the head of communications for Yahoo, and she was calling with a request from Charlie Rose and CBS News. They wanted me to swing by the studios and comment on the incredible legacy of Mr. de la Renta for the following morning's show. Of course I had to say yes.

My night might have been crazy and surreal enough (and busy enough) but still, I ran to my apartment, grabbed a suit jacket, and sped over to the CBS News studio, which at 11 p.m., was completely deserted, except for the night crew. I filmed my interview with Charlie and left and made one last pit stop for the night: a drink with my old *Elle* colleagues at the Four Seasons Hotel, where they had hosted their annual Women in Hollywood event hours earlier. I remember arriving there close to midnight and falling into a chair at their table with exhaustion, but also exhilaration.

*All this has happened*, I thought, *and it was just six hours in my life*. In that short time, I had been a reporter/investigator/TV commentator/pundit/copy editor/former magazine guy. What would the next day hold?

More of the same? Something unexpected? More obstacles to jump? New hats to wear? Potholes to maneuver around or even new successes to champion? Yes, to all of the above, and that's why I do—and obsessively love—what I do.

Kat, my editor for this book, knows this so well about me, and she has been incredibly patient as I've pushed the deadline and publishing dates for this book three times.

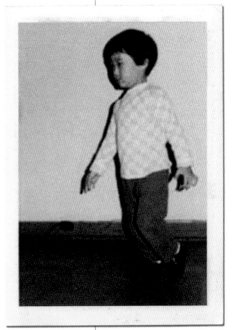

{ ABOVE }

Running late for something again, even at an early age (1972).

I would constantly write/call/email/text her: I have one more thing to add! Let's wait for that next big thing coming up!

There was always more and there was always something else I was doing. Finally I had to say to myself that any more slashes can wait. I was ready. I wanted to share my rules, my life, my lessons, my insider stories, my tips, my tricks, my triumphs, and my tribulations from the crazy, silly, zany, screwed-up but incredibly creative industry known as fashion. This business didn't just teach me the beautiful and the glamorous rules, but also the ones that allowed me to do and tackle everything I ever wanted to do. Nothing was impossible. I sat at a diner when I first moved to New York in 1990 with a friend of a friend who told me, under no uncertain terms, that I would never make it as a fashion editor, nor would I even be given that opportunity. Those spots, he very firmly declared, were reserved for blond privileged girls, and I was none of the above. There was no room at the table for a middle-class Asian boy.

Well, good thing I don't sleep and good thing I don't stop because I think I've proved him wrong. Even the sticker on my laptop, which is permanently opened, has a motto: #NeverNotWorking. And not that I'm preaching, because that's not me, and I know that everyone approaches their passions in a different way, but this book is my personal journey, how I got here, and that's what I want to share with you. It may chronicle all my crazy fashion adventures with all the crazy nonstop teachings but what I hope you take away from this book isn't just how my business works, but how you can make fashion—or any other business—work for you. I've made those mistakes, I've proved those naysayers wrong, I've accomplished things I never thought I would in my lifetime, and I'm grateful every day. This book is by no means a final exclamation point on my career. In fact, even as you read this I am still out there tackling. I do hope you like what I have to share here (hit me up on social media and let me know) and even if, like me, you end up doing a hundred other things at the same time while reading this, that's okay. I got your back.

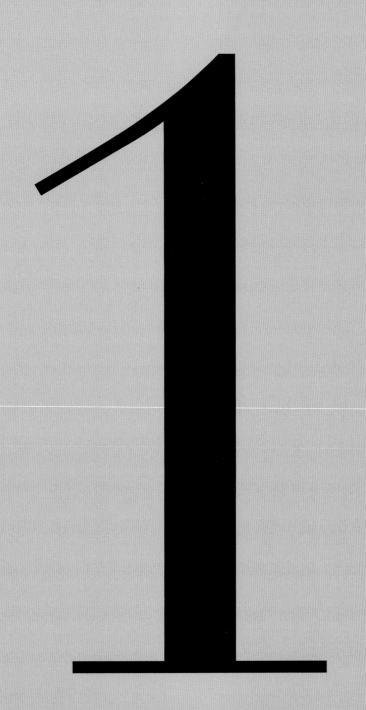

# BOY GEORGE

## WAS MY BIEBER

**Y EARLIEST FASHION MEMORY:** I'm six years old and sitting at a makeshift desk I've dragged out into my family's sparse living room in suburban Toronto, getting ready to dispense wardrobe advice for 10 cents per question, *Charlie Brown*–style. I'm wearing oversized Jackie O shades salvaged from the back of my mother's closet, short shorts (fashionably shrunken pinstriped Osh-Kosh from two years earlier, probably), and leather sandals. Ironically, now, as a grown-up, I loathe man sandals more than any other shoe because I really hate seeing men's gnarly toes creeping out of fancy leather. I can live in a world with Uggs. I can get over Crocs. But I'm sorry: I cannot live with mandals. Even the name gives me shivers.

To safekeep my earnings, I have with me my newish Mickey Mouse handbag, a prized possession my grandmother broke down and bought me after an unfortunate incident at the mall that had me lying on the dirty floor in front of the store window,

{ BELOW }

The Mickey Mouse bag I had to throw a tantrum to get. It was worth it; it went with me everywhere (1974).

screaming for someone to buy me the bag right now, right that instant. I was always a total brat about fashion.

But I really, really wanted that bag.

This little wardrobe advice business was my first foray into earning a living in fashion, and quite a promising one at that. In just one hour on the job I netted 30 cents, which was 30 cents more than my average *monthly* income at the time, given that I was six and unemployed. So I was pretty pleased with myself. Who cared if the entire sum came from my friend after

## "Everyone in my family thought fashion was an eccentricity, SOMETHING I'D GROW OUT OF."

I'd bullied her into paying me to say that her knee socks made her look like a baby? She needed to hear it.

Everyone in my family thought my love of fashion was an eccentricity, something I'd grow out of. They didn't exactly know or, maybe more to the point, care to know about style or clothes. Not like I did, at least. They did a good job of humoring me, though. I got a lot of "Isn't that cute?" But my mother, a Tiger Mom before Tiger Moms had a name (I call her a Lion Mom in my head now), always expected me, in true Asian fashion, to grow up to be a doctor or a lawyer, even though I clearly showed far more interest in shoes than in science. Even, too, after the Christmas I convinced my brother and sister that we needed to pool our savings to buy Mom an entire Gloria Vanderbilt outfit I'd seen in the local mall's holiday catalog. The corduroys were fuchsia, my favorite color at the time, and the sweater was, too, and it was on-trend perfection.

( OPPOSITE )

One of my first school photos (1972).

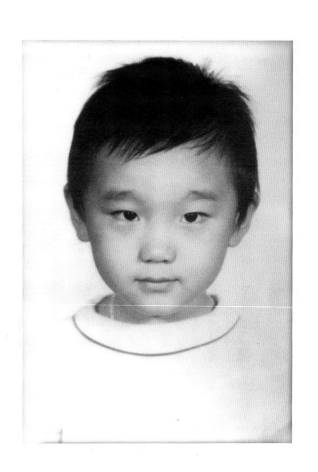

"This woman is so fashionable," I told my brother and sister, shoving the catalog at them, where the photo in question ran full page. The model stood with her hip cocked, incredibly beautiful with long, dark hair. The iconic Vanderbilt swan logo sat neatly on her chest, and to me it screamed status and elegance. "We *have* to buy this for Mom," I insisted. We each threw in $22—a lot for me as a ten-year-old, but I was always very good at saving.

This was my first failure as a stylist. In the days after Christmas, Mom took the outfit back to the mall without even trying it on. I was upset, but it

"... a very important lesson:

# KNOW YOUR CLIENT."

also taught me a very important lesson: Know your client. My mother was very practical. She didn't see the point in spending $65 on an outfit, never mind a hot-pink one, even if it was a gift.

But I wasn't discouraged permanently. A few years later, during high school in Toronto in the 1980s, I made a name for myself by dishing out fashion advice between periods. Kids stopped by my locker with serious inquiries: "What should I wear to the prom?" "How can I peg my jeans like they do on TV?" "Does this turtleneck make me look fat?" And I'd answer them, then send them off with magazine tear sheets as supporting affidavits. I was a master at coiling the laces on the Sperry Top-Siders everyone wore, and I'd stand there between periods, twirling away at my classmates' shoes while spewing out aphorisms I'd mainly picked up from reading magazines: Say no to horizontal stripes. Never dress like a side dish (no green and orange, which look like peas and carrots, or red and yellow, which would make you look like a hot dog condiment station). I was positive I was performing a great service, saving all these people from future mortification when they looked back at the acid-washed jeans and strapless floral taffeta dresses they'd surely have picked if it had been up to them. What's most amazing is that I can't remember anyone ever questioning my edicts or disagreeing with me, though I think there was probably some astonishment at my definitiveness and more than a few sarcastic smirks besides. In hindsight, I'm sure people were laughing at my total earnestness—if I weren't me, I'd certainly have been laughing, too—but at the time I never noticed. I was too focused on my task at hand: saving my classmates from their own bad fashion choices.

{ BELOW }

The last time I rocked a tank top (1979).

I wasn't what you might call an obvious style guru, or even a guru at all. Yes, I read all the latest fashion magazines cover to cover the second they arrived in my mailbox. And yes, I did go through a major Barbie phase (pretend you're shocked). But on the surface, I was a nerd: a classic, textbook, over-achieving, hyper-hand-raising, front-row-sitting Asian kid. I taught myself how to play the violin—and then the viola, the cello, and the stand-up bass. I would put on my Vivaldi *Four Seasons* record and play along, stopping and starting it until the thing was more scratched than a cat tree. I liked math, science, history, you name it, a bona fide Tracy Flick (not to mention a one-man string quartet).

My obsession with fashion and magazines was executed in typical type A style. I didn't just read them. I studied them. Every page, every ad, every piece of text and every photo, and even the credits pages—literally, I would know that issue front to back, top to bottom by the time I was done with it. The people on the mastheads became my imaginary friends. I'd notice if they got married and changed their names, or if they no longer worked there, in which case I'd go check the latest issues of my other magazines to see if I could figure out where they'd landed. I'd obsess over the fashion photos and quiz myself to see if I could identify the designers and photographers without looking at the captions. Like, "Is this Louis Dell'Olio for Anne Klein? Is that Claude Montana?" Then I'd look at the credits and go, "Yes! That is it!" Afterward, once I was done annotating and memorizing and ripping out pages, I'd be devastated to remember I'd have to wait an entire month to get the next issue.

\* \* \*

**S**OMEHOW, EVEN WITH THE SCHOOLWORK AND the music making and the magazine OCD, I still found time to watch eight hours of TV a day—yes, eight hours, not exaggerating even a little—racing home after school at exactly 3 p.m. to escape into the soft-focus world of *General Hospital*, *The Price is Right*, and, every night at 6 p.m., for reasons I still can't explain, Buffalo, New York's *Eyewitness News*, even though I didn't even live in the country those poor overcoiffed anchors were reporting on, and then primetime shows all night. I got up hours before I needed to go to school to watch more. TV was my best high school friend, one I never got bored with because I always found something new to marvel at, or a different way to watch a particular show. I loved *Charlie's Angels*, for example: The average kid might look at the show and say, "They're so beautiful and glamorous," and I thought that, too, but I also remember thinking, *Boy, that Aaron Spelling has really got it together*. My mind was already on the marketing genius behind the show, and the pop culture moment creator Aaron Spelling had tapped into. Second-level stuff. I don't think I was trying to be that way. I was just an old soul. I watched *Dynasty* and *The Colbys*, which I loved for their entertainment value but also because I thought, *They're really nailing the TV market*. I've always appreciated creativity, but somehow, even early on, I had an even greater appreciation for creativity that *sells*.

Growing up, I especially loved to watch musicals (cliché, I know). In primary school, I'd insist my mother drive me to the library so I could check out old song-and-dance films: *Top Hat* and *Swing Time*, Gene Kelly and Judy Garland's *The Pirate*, *The Sound of Music*. I adored Fred and Ginger, not to mention the dashing style of a curtain-clad Friedrich. I'd watch them over and over again, singing along in between vocabulary homework, snapping to the beat of my long division, pulling my grandmother out of her chair to try a little side step with me. My entire junior year, mornings before school were spent getting ready with the Gene Kelly–Frank Sinatra musical *On the Town* running on VHS. These musicals were my morning news while everyone else was watching the *Today* show.

What I liked about musicals, beyond their visual magnificence, of course, was that there was never anything too heavy or serious going on. No one really got bogged down in silly details like "plot" and "character development." Everyone wore amazing clothes. But mostly what I loved, especially as I got older, was the life lesson the films and TV shows imparted: that there's no problem that can't be fixed with a little song, some soft-shoeing, and a dance-floor-ready outfit. It's a mantra I find endlessly comforting to this day.

High school is rough; every insecurity bubbles to the surface. But when you're living it, you can't understand what it means to be different, or why you'd ever want to be that way. You try so hard to fit in, or at least I did. For me, fashion was one way to find my place as a middle-class Asian kid in a mostly upper-class Jewish school where everyone seemed to have so much more than I did. Clothes were the easiest and most functional way to change your appearance. They become your armor, and the thing to set and define you. What you wear, I learned, immediately says who and what you are. It determines where and with whom you'll be sitting at lunch. This explains how I might have been dressing as a prep on Tuesday but trying out Goth by Friday. I spent much of high school figuring out who I was, and where I fit in, through clothes.

In my high school, the preppies ruled, and for a time I was one of them, donning Polo ponies and Lacoste alligator shirts (collars popped, naturally), V-neck tennis sweaters, carefully rolled jeans, and the aforementioned Sperry Top-Siders. In seventh grade, I saved all of my lunch money for a month—I got $10 a week—so that I could buy a pair of Jordache jeans at a Toronto denim store called Thrifty's. I remember my mom and grandparents asking me why I'd spent so much money on a pair of jeans, but I wore them *every single day*. I would put them on and feel like a different person. I was obsessed with the triangle design on the back pocket, which was a status symbol for a teenage kid. In hindsight, that was the first time I

Michael Pataran
Monica Freedman
David Dalglish


Debbie Hale
Debbie Holmes
Sarah Matheson


Aimee Debow
Natalie Greenbaum
Calvin Eng


Collin Shuman
Robbie Spector
Noriko Maekita


Dahlia Rotman
Martin Himelson
Joe Zee


Britta Eckmann
Oscar Toledo
Karen Pettingill

# ARM

Brad Buss
Natalie Greenbaum
Danny Kroll
Calvin Eng
Karen Pettingill

James Brotman
Rebecca Goldfarm
Tasleem Khan
Britta Eckmann
Perry Melzack

Leslie Bernstein
Joel Gardner
Michael Kalchman
Mark Dubowitz
Sarah Matheson

Linda Austin
Kathy Gale
Debbie Holmes
Aimee Debow
Deborah Mason

Joe Zee
Monica Freedman
Martin Himelson
David Dalglish
Noriko Maekita

Oscar Toledo
Joanne Freedman
Debbie Hale
Michael Charendoff
Emma Louie

Robbie Spector
Dahlia Rotman

22

{ ABOVE LEFT } Me in seventh grade.  { ABOVE RIGHT } Me in eighth grade.

GRADE 8 STRING ORCHESTRA
Back row - Deena Ginsberg, Debra Hamilton, Marla Brown, Lara Pulver,
  Elizabeth Finney, Andrew Rothblott, Beth Posen, Dahlia Keen, Beth Matenko,
  Amy Barkin, Cynthia Rosenberg, Steven Hall.
3rd row - Robbyn Draimin, Vinita Srivistava, Karen Wirsig, Laura Wong,
  Sean Meggeson, Tracy Bennet, Lisa Beaumont, Debbie Schwartz, Veronica Crane,
  Mary Kelenjian, Connie Econcay.
2nd row - Shadi Dastranj, Tony Chiu, Josh Cooper, Donna Winters,
  Jordan Greenberg, Tomoko Myint, Colleen Dalos, Simone Jubas, Mara Heiber,
  Mrs. Albert.
Front row - Elizabeth Goldstein, Ellen Sandler, Marni Sky, Ilan Soudack,
  Heather Hossack, Serena Eng, Jackie Klein, David Ospalak, Adam Minsky,
  Jamie Hewlitt, Helena Pavlovich.
Absent: Jeremy Jacobs, Neil Sequeira, Nancy Malcolm, Jenny Raphael,
  Erin Burke, Chris Vozoris, Kyle Genga, Kim Manchester, Chris Fleck,
  Elizabeth Brown, Christine Kaarsberg, Kamran Kasvavi, Mitchell Fain,
  Jennifer Haffman, Jill Klein, Rudy Amid, Pauli Schachter, Paul Chang,
  Isaac Chen, Paul Zuker, Shaundra Paul, Leslie Drevnig, Wayne Deitel.

*there's Joe!* →

STRING QUARTET
Adam Minsky, Sue Motahedin, Debra Sheehan, Joe Zee.

53

Marla Ash

Elaine Cruise

Calv

Andrea Gliserman

Steven Humanski

Lisa Nemish

Mrs. Slacer

*for...*
*...pl...*
*...have...*
*in m...*
*Good...*
*...m...*

SLA

Kelly Ritson

Joe Zee

{ ABOVE LEFT } My ninth-grade string quartet photo.   { ABOVE RIGHT } Me in ninth grade.

realized that clothes could create an image for people and create confidence and allure—that they could be a secret signal to those who are "in the know." Those jeans were everything to me. Of course, I realize, looking back, I was wearing women's jeans the whole time.

Then I saw *Pretty in Pink* and decided that Duckie's look, with the porkpie hat and mismatched pattern worship, made him more intriguing than James Spader's preppy-posh Steff, even if Steff was objectively far better looking. But that didn't last too long, either. When it came to fashion, my tastes changed on a dime, but there was a reason for that. Part of it was about acceptance and part of it was about rebellion. As a teenager, I wanted to tag it as rebellion, but I really just wanted to be *accepted* by the world of rebellion. Everyone wants to be sitting at the A table at lunch, and everyone wants to be invited to the party—I was no different. I remember overhearing the group of kids who hung around the smoking area saying they'd bought their long black trench coats downtown and thinking, *Downtown?!* It was so cool to me, the idea of going *downtown*, instead of the mall, to buy your clothes.

That's how I was introduced to what became my longest adolescent fashion phase, a fascination with the excess-is-best stylings of New Romanticism and new-wave music. This began sometime around junior year. In addition to my fashion magazines, I now devoured *Record Mirror* and *New Musical Express* and found inspiration in the British bands of the '80s: Culture Club, the Smiths, and Tears for Fears, which I'd listen to on my Walkman the size of a brick. My style god was Robert Smith from the Cure, so I set out to emulate that look, but with things culled from my local mall, which was the best I could do since I had no way to get downtown on my own. I bought skinny black jeans, pointy women's flat shoes from Le Château, and Aqua Net hair spray, which I consumed in vats until one school trip to London when I stumbled into a barber and asked to have my head shaved in a checkerboard pattern. That was also the year I ditched afternoon classes to wait in line at the Music Express on Yonge Street for a meet-and-greet and record signing with Spandau Ballet. I was probably the only boy in line that day, and most definitely the only boy wearing a ruffled blouse and a rhinestone brooch.

These days, I don't love lines. But as a teenager, I was thrilled to wait for something I was excited about. Waiting, the anticipation, was part of the draw. It was having something to look forward to. Once, on a mission to score tickets to a Culture Club concert, I brought a sleeping bag and my best friend to camp out inside a mall, the same mall where I'd spotted Mom's fuchsia Vanderbilt getup, so that I could be there as soon as the sales window opened. I dressed up for the occasion, of course, and not halfway: skinny black pants, black overcoat, fingerless gloves, fedora, and, I'll admit it, eyeliner. If my hair had been long enough, I'd have done it up into a braid. My popped-collar days were long behind me, at least in spirit. But what can I say? Boy George was my Bieber. And the competitive streak that was just beginning to emerge served me well: My friend and I were sixth in line and got seats so close to the stage we could literally see every pore on Boy's face under his makeup.

When I commit, I really commit. Often, I drag everyone else down—er, along—with me. The next day, the same friend and I staked out the Four Seasons Hotel in downtown Toronto. We'd heard that's where Boy would be staying, and I decided that we had to catch a glimpse, even though I'd never before been in that hotel and it scared me with all its snooty fabulousness. My friend and I canvased every single hallway until we found a room with security posted outside, then stowed away in a nearby electrical closet. For real. I can't imagine people doing that today. It was like we thought we were starring in some after-school sitcom plotline, though of course our outfits—oversized button-downs, leggings, and matching fedoras, obviously—were dead giveaways of just what business we had being in that hotel, which was none. We opened the closet door just enough to give us a view of the room and waited until the guard took a break to pee. That's when we made our move, practically tripping over each other as we lunged toward Boy's door.

{ OPPOSITE }

High school in Gaultier and mom jeans (1987).

# DRESS FOREVER YOUNG

## (BUT NOT TOO YOUNG)

**B**ECAUSE EVERYONE'S OBSESSED with eternal youth, one of the most common questions I get is "Can my clothes make me look younger?" And I always answer: honestly, no. I really believe that looking younger is just a state of mind. Age is just a number.

That said, the wrong clothes *can* make you look older. But youthful dressing is not about reliving your past (put the flare jeans down) or looking like a teenager. It's about avoiding the common mistakes that can pile on years as easily as bangle bracelets.

### ✓ OUT WITH THE OLD!

You can't expect to look modern when your clothes are older than a boy-bander. Some pieces come back. Others never should. Though vintage has a certain cachet in Hollywood, it's opened the door for people to think that clothes never go out of fashion. That is not true. Nor are vintage clothes an excuse for the ill-fitting or stained. I find it hilarious that some career suit from Bonwit Teller in the '50s is now a rarefied collectible in the world of fashion. It's like saying an inexpensive shirt from H&M will be museum-worthy in fifty years. Clothes, like canned goods, have an expiration date.

### ✓ PAY ATTENTION TO COLORS

Right now, we're in the middle of a color love fest. Patterns are mismatched and anything goes, and while black will always be chic there are plenty of great alternatives: navy, forest green, charcoal gray. But while color can be youthful and current, it can also make you look like a kindergarten teacher or your sister's hippie therapist. Context matters. A bright yellow pop of a handbag works. Bright yellow cords, on the other hand, scream, "Time for finger painting, kids!"

**X DON'T GET BORING.**

I had a college professor who told me that my obligation to my friends and family was to continue educating myself, in some form or another, throughout my life, so that I'd never bore them with banality and always have something interesting to share. The same goes for how you look. Looking exactly the same every day is monotonous, and monotony is aging. Experiment with your haircut or color on the regular, or at least try out a new lipstick. You can play around with nail color (yes, you can wear blue) but keep nails short.

**✓ WOMAN UP AND WEAR HEELS ALREADY.**

Flats can be very stylish, as any Charlotte Olympia fan knows. But heels will always be more youthful—and more flattering. A pointed black pump, like one from Manolo Blahnik or Jimmy Choo (Zara will offer a more affordably priced version), is reasonably high, goes with almost everything, and isn't super trendy, which means you'll get a few seasons out of it.

**✓ WEAR WHAT FITS.**

Got your eye on that sale item that's two sizes too big? Step away and don't buy it, even if you think it looks boyfriend chic (it doesn't). Or have it taken in. Similarly, don't try to squeeze into your high school jeans just because you can. Remember how tight Steven Seagal's acid-washed denim was in *Hard to Kill*? Do not look like that.

We'd already knocked, and rather disruptively, when we heard the singing. Then we heard it stop. Boy George—that makeup-wearing, braid-swinging Karma Chameleon—opened the door himself and, no joke, invited us in! He didn't even look mad. We realized pretty quickly that what we'd interrupted was a private mini-concert for some sick kids from the local children's hospital, but we got over the guilt and shame pretty quickly. Because, hello, private concert!

There we were, sitting on the floor of Boy George's hotel room, five feet from the man's perforated black leather boots, which I was coveting, when I thought, *I am so quitting school*, though I knew I was never going to be a big enough rebel to pull that off, and it would never fly with Lion Mom.

So instead, I put my energies toward making my own music and cultivating my own fashion sense. My band-geek alter ego was busy tearing up the string sections all over town; I'd started playing my violin with the Toronto Symphony Youth Orchestra, and earlier that year, we had traveled to New York to perform somewhere. I remember walking around Midtown and stopping to gape at the windows of Bloomingdale's. I walked into the Fiorucci store and it was literally pulsating with energy, with a bank of TV sets at the back of the store and some of the coolest people I'd ever seen. That's when I knew I wanted to live in New York. I knew, though, that it wouldn't be music that brought me back. It would be fashion. That certainty began my obsession with fashion and New York. You might even say it began my obsession with obsession.

\* \* \*

MY FASCINATION WITH TRANSFORMING how I looked grew into transforming how other people looked. Watching those nightly news broadcasts, I was dumbfounded by the lack of imagination in their style and became fixated on the fact that these female anchors could look so much like plastic versions of themselves. If your job requires only that you look amazing from the waist up, I figured, shouldn't it be half as difficult to look good? Meanwhile, the male anchor

# BE OBSESSED

L ET'S TAKE A break from my Canadian youth to paraphrase a little Thomas Edison. Lesson no. 1 of this book: Making it big in fashion—or any industry, really—is 1 percent inspiration and 99 percent obsession. You have to *live it* in order to, well, live it. I firmly believe that if I hadn't been the sort of kid so hopelessly devoted to fashion and to my musical heroes—dressing like them, stalking them—I wouldn't have gotten half as far as I have in this business. There are plenty of talented kids who want to be designers or editors or celebrity stylists. But the people who succeed often do because they're just unwilling to fail. Failure is just not an option.

Super-blogger-brander-everygirl Leandra Medine, also known as the Man Repeller, knows a thing or two about being hell-bent on making it big. Leandra built an online empire while an undergrad living in her parents' apartment purely because she was so committed to fashion, and to helping people find their own modes of expression. I asked her to give us a few quick and useful tips on how to be obsessed.

✓ **START EARLY.**

"As a kid, I really liked style. For as long as I can remember, I really, really appreciated not a nice piece of clothing but the way a woman put together an outfit. That thinking process—locating the style first and then deconstructing the items she is wearing—seems to reveal itself in all of my writing now, which tends to be much more about the way clothes make women feel as opposed to just about the clothes point-blank."

✓ **GET EXCITED—
AND STAY THAT WAY.**

"I think the word 'obsession' is overused, so I'd prefer to replace it with 'excitement.' I think excitement has to factor into the way I work in order to keep what I put out compelling for whoever is taking it in. If I am feeling uninspired or like I'm just moving the needle, I try to stimulate myself and turn the anxiety of uninspiration into excitement. That's often by way of a book (I really like Nora Ephron for this cause) or a movie (I like Nora Ephron for this cause, too), and, because I'm lucky enough to live in New York, just sitting outside on a densely populated sidewalk for a few minutes and watching the people walk past me really helps."

✓ **GO BIG OR GO HOME.**

"As far as advice for being noticed in fashion or in life without being perceived as having gone too far, I have to say that I don't think, at least in fashion, that there is anything wrong with going too far. What is too far?"

looked consistently debonair in his suit, crisp button-down shirt, and patterned tie.

A hard truth from a male women's fashion editor: It is so much easier for a man to look polished than a woman, and I know that's unfair. When I want to look professional and pulled together, I put on a suit. When I want to look cute and casual but put together, I pull on jeans and a T-shirt. It's just never that easy for women. When a woman wants to pull on a pair of jeans, she has to decide between skinny, straight, boot cut, ripped, or waxed, and she probably won't think she looks good enough in whichever one she chooses. Many women spend entire lifetimes looking for their "best" denim, like some impossible scavenger hunt. Designers of the "perfect T-shirt," meanwhile, can, and do, charge obscene amounts for something Hanes has been doing for decades.

As much as I thought that women were more harshly judged on what they wore, this also meant that there were so many more options for how to be creative in the world of women's fashion. If watching one Buffalo news anchor sparked that thought in my head, I knew there would be a bigger world out there to style.

And that world was New York City.

# SHOPPING CART
# CONFESSIONS

I STARTED MY COLLEGE CAREER AT THE University of Toronto, but Toronto was never really part of the plan. I had a very specific plan. After being completely seduced by New York City during that school trip a few years back, I knew that New York was where I wanted to be. And I knew I wanted to work at a fashion magazine. Beyond that, I had no other plans. There was no "I'll give it a try" or "fingers crossed." "Fashion magazine in New York" was my plan A, B, and C.

There was a hitch, of course. Working in New York required a visa, even for a Canadian. Through hours of research in the Toronto Public Library (this was pre-Google), I learned that I could get a one-year student visa after graduating from an American college. That sticky little point made the decision for me. I would go to school in New York and get the quickest degree I could while jamming in some practical experience along the way. I would save enough to live for the two years—frugally, of course— and I would not waste a single second of it. Time was crucial.

Of all the different schools in NYC, I set my sights on the Fashion Institute of Technology. Once called the "MIT for the fashion industries," FIT had a long list of illustrious alumni, including Michael Kors, Carolina Herrera, and Calvin Klein. Just as important, FIT was subsidized by the state, which meant that tuition was one-tenth that of the more prestigious Parsons School of Design, which catered more to aspiring designers anyway. I knew I didn't want to be a designer. The summer before, I visited New York for a week to stay in the FIT dorms and check out the school. I ended up getting the full experience in three hours and spent the rest of the time exploring the city, from the storied floors of Macy's to underground nightlife like that at Undochine, a club hidden beneath the hip restaurant Indochine that you accessed through a sewer grate. It was 1989 New York, the days of Nell Campbell and Café Tabac and supermodels. Everything—and I mean everything—was titillating to me. I couldn't sleep at night because I was that excited.

Back home, I pestered the admissions people at FIT until they accepted me. A few days before the freshmen were scheduled to arrive on campus, I loaded everything—and again, I mean everything—I owned into the back of my dad's station wagon, that's how sure I was that I would not be coming back to Canada. Off we went: me, my dad, my grandmother, and our car full of crap—but my crap, which felt liberating. Even getting lost in the Bronx in the early-morning hours of the final leg of our trip, a worrisome detour into a neighborhood of boarded-up doors and textbook New York graffiti, couldn't dampen my excitement. My new life was about to start.

As I had vowed, I did not waste a single second. On my second day of school, my clothes hung up and my new bed made, I walked into the career services center of FIT on the second floor of the C building on 27th Street and told them I was there to be set up with an internship, please. "Magazines," I added. The woman behind the desk told me politely, but in no uncertain terms, that freshmen didn't "do" internships—I had to wait until my third year—and that I should just go and get acclimated first, explore the city, find the cafeteria, bond with my roommate, etc. "Go be a freshman," she said. "Have some fun." I was horrified. I had no time for any such thing. I'd already had my freshman fun back in Toronto. This was not the time.

Dejected but not deterred, I set out to find a solution. Problem solving in this practical sense would become the hallmark of every fashion job I would go on to have in my career. Roaming the hallways and escalator banks, I noticed a hot-pink flyer pinned to a bulletin board advertising the school newspaper, called, at the time, *Revelations*—yes, just like the scary End Days part of the New Testament. Exactly what you'd name the student paper of a fashion school in the heart of New York City, the hedonism capital of the Eastern Seaboard. Anyway, there was to be a meeting for interested new *Revelations* staffers held later that week in the student center. I decided, fine, no internship? I'd go work on the paper instead. I could at least start there.

Friday couldn't come fast enough. A good thirty minutes before the meeting even started, I had already arrived, notebook and binder in hand, pen flipped, ready to pitch ideas, classic Tracy Flick style. God, I think I even annoyed me. (Well, at least the now me.)

When it turned 5 o'clock, there were still only four people at the meeting, including the faculty adviser, Richard Balestrino, who would later become one of my professors, and me. Another guy—this tall New England–by–way–of–the–East Village–looking kid named Carter, in L.L. Bean boots and a grungy gray tee—was also there, with his friend Michael. They both wanted to be photographers. Without even being asked, I immediately reeled off all my ideas and finally someone—I am assuming it was Professor Balestrino—interrupted. "You've got the job," he said.

"Excellent!" I replied. I had the job! I'd be the new fashion editor of *Revelations*, which was full

{ ABOVE }

Me and Carter Smith at FIT (1990).

of irony since the paper, up till that point, had contained no fashion whatsoever. And I'd beaten out, well, myself to get it. Carter and Michael, meanwhile, were going on and on about how the magazine's photography could be so much better. I agreed, even if there was absolutely no point of comparison. Instead of fashion or photography, the content was driven by campus news (even though there really was no campus; FIT is a true concrete slab of a city school) including such inanities as what the volleyball team was up to, as if anyone really cared or even knew FIT had a volleyball team. The only photos that existed in the school newspaper were snapshots of events around campus. We were at a fashion school. Where was the *fashion photography*? No one read the paper, at all, except for maybe the current editor in chief's grandmother. And that's still a big maybe.

After a long, drawn-out conversation, Michael left and Carter and I stayed there for hours, dissecting what we would do with this school rag. We had much to talk about, given our shared obsession with fashion and photography, and became fast friends. Carter and I teamed up on a novel concept: Let's bring some fashion to the fashion school paper. I also decided that even if I wasn't the person in charge, I would be the person who pushed for every single change I thought the paper needed.

I had my work cut out for me.

## "I wanted it to be the WOMEN'S WEAR DAILY OF SCHOOL NEWSPAPERS."

{ OPPOSITE }

The very first cover of the FIT school newspaper that I styled. Carter shot the picture (1991).

First: We just had to change the name, *Revelations*. If, I said, this isn't a pamphlet detailing the dates and times of when we will be struck dead or saved—hopefully with plenty of bright light along the way—then I think we're misleading our reader here. And, yeah, blasphemy was probably rampant at school, but I had no interest in covering it. That's called dorm-room gossip.

The newspaper was a broadsheet. Let me explain how newspapers work. There are generally two types of newspapers: The broadsheet is folded in half and has no cover but instead columns of news, where visuals are secondary. Think *New York Times* or *Washington Post*. Smart-people reading. Then there is the tabloid, which is folded like a book with a cover and pages that usually are devoted to a different spin on subjects and can be more feature-based. Think *New York Post* or *Women's Wear Daily*. Fun-people reading. Guess which one I was gunning for. Yeah, fun reading. *Revelations* was a broadsheet

A PUBLICATION OF F.I.T.

# W27

OCTOBER 8/91 · VOLUME 47 · NUMBER 1

## GET STONED!
The new way to wear those rocks

## ANNIE GET YOUR CAMERA!
20 years of Celebrity pics

## HIGH SCHOOL CONFIDENTIAL:
F.I.T. 90210

## RIGHT HERE! RIGHT NOW!
All the news on West 27th Street

**FALL PREVIEW...WHO'S SHOT · WHO'S HOT · WHO'S CAUGHT**

where the most exciting thing was a campus visit from a textile manufacturer. Snooze. I wanted it to be the *Women's Wear Daily* of school newspapers: great photos, lots of trends, but news, too. Important. Essential. And, most of all, beautiful. Which meant, of course, real fashion stories.

No one wanted to work on this. I didn't mind doing everything (hint: control freak here and probably the beginning of my slashie phase), but I needed them to care. At least if I was going to make this a success.

After some heated debate, *Revelations* was renamed *W27*, after the block between Seventh and Eighth Avenues where FIT has most of its buildings. (It's what the paper is still called today.) The format was changed to tabloid, ditching the newsy look. Carter and I spent hours in bookstores, strategizing and scouring our favorite fashion magazines for inspiration, analyzing Italian *Vogue* and French *Glamour* and *Per Lui* like they were the Bible: How could we re-create this or interpret that in a way that was right for our readers (even if there were only three of them)? Often, Carter and I would go to our local Gristedes supermarket and push a shopping cart around with issues of international *Vogue*s, going up and down the aisles, slowly studying them. Sometimes—only when it was totally necessary, we told ourselves—we might slide a magazine we wanted to take home in between the pages of the oversized *New York Post*, which at only a quarter was far cheaper than those fashion magazines, which could set us back at least $20 (the cost of a week's worth of food). We justified this petty theft as a crime in the name of good fashion, and of the proper education of our peers. Steven Meisel would want us to savor his pictures properly, we convinced ourselves, not hover over the meat freezer.

Armed with inspiration, Carter would take the pictures for the cover and I would style them. I styled shoots by going to stores, buying up clothes using a credit card (that was so easy to get, even though I had zero credit), and returning them after we were done—or by lying. I remember phoning up the Dolce & Gabbana showroom (as a student) and asking to borrow one of their famous jeweled bodysuits to shoot for a fictitious Canadian magazine—and getting it. That's something you can't do now, when everything is traceable and the Internet can pretty quickly tell you which companies do and don't exist. This process almost always went smoothly, with minimal

dirty looks and zero of my own money expended on what I thought seemed like magazine-quality fashion spreads (or close enough, anyway). Better than average, let's say.

There were exceptions, of course, like the time I was styling an Audrey Hepburn–inspired shoot and bought and returned a pair of white gloves from Macy's and got the fingertips dirty (well, blackened them, to be precise) because that's what happens with white gloves, the least practical

# MASTERING THE "BUY AND BORROW"

NOT THAT I would *ever* advocate what is often called "wardrobing"—that is, buying an item, wearing it, and then returning it—but sometimes the only way to know that a pair of jeans is right for you is to wear them around for a day. Or two. Or you find out that the dress you spent hundreds on really doesn't look so great outside of the dressing room . . . which you learn when you're already wearing it while out on a date. Hey, we're all a little guilty of this. Some department and online stores—where you never even have to worry about being confronted by a scowly salesclerk—have amazing "no questions asked, satisfaction guaranteed" return policies, while others are starting to implement strategies to prevent wardrobing, like extra-large hang tags that cannot be reattached once removed. If you're going to practice the "buy and borrow," there are a few musts:

✓ **GET A GOOD EXCUSE.**
Many shoppers prefer to try things on in the comfort of their own bedrooms, with a familiar mirror and better lighting. Explain to the salesclerk accepting your return that this is you, and that you're committed to trying on clothes at home. Say, "I know it's more work. But I find I return far fewer things that way." Even if it's not entirely true . . .

✗ **AVOID RED WINE.**
Duh. Because the rule of wardrobing is that if it can spill, it will spill. If you're wearing a dress that might possibly be borrowed, stick to clear liquids and don't get sloppy.

✓ **FEBREZE, FEBREZE, FEBREZE.**
Febreze is a stylist's good pal. Also, don't forget to wear deodorant (and make it the clear kind, please).

✓ **RETURN IN A TIMELY MANNER.**
You're likely to have fewer raised eyebrows if you return a purchase within a few weeks rather than three months later.

✗ **DON'T MAKE A HABIT OF IT.**
Or at least spread the wealth. If you're routinely hauling away bagloads of goods from the same store on a Friday, and then hauling them back two weeks later, someone will catch on, and it will be embarrassing when they confront you. Remember that the point isn't to get a free wardrobe but to have a little leeway in seeing how your clothes work in action before fully committing to them.

item ever. The salesgirl refused to let me return them, while I tried desperately to convince her that I had no idea how they got like that and that was precisely the reason I was returning them! "You didn't notice before buying them?" she quizzed. "And whom exactly are you buying them for?" I guess the market among college students for white, wrist-length cotton Easter gloves wasn't particularly big. We were busted. She refused to accept the return, and both Carter and I freaked out. I bet they cost something like $40, but that was a fortune to us at the time. We barely had money for lunch in those days. School lunch back then was a can of Slimfast, which we'd opt for over a slice of pizza because Slimfast was 15 cents cheaper. Pizza was reserved for Friday "splurge days." And on very special days, with the spare change we'd tossed in a can, we would have a bigger splurge at the local diner. A real restaurant with a waitress and everything.

That jeweled Dolce & Gabbana bodysuit pic became the cover of our first issue together. The destroyed-white-gloves shoot never saw the light of day. Already I was learning about a killed shoot.

* * *

I FINISHED THAT YEAR AS FASHION EDITOR. Eventually, my opinions, and my bossiness, landed me the job of editor in chief, as I'd intended. When I took charge, I made a few more changes. I elevated the paper stock to make it whiter, less gray. I created sections, like a real magazine, keeping the school "news" at the front, to minimize the complaints from traditionalists (and faculty), but I gave the section a catchy name—"Right Here, Right Now," inspired by the 1990 Jesus Jones song that was a top-ten hit—and incorporated as many photos as I could. After that was the style section, and then arts and entertainment at the back.

It was exhausting but surprisingly exhilarating work. Carter and I were far more into the newspaper than anyone else on staff, and our faculty adviser more or less left us alone. (God bless Professor Balestrino.) Morning, noon, nights, and weekends, I'd sit in this little room on the top floor of one of the more nondescript buildings, writing, planning shoots, laying the

{ RIGHT }

Carter and me doing a
test shoot in Coney
Island when we decided
we wanted to be a
photographer and
a stylist (1993).

paper out, and doing things like researching and pricing out paper stock, while balancing a full course load of magazine journalism and fashion communications classes and, later, an internship, too. So I was an editor/writer/publisher/student. On the weekends, I might be there from nine in the morning until ten o'clock at night. I put in requests to interview real industry people—Diane von Furstenberg, for example, and Ralph Lauren—and some people even said yes. After a while, I had to stop running stories with my byline because "By Joe Zee" accompanied every single story. And perfectionist that I was, I'd even outsource the design, calling in favors from my friend Stephen, who had moved from Toronto the same time as I did and who was an art director at Macy's, to help me lay it out in a professional way. I was counting on using the newspaper as a sample of my work when I applied for jobs later, so it was important that it represented the best I could do. Besides, isn't this what a magazine editor does? Isn't this why I came to New York even if a woman behind a desk said I couldn't do it—yet? No, this was vital. I meant business.

And I didn't stop there. Every week, after we got in new issues, I'd haul stacks of them around the West 20s, begging the owners of every store, bodega, restaurant, and deli to put a few copies at the register, or in a corner near the door—not content to limit the circulation of our free student newspaper to mere students. All the local business owners thought I was crazy, but because they took the papers, I was able to say on my résumé that, under my tenure, we increased circulation by 500 percent. And it was true.

\* \* \*

IN MY FIRST YEAR AT FIT, I EVENTUALLY DODGED the rules about internships not being open to freshmen by contacting magazines directly. I scored an internship at this small trade magazine called *Sportswear International* that was big and colorful and glossy but had a very small operating budget. People in positions of power are always going on and on about "paying your dues," blah blah, by which they mean spending time performing the sometimes menial tasks assigned to interns and assistants. When I was an intern, I fetched coffee and dry cleaning and I made dinner reservations and I was glad to do it. I compiled the "gossips," xeroxed versions of the celebrity and society gossip columns of all the daily papers, like the *New York Post* and the *New York Daily News*, and distributed them to all the editors. I reorganized bookshelves and sorted mail. I weaseled hard-to-get invitations for my boss, and I found the most reliable drivers so she was never late to an appointment or dinner. I understood none of this was beneath me. That's because I also got to spend twenty hours a week at a real fashion magazine, making real connections who, with any luck, I'd be able to work for one day. When I was at *Elle*, we had full-time assistants whose jobs included mindless tasks like taping receipts to sheets of paper so that an editor can submit them to accounting for reimbursement or alphabetizing clothes or cleaning up the fashion closet. Not every day is the fun learning experience you might expect, but it's a learning experience nonetheless. Sometimes, it's just about helping keep the trains running.

At *Sportswear International*, my job included bagging up and then returning to various showrooms all the clothes we'd borrowed for fashion shoots, like a glorified messenger. The magazine had an office in Manhattan's Garment District not far from FIT and in walking distance of most of the showrooms. Every Monday, Wednesday, and Friday, I'd spend hours

# GLORY

FEBRUARY 1992 • VOLUME XXIV NUMBER 1 • $2.95

## The Trouble with Harry

### BY BRET EASTON ELLIS

## The Geffen Empire

### BY RACHEL URQHART

## Chanel Revisited

### BY TAMA JANOWITZ

Joe.

great! well executed —
(cover is finely developed as
in the entire book.
Ck out p. 20 contents p synopsis —
"... on the opening of her reincarnation
"... is not English.
Overall — a pleasure !!

(A)

Layouts particularly are Pro so B's !

Pro    ✓✓ +
14    ✓✓ +
11    ✓✓ +

Literate — intelligent, good grasp of

language — ads are especially well

defined (as for as you go). A pleasure

to read

pushing a supermarket shopping cart piled high with garment bags up and down Broadway, going from showroom to showroom, looking like a homeless person, returning clothes. We would always work in pairs so that one of us could wait downstairs and guard the shopping cart while the other ran upstairs and returned the bag. I always did the up-and-down part because, in my head, I wanted that experience of *being* in the showroom. I loved this job because I learned where every single showroom was and *I got to see inside*, which is more than I ever did working as a buyer for the largest luxury department store chain in Canada. I look back now and I think, *I can't believe I pushed a shopping cart down Broadway*. How mortifying! But at the time I thought this job could not be more glamorous or exciting. I was like, "I can't believe I get to go to these showrooms! This is why I came to New York. I'm here. I have arrived!" Even if I did only meet the gum-smacking receptionists, still I loved it. They were the epitome of glamour, those shopping cart adventures. Though today, times have changed and interns have a different level of expectations and entitlement. Pushing a shopping cart and returning clothes was fun for me back then. For someone else today, it could be justifiable cause for a class-action lawsuit, as has been the case for some interns in my industry.

To be an intern is a curious thing. It can mean different things in different vocations. I am assuming that an intern in law or medicine or finance involves a different kind of hazing than in fashion, but somewhere in there is probably a universal thread of running personal errands. But I still think you earn your opportunities, no matter the industry. Surgical interns can't dictate when they scrub in, and fashion interns shouldn't be able to dictate when they go on photo shoots.

When I was the fashion director of *W* magazine in the mid-'90s, an intern came up to me on her first day—she hadn't even done anything yet, including introducing herself to me—and just said very directly, "I just want to ask—if you have a photo shoot with Gwyneth Paltrow, I'd like to come. She's my favorite. Same with Madonna." Half of me was like, "I kind of like that tenacity," and the other half of me was like, "Why don't you do what we need you to do here first instead of putting in your order for which actress you'd like to meet?" During those months that I crammed my entire class schedule into two days so I could spend the other three pushing a shopping cart through the Garment District I never once said, "You know, I prefer to go to only the best showrooms and not all of them. I'll go through the list and let you know which ones work for me." The fact is that the returns had to be made, regardless of destination or delivery guy, and I was performing a crucial job by making them. And if I didn't, there was a line of kids who would.

I also did it because I knew that good interns are remembered. And they're hired. An internship is about seeing how a magazine works, for sure. But it's also about making connections, showing people that you're a team player and eager and interested and that you really, really want this. An intern willing to put aside her Princeton education to spend an afternoon enthusiastically steaming wrinkles out of clothing or taping the bottoms of shoes so that they don't get scuffed during the shoot says, without saying it, "I am a team player." If an intern is "too good" to do these sorts of tasks, who else should do them? (And PS: That *W* intern never made it to any of my shoots. Including the cover shoot of Gwyneth I shot that following week.)

After a semester working for *Sportswear International*, I applied for and got an internship at *Mirabella*, which was a major coup. Grace Mirabella, the magazine's founder and editor, had been the editor of *Vogue* for seventeen years, taking over from Diana Vreeland in 1971. After she was fired and replaced by the much younger Anna Wintour in 1988, she started her own magazine with the backing of Rupert Murdoch. *Mirabella* was a big deal, and a dream job for me, the equivalent of going to work for Anna Wintour right after she left *Vogue* to start a new magazine called *Anna*.

That is a *lot* for a Canadian kid at FIT.

I thought I wanted to be a writer, so I asked to work with the magazine's fashion department. The person I was assigned to was also working on a book project, so I'd be helping her research that, too.

My internship was supposed to last one semester but instead it continued for a full year and a half—far longer than I'd anticipated, or maybe even appreciated, but I was glad. I knew that a year and half would ultimately look better on a résumé than six months. My boss worked out of her apartment and that's where I worked three days a week, doing everything she needed. I'd make the seventy-block trek north from my shared student apartment in Hell's Kitchen to her place in the East 80s. When I could, I'd walk. It was New York, after all, but also walking was free. The subway wasn't particularly expensive—$1.25 each way back then—but I was broke. Carter and I were roommates by then, and we'd regularly share a $1 box of Rice-A-Roni for dinner, which meant $2.50 a day for transportation was more than twice my food allowance. It was expensive to intern, and I know a lot of fashion interns will agree with that. Working for free ain't easy—or cheap.

But I was willing to make sacrifices and I told myself I was collecting invaluable experience and a great résumé line item: After all, I'd be instrumental in having researched an entire book about one of the most iconic women in fashion. My boss tasked me with finding obscure information and I enjoyed being resourceful. When I was told to go to the Columbia University library and xerox an entire three-hundred-page book, cover to cover, even though as a nonstudent I was not allowed to even enter the library, I didn't question why or ask how I would make that happen. I just figured it out. I talked my way in. I made friends. I got it done. And I found that aspect of the job incredibly fulfilling. It seemed very journalistic, being able to get myself into places I wasn't invited and uncover information I shouldn't have been able to access.

I was a fashion detective of sorts. Sadly, this woman was also shamefully cheap. I'd get back to her place, proud of myself for having gotten what she needed, but having spent 5 cents per page to copy a freaking book. My time might have been worth nothing, but I wasn't about to pay out money I didn't have. "Just keep track of how much you spend and I'll reimburse you," she told me, though she never did. And yet I didn't quit. Instead, I started walking to work every day. I cut out pizza Fridays. The experience meant more than anything to me, so I kept going, even when I was upset and devastated and tired—and, in the middle of February, freezing my ass off.

\* \* \*

**T**OWARD THE END OF THE YEAR AND A half, as I neared graduation, I began to look for a full-time job. I sent out a bunch of résumés that listed all of my relevant experience, including the research on the book I'd been working on. I was pretty quickly called in for an interview at a major teen magazine. There was no job for me there, but one day not long after, one of the top editors was looking to get in touch to see if I could help out with a story they were doing on recent college graduates. She tried to track me down through my work experience on my résumé.

Later that week, when I arrived at the apartment of the woman I was interning for, she was really upset that I'd listed all of my duties on my résumé, and maybe in hindsight, she felt that I had blown out of proportion the work I'd done on the book, when really I was just proud of my work experience and eager to find a job.

Some fifteen years later, *WWD* ran an announcement that I would be leaving *W* to become the editor in chief of *Vitals*, a new magazine being launched by Fairchild and Condé Nast. I was cleaning out my cubicle at *W* when I got a phone call: It was her, my old boss, the first time we'd had any contact since the end of our intern-boss relationship.

She wanted to know if she could contribute to or work for the magazine(!).

Certainly, I think the logical thing would have been to remind her of the past and our conversation about my résumé all those years ago. Perhaps I might have mentioned the subway fare she still owed me. But no. That wasn't how I felt at all. Instead, I sat at my cubicle, speaking with her, and I thought about how difficult it was for her to call me (or perhaps not). Either way, it wasn't my place to judge. I'm not her, nor am I all the different types of bosses I have had and worked for in my career. Yes, I've worked for some insanely great people, but in the end, we are all unique in the way we do things. The best that I can do is be me. And my "me" always opts for grace over snark. That internship had taught me many things and she was really right: I was richer for the experience, so in some ways I am grateful. It allowed me to really understand a side of this industry that people always see and fear (especially now that it's been immortalized on film), but it also says to me that this isn't always the case. I'm me; I'm not a character. Maybe she wasn't even aware of the way she'd treated me and that's also okay. I blame no one. It's all part of life's lessons.

I sat on the phone and really, *really* wanted to help her. I was thinking of ways that she could contribute, but our staff was small and budgets were even smaller. Interns were writing things for me, so it was tough—and strangely ironic—to ask her to write for free. I couldn't do that. And I didn't have any positions to fill. I told her that but said I would get in touch. That was the last time we spoke.

I don't tell this story as a lesson in karma. I mean, I do a little bit. But I think what I really want to say is that while the impulse might have been to point out to my old boss how the tables had turned, doing so was not necessary. She already knew. It was just as easy for me to turn her down politely than to tell her where she could go shove her résumé, and made me feel better, too. Just because it's fashion doesn't make that age-old lesson any less valid: Treat people as you'd want to be treated.

And maybe it was that one horrible experience as an intern that helped me realize that every voice needs to be heard—and I'm glad I did, because these days, the assistants and interns are some of my favorite sources of information and inspiration. They're excited, they're enthusiastic, they're earnest, and, let's face it, they also see and hear things that I may never know about. As editor in chief at *Vitals* I'd invite everyone—including the interns—out for drinks or to my house for meetings and takeout or even group movie outings. People loved to ask, "Why are the interns hanging out with us?" To which I'd reply, "Because I like the interns. Interns are people, too."

And because you never know if you're going to end up working for them one day.

# LANDING THE INTERNSHIP

THE INTERNS I'VE hired over the years have had the following things in common:

### ✓ SMARTS.

They love fashion, but it's not their life. You might think it's cute to say you have a passion for fashion—maybe you do, and hey, it rhymes—but your love of the latest trends won't get you the job. A fashion editor will be less impressed by your ability to rattle off Phoebe Philo's career trajectory or the name of Karl Lagerfeld's cat than by your willingness to learn and be taught, and to carry on a conversation on a number of topics. Also, be flexible: Don't be so sure you know exactly what department you want to work in and insist that only that department will do. Internships are about exploration. Remember that I went into at least one internship convinced I would become a fashion writer and now I'm clamping dresses to supermodels. In the end, some of the best interns I've hired were political science majors who didn't know the difference between Olivier Theyskens and Laurence Olivier.

### ✓ CLASS.

They know appropriate (dress, attitude). Resist the urge to throw on every single one of your designer items. Practice a bit of restraint. Look put together, but not like a showroom exploded around you. Along those lines, don't be a bitch. Even if fashion breeds mean girls, snobbery will never, ever get you the job. In all ways, just be yourself, not what you think the fashion industry expects of you.

### ✓ CURIOSITY.

They read. An editor might ask you about your favorite magazine. Make sure you can cite one other than the one you're interviewing at, and be able to explain what you like about it. "I like the fashion" does not count as a viable answer.

### ✓ WIT.

They have a sense of humor. No one knows tunnel vision commitment to succeed like I do, believe me. But if you appear too intense in an interview, you risk scaring everyone off. Fashion is business, but it's also fun. Show you can have some of it. Some of my best friends are my former interns, which means they let me get to know them as people. Do that. Trust that you're worth knowing, because you are!

WWD — Edward Nardoza
        Editor
        Patrick McCarthy
        Executive Editor, Fairchild

DNR — William Taffin
        Editor
        Kim Cihlar
        Fashion (M + DNR)

Human Resources — Sharon Thorn
            Director, H.R.

Polly Mellen        André Leon Talley
Linda Wells
Elizabeth Saltzman
Jane Hsiang
Liz Tilberis
Fabien Baron ————
Nancy Axelrad Comer ————→
Jade Hobson Charnin ————
Hearst Personnel — Kenneth Feldman
Hachette — Joan Fila
Ingrid Sischy ————→

{ RIGHT }

Sneaking into the
FIT internship office,
I had to copy this
info down secretively to
try to get internships.

{ OPPOSITE }

If I couldn't get an
internship, I was going
to try to be a waiter.

PICTURE COLLECTION of NY Public Library
3rd F/L of Midtown Branch.

1) New Club Promo   727-8841/8840
   1-5 pm M-F   20 W 20th St.

2) Waiter — P/T   M-F 2-5 pm
   Ottomanellis Cafe — in person
   538 3rd Ave (36th St.)  686-6660

3) Waiter — P/T   W-F 2:30-4:30 pm
   FIASCO! — in person
   358 23rd St. (bet. 8/9 Ave.)

4) Waiter — W-T 3-5 pm
   12 E 22 St.
   Mary's 13 Feb:  Pamela Halock!
   Publicity Coordinator
   Special Events

Kim Hastreiter
David Hershkovits

# BE A GREAT INTERN

FANS OF *THE Hills* and *The City* are familiar with one of fashion's most famous interns, Whitney Port, now an established designer in her own right. I met Whitney after she'd graduated college and was working for Diane von Furstenberg. And though her internship at *Teen Vogue* was largely captured on camera, it was still very much a real internship—one with both upsides and downsides, but one that Whitney obviously made the most of. I asked Whitney to share her thoughts on what makes a great intern.

*The most important thing I learned as an intern was that you have to be willing to do the smallest and most remedial-type tasks in order to land the position you're working toward. Whether that's learning how to properly steam clothes, or organize the hangers so they're all pointing in the same direction, the job is really about respecting the boss, learning how to work under them in the most efficient way, and not taking anything personally. I learned many things that come into play in my professional life now, like prepping for a photo shoot. Look book shoots are easy-peasy for us because of my background. My internships also helped me gain confidence. People knew I had a good work history so they were able to trust my taste and expertise.*

*Now, as a boss, I hire interns. A good candidate has a positive attitude and a willingness to say yes to*

{ OPPOSITE } Whitney Port and me at a BeautyCon conference (2014).

whatever is being asked of them. He or she is strong enough to share an opinion but knows the right time and place—when to speak up and when to just take direction. I have an intern right now whose fashion instinct I trust, and that is majorly important as well. She's someone who gets what's going on and can help me translate that into my collection. I feel too guilty asking my interns to do anything too crazy, but that's just me. A good intern is prepared for it all!

—W.P.

# BREAKING IN

N OT THAT LONG AGO, WELL INTO MY
career, I went to Japan to help style Julia Roberts for the Tokyo premiere of *Eat Pray Love*. It
was my first time there, and I was *so* excited.
Japan is like this fashion fantasyland, and I was

{ BELOW }

An on-the-red-carpet
selfie with Julia Roberts
in the middle (2014).

dying to see whether all the legends were true. Did the Harajuku girls really
exist? (They do, and they're adorable.) Was the sushi really that much better?
(It is! Even at 6 a.m., eaten literally minutes after being unloaded from a fishing boat.) I stayed on a bit longer to investigate, eat, and shop. (One thing you
might not know about Tokyo: The vintage shopping is outstanding.)

Because I would be away for more than a week, I'd also
decided to have my apartment floors redone while I was
gone—a three-day project at the most, I was told. Of course,
nothing in New York City is ever just a "three-day project,"
and when I called my architect from the runway, exhausted
and desperate for a shower after what felt like a three-day
flight, he told me the floors were still drying and that I could
not go in. "Tomorrow," he told me. "Sorry."

I have a second house in the Hamptons, so yes, it could
have been much worse. But Sag Harbor was two hours away at

least, and after a fourteen-hour journey I was beyond jet-lagged. I lugged all my luggage with everything I'd bought to my garage and loaded it all into my car and drove myself to Sag Harbor. By the time I got to the top of my street, my house in sight, I could already feel the pillow under my head.

But wait—was that *trash* all over the front lawn?

It was.

Inside was worse, a scene ripped out of "Goldilocks and the Three Bears" as I crept through my place, careful not to disturb . . . who, exactly? Whoever he was, he had literally been sleeping in my bed, and pretty recently. The shape of his/her/its head was still indented in the pillow—*my*

# "EVERYONE WANTS TO BREAK INTO FASHION.

## But literal—actual—breaking in is not the way . . . "

pillow—and the comforter had been thrown open in dramatic fashion, as if someone had yelled "Fire!" and everyone had run out in a panic. Upstairs, there were crumb-filled plates strewn about, and two glasses of red wine. One had a lipstick mark on the rim.

I called my friend Keith. "Have you been here?" I asked. He hadn't— but, he told me, my assistant had. "She called to ask where the key was hidden," Keith said. "I figured she just needed to drop something off." After some investigative reporting, I found out that my assistant had, in fact, been at the house: eaten my crackers, drunk my wine, and, though I did not ask for details, for all I know had gotten it on in my bed with some boy she was looking to impress. When she'd heard I would be heading to the Hamptons house rather than staying in my city place, she'd scrammed out of there.

"I did not give you permission to let yourself into my house," I shouted through the phone as she sobbed. "I am your boss. You do not do this to your boss. You don't even do it to your friend." Except I couldn't tell if I was angrier at the fact that she'd broken into my house or at her confounding inability to see that she'd all but guaranteed she'd get caught, what with her trail of bread crumbs—literally—and her call to Keith. Where was her common sense? How had I hired this person? I understand the impulse to do something crazy to impress a boy—but at fifteen, not twenty-five. "I'm going to call the police on you," I said, and I meant it. She wailed.

But I didn't call the police. I didn't make her come back to clean up all the trash that had been sprinkled across my lawn. And I didn't even fire her because I thought, *You know, she's a decent assistant. She's young. Something must have short-circuited in her brain for her to pull a stunt like this.* And maybe, well, was it a little funny? I mean, *she broke in.* I wondered if I was to blame. I do have a tendency to become too close to my assistants—something about all that time spent together and, well, I tend to hire people I like, and so we become friends. And I think when you're young, that can be misinterpreted. It's hard to know where the uncrossable line is.

The lesson here: Everyone wants to break into fashion. But literal—actual—breaking in is not the way to go about it. That should be obvious, but apparently it's not to everyone.

* * *

**A** FEW MONTHS BEFORE I GRADUATED FROM FIT, I began sending out my résumé to magazines—seventeen in all, which was probably the total number of fashion magazines based in New York at the time. I got sixteen interviews. *Harper's Bazaar* was the only one that didn't give me an interview, but they did send me a nice rejection letter, which I still have. I was convinced that someday I would work there, and I'd hang the rejection letter, nicely framed, of course, in my office (though that hasn't happened—yet!). The rejection, though, was extra painful because

# COMMON SENSE

**F**ASHION IS MORE democratic than ever before. That's because it plays a more significant role in the world than ever before, from sports to literature to, of course, Hollywood and entertainment. Designers are celebrities, and celebrities are designers. And it's changing. Think about it: Do we value the veteran fashion journalist, or is the blogger the new critic? Is it all about the girl on the runway or the girl on the street? Do we value the quick turnaround of H&M fashion or the long-established craft of couture? Fashion is fluid these days. Stylists rarely dress anyone in head-to-toe anything anymore. Now, high-low is expected for even the most dedicated followers of fashion. Things are evolving, and quickly.

It's a different world from when I started out. Back then, in the early '90s, the structure of the industry was easy to understand. Editors ruled. Models dominated magazine covers. Reality TV—it didn't exist (imagine). In those days, you couldn't talk to your idols through social media. They were removed from your existence. They *were* the elite. Now, the rules are changing. Sure, you've got your girls who were manor-born into the business. But you also have bloggers, girls like Leandra Medine and Rumi Neely, who made their names on their own with little more than a laptop and a serious love of fashion. Fashion is the epicenter of fame. And it's big business.

One thing that remains unwavering, however: You've got to have common sense. This is not optional.

In a way, I came to think of the Great Hamptons Break-in Incident as something of my own doing. I've had some great bosses throughout my career. And one thing they all shared that has really made an impact on the sort of boss I became myself was their understanding of the value of hiring good people. They taught me that the best way to lead is to resist micromanaging and to let people do their jobs. But the only way to do this is to make good hires. Because I make a point to do this, the people I hire often become friends. For an assistant, maybe it can be difficult to know when we're friends and when we have to work. That requires a level of maturity. It also requires common sense.

What I have learned is that I can teach people—interns, assistants—everything about the job, but I cannot teach them common sense. I still try, though. When I walk into the fashion closet to find an intern with her feet on the table, gossiping really loudly with her friend on the phone, and she doesn't immediately hang up and at least pretend to look busy, I can't help but want to say, "It appears we are keep-

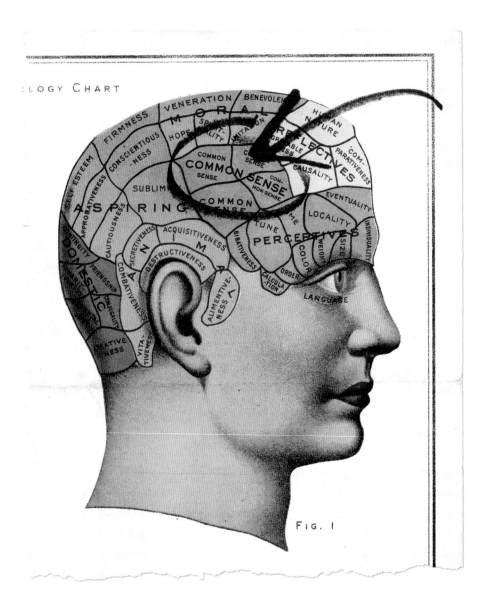

FIG. 1

ing you from something much more important." Do I sound like a crabby old man? Maybe. Maybe it seems harsh, but when I was an intern, I was determined to learn, and I think interns and assistants today should be, too. Putting your feet on the table and telling me to hang on as you chatter away loudly about your plans for tomorrow night leads me to believe that you have no common sense. Which means you're wasting my time and yours.

# Hearst Magazines

Kenneth A Feldman

224 West 57th Street
New York NY 10019

NEW YORK
APR 21 '92
NY

Mr. Joe Zee
201 East 12th Street, PH2
New York, NY 10003

## Hearst Magazines

Kenneth A Feldman
Vice President
Director of Human Resources

224 West 57th Street
New York NY 10019
212 649 3660

A Division of The Hearst Corporation

January 20, 1992

Mr. Joe Zee
201 East 12 Street, PH2
New York, NY   10003

Dear Mr. Zee:

Thank you for your letter and resume regarding a
position with Harper's Bazaar.  I am forwarding
your information to Ms. Elizabeth Tilberis so she
will have the opportunity to review your
background and experience.

At the present time, she is in the process of
determining what her actual staffing requirements
will be.  We are also maintaining your resume in
our active files should she determine she would
like to further consider you for an appropriate
opportunity at Harper's Bazaar magazine.

May we request that if there is any change in
either your home or business location, that you
contact this office in writing so that we can
update our files should we need to contact you at
some future date.

On behalf of Ms. Tilberis and Hearst Magazines, I
would like to thank you for your interest.

Cordially,

KAF:dg

{ ABOVE }

When model
Carolyn Murphy and
I thought we should
work in the fashion
business (1993).

*Harper's Bazaar* was, at the time, the magazine I really wanted to work for. Liz Tilberis had become the editor a year earlier and, along with now legendary creative director Fabien Baron, changed the entire magazine. I wanted to be a part of that.

I had a decent résumé—I'd kept the *Mirabella* stint on there after all; I figured I'd take my chances that my old boss would never find out—but there weren't many jobs, so most of the interviews were purely informational. This was 1992, the beginning of that recession. A few people told me they'd called me in mainly because they were fascinated by my name and were curious to meet me. "Is it an alias?" more than one person asked me. "What's it short for?"

As planned, I brought along to each interview all my issues of *W27*, my school paper, along with one of the old versions of *Revelations*, so that people could see what it had been like originally. One of the first interviews I went to was for a job at *Women's Wear Daily*. I wasn't entirely sure what I was applying for; I thought maybe I wanted to be a writer or maybe a stylist, but I didn't really know either way. To be honest, I would have cleaned the windows—anything to get in.

The *WWD* interview went well enough that they offered me the chance to do a styling test, basically to try out for a job as a fashion editor. I was asked to stage a photo shoot to produce what *WWD* called a "page 1 and double"—which was a cover and then a two-page inside spread—on a current fashion trend.

Pretty much everything that could go wrong that day did. First, the location flooded. Then a light fell, exploded, and caught on fire. My model didn't show up. She had a family emergency, but no one bothered to call to tell me. By the time I found another model to fit the clothes, we had one hour left before being kicked out. We rushed through the photos, and needless to say, they turned out god-awful.

# "IN FASHION NO ONE CARES

## about roadblocks, obstacles, or dilemmas . . ."

Obviously, I did not get the job, and I knew I wouldn't from the moment I left the set that day. And I don't blame them—I wouldn't have hired me, either, even if most of the mishaps weren't my fault at all. In fashion, no one cares about roadblocks, obstacles, or dilemmas that you have to overcome along the way, or the floods, fires, and family emergencies that always come up. It's a simple question: Did you get the story? I didn't get the story. And I didn't get the job.

The irony, of course, is that these days I can put together a photo shoot in half an hour and have it turn out amazing. The difference is that I have experience now, and confidence, too.

The week after that disaster, I went back to Toronto to visit my family, and maybe wallow a bit. I remember curling up in the fetal position in my childhood bedroom, thinking that perhaps I wasn't meant to work in fashion, or in New York City, after all; that everyone was right and if I wanted to get hired at a magazine, I needed to be a woman, and blond, with family connections. And I was none of those three. Three strikes—I was out.

Then I got a call from Condé Nast, from an HR person phoning to say that Polly Mellen might have a position opening up, and might I be available, say, tomorrow, to come in and meet with her?

I could not have been more available. Polly Mellen was one of my all-time personal icons—a longtime stylist at *Vogue* who had recently become the creative director of *Allure*, Condé Nast's new beauty magazine. I'd previously told this same HR person that I *only* wanted to work for Polly Mellen, although I was being my usual hyperbolic self and in reality I would have taken any number of jobs at Condé Nast. Still, it felt like an amazing event of serendipity. A few hours later, I was on the train back to New York City. I spent the entire twelve-hour ride fretting—not over what I would say to Mrs. Mellen but over a more vital dilemma: What exactly was I supposed to wear? I had a student wardrobe and, with no job, zero money. Everything I owned was all wrong. All wrong.

Around hour eight, I settled on a pair of black, paper-baggy pants I'd owned since I'd bought them from Demob during a high school trip to London. This was during my New Romanticism phase, and Demob was one of the purveyors of the sort of clothing worn by bands like Culture Club and Spandau Ballet. These were some pretty crazy-ass statement pants, with a drop crotch and buttons all up the sides. I paired them with a white shirt, buttoned all the way, and a cheap leopard-print vest because I thought, well, Mrs. Mellen had worked for Diana Vreeland and Diana Vreeland loved leopard.

I knew a lot about Diana Vreeland and, in fact, Polly from having spent all my internship months researching both of them because Polly had worked for both Diana Vreeland and Grace Mirabella for many years. She had worked with everyone I admired, really—three *Vogue* editors and every top photographer imaginable, including Helmut Newton, Arthur Elgort,

Avedon, Penn—and was arguably as influential as the *Vogue* editors she'd worked under. It was Polly who discovered many of the girls who went on to have the most incredible modeling careers, girls like Lauren Hutton, Patti Hansen, Naomi Campbell, and Penelope Tree.

I knew from researching Grace that, as a stylist, Polly liked things a certain, sometimes unpredictable way. I also knew that she valued enthusiasm, and was particularly enthusiastic herself, especially when she was pleased with someone's work, whether it be that of a fashion designer or someone she employed. If nothing else, I figured, I had enthusiasm going for me. I told her about the research I'd done, and she seemed genuinely fascinated. She was impressed I knew so much about fashion, and about her own career in particular. Also, she told me she liked my vest.

The next day, I got another call from HR. Mrs. Mellen had enjoyed meeting me, and would I be available to come back that week to meet with Linda Wells? Linda is the editor in chief of *Allure*, and is known for being young, cool, and very smart. She'd already put in time at *Vogue* and the *New York Times Magazine*. *Now* what was I supposed to wear?

But then I figured: Why not repeat the outfit that had so impressed Polly Mellen? I was meeting with an entirely different editor, after all. Problem solved, the day of the interview, I dressed in my button-up pants, white shirt, and leopard vest. For an hour, I sat with Linda, who was as enthusiastic about me as I was about her. "Polly thought you'd be fantastic," she told me. "And I agree. So we'll be in touch. Let me walk you out."

As we headed toward the exit, Linda suggested we stop by and say hi to Polly. "I'm sure she'd love to see you again," Linda said, sweetly, and I died inside. What was I supposed to say: "Not today, thanks"? "*Pass*"? I had no choice but to act like nothing was wrong, that I wasn't worried about looking like a Boy George groupie, or worse: like a kid with only one outfit. *Please don't be in your office today, please don't be in your office today*, I repeated over and over to myself as we plodded down the hall toward her office, where all the lights were on.

She was in; of course she was. And she was amazingly gracious and elegant and, it seemed, happy to see me, though I was positive I heard her chuckle ever so softly as she stood to shake my hand. The entire way home

# allure

LINDA WELLS *Editor in chief* August 12

Dear Joe,

I just wanted to write you a note to thank you for always thinking and contributing ideas. It's so important, and such a great addition.

Best,

360 Madison Avenue New York New York 10017 Telephone 212. 880 5551 Fax 212 370 1949
THE CONDÉ NAST PUBLICATIONS INC.

{ ABOVE } One of my first notes from Linda Wells at *Allure*.

# allure

POLLY ALLEN MELLEN ~~Creative Director~~                    5/9/95

Dear Joe Z :-
    We (Henry & Pam) are having a few people
for drinks on May 11th. and we would love To
have you join us.      7pm ish —
            405 East 54th. St. - Apt. 14B.
    R.S.V.P. 880 - 5569        Love, Polly.

360 Madison Avenue  New York  New York  10017  Telephone 212. 880 5569  Fax 212. 880 2282
THE CONDÉ NAST PUBLICATIONS INC.

{ ABOVE } An invitation to a dinner at Polly Mellen's house with her husband, 1995.

I was convinced that I had just ungotten myself my dream job. Damn unforgettable leopard vest.

Two days later, I got the call. I was hired. The first thing I did, even before calling my mother or my best friend, was to go shopping for a whole new wardrobe.

At some point over the years, the vest was lost, or given away. Hopefully, it went on to bring some similar good luck to someone else. But I will always be grateful to that little swath of leopard.

* * *

IT WAS WHILE WORKING FOR POLLY THAT I realized that being a stylist—and not a writer, or an art person—was my calling. I loved everything about clothes: looking at them, touching them, and especially telling stories with them. On my very first day at *Allure*, I remember walking into the fashion closet and seeing heaps of expensive dresses and piles of mismatched Manolo Blahniks on the floor. I had gone into the closet to pick up some bags of stuff to bring to Polly, who was prepping for a shoot with photographer Steven Klein and Kate Moss, two virtual unknowns at the time, though of course they would go on to become one of fashion's most sought-after photographer-model collaborators. Girls were rolling clothing racks right over the clothing and I was freaking out: How could they treat these beautiful things so carelessly?

As one of Polly's assistants, I learned to see and appreciate fashion. She taught me to try hard to always remember to value the work; that it's not just clothes and shoes and accessories, disposable and replaceable, but someone's art, which should always be treated with reverence and respect. The job itself was a typical assistant-level mishmash of important, exciting work and administrative tasks. I answered her phone. For nearly a year, I called her Mrs. Mellen until she finally one day said, "Joe. Call me Polly, *please*." Polly wasn't demanding, but she did expect a certain level of excellence. She was always the first one to arrive at the office—no matter how early I got there, she was already sitting at her desk—and the last to leave, even on a Friday, when her husband, Henry, would be downstairs, waiting

'93 4 9

to pick her up. But though she had come up in the industry during a time when women didn't really work, and had fought to earn a certain level of respect, she was never mean or belittling. She just wanted you to do the best you could, even if the best was always just a little bit better than what you were doing (and if often was). She had an incredible work ethic. I think ultimately that's why she hired me; she could tell I did, too.

We worked long hours (although never weekends—Polly had a strict policy of never working on weekends). As a stylist, Polly was precise and particular. She had impeccable taste in clothes—for herself and for others—but she was not "fancy." She taught me how to tell if a garment was well made, and how to talk to models about taking care of themselves (which is important because a stylist's worst nightmare is a beautiful girl who looks like she's been up all night and living on secondhand cigarette smoke). When Polly prepared for a shoot, she really prepared, bringing along a very tightly edited selection of clothing—no excess. She'd have me call in specific looks—look 13 from the Isaac Mizrahi runway show, for example—and she'd want all of it, precisely as it had appeared on the runway. So if a girl wore pantyhose in the runway, she'd want that exact pair of pantyhose. Clothing to be transported was bagged the Diana Vreeland way. Everything was hung the way it was worn, from the outside in and from top to bottom: coat over shirt over T-shirt over underpinning, all assembled together, each on its own uniform hanger, with the hangers all facing the same way. The accessories would be bundled together in a clear bag and hung with the outfit. A photocopy of the look was taped to the first hanger so you could see how the outfit was styled. This is the way it was done every time, for every look, without exception.

\* \* \*

LORI GOLDSTEIN, MY OTHER MENTOR FROM that time, could not have worked more differently. Lori and I met for the first time at the company Christmas party. She was *Allure*'s senior fashion editor but technically a freelancer, so she didn't work from the office, but I knew who she was because I'd been growing ever more obsessed with her work. As soon as I spotted her at the party, I went over to introduce myself, citing a

{ OPPOSITE TOP }

Working hard at a photo shoot on Pantelleria, an Italian island near Tunisia (1993).

{ OPPOSITE BOTTOM }

Assisting Lori Goldstein on a photo shoot for *Allure* with photographer Wayne Maser in Lake Powell, Arizona (1993).

recent story photographed by Steven Meisel that she'd styled for Italian *Glamour*. "Oh my God," I gushed, "I'm a huge fan of yours. That story with the girls in the blow-up swimming pool wearing the bathing suits with the grunge hats . . . Everything was, like, genius." I'm sure I made zero sense.

But flattery, people, will get you everywhere, especially in fashion. "Wow, thanks," she said, eyeing me up and down a bit, in the nicest way possible. "Do you want to come work with me?"

I started working as Lori's assistant on various shoots she did for *Allure* as well as freelance jobs she took on. Since she wasn't full-time, this was fairly easy to do along with the work I already had for Polly, although these side jobs definitely had me working weekends. (This was the start of what would become a lifetime of multiple gigs at once, my start as a slashie. Back then, I was a rare bird in the fashion industry for working more than one job because I wanted to and not because I had to. These days, though, this is how kids want to earn a living—by working for themselves, essentially.)

And I loved it. I learned a lot, and fast. One of my first big jobs with Lori wasn't even for the magazine. She was shooting a Karl Lagerfeld fragrance campaign with Peter Lindbergh in the South of France. My job on that shoot was very important: to pick up a dress from Karl's apartment in Paris and chaperone it, on my lap, to Karl's apartment in Monaco, where we would be shooting. I'd be transported between the two locations via private helicopter. I remember sitting in the backseat of that helicopter—a glorified messenger, really—wondering how exactly I'd gotten so lucky.

The high lasted until the next morning when I decided to get up early before the day started to go explore. Monaco was one of those places I could never have afforded to get to on my own and I figured I'd never be back, so I wanted to try to see as much as I could. No more than twenty steps from the hotel I was stopped by local police, who demanded, in French, to see my ID: "Where are you staying? Who are you with?" I told them, then stood by as they called the hotel to verify. An Asian kid in jeans and sneakers, it seems, was just too shady for a place like Monaco. And I was right: I have never been back.

Unlike Polly, Lori was about creating in the moment. She did not want exact looks, and she did not want to plan ahead. "Let's just get everything,"

# MIND THE
# DETAILS

Dear Mr. Zee,

I have always been a fan of your work. and yovvvvur magazine W is
the best magazine, and your stories are the first ones I look for. I'd be
honored to have the opportunity to come work for you at Vogue.

*[handwritten annotations: ✓ !, SP, Really?, NO!]*

Hmm.

I understand that it is a tough world out there—even harder than when I was
starting out, because there are fewer magazines and staffs are smaller—and that to
land one job you might need to send out a hundred résumés. To that end, I understand you may be inclined to put together a form letter of sorts. But if you can't even
be bothered to proofread that letter or email before you send it to any potential
employer, you have no business working for this, or really any other, magazine, where
words and attention to detail actually matter.

Back when I'd get these letters through snail mail, I used to circle all the mistakes
on the cover letter and mail it back to the sender. Not being able to do that is the
worst part about email, as far as I'm concerned. Hopefully, those would-be assistants
used what I taught them to find a great job with someone else.

she liked to say. "Let's see how we feel in the moment." There would be a theme, of course, but it would be very broadly interpreted, at least until the actual minute we were shooting. She was about having tons of stuff to play with and about having fun—carefree and crazy to Polly's calculated and meticulous. This resulted in us bringing trunks' and trunks' and trunks' worth of stuff to shoots, no matter how minor. Even if we just needed one shot for a single page in the magazine, we took what amounted to dozens and dozens of outfits.

One approach was not better than the other, but I found I gravitated more to the loose, go-with-it method practiced by Lori. Maybe it was an excuse to procrastinate, or be excessive, but to this day, I am not organized and I don't plan in advance. I find that my best ideas are the ones I have when under at least a little pressure, while some willingness to be flexible comes in handy when working with celebrity models, which Polly only occasionally had to contend with in her day. She dressed celebrities like Nastassja Kinski, Barbra Streisand, and Judy Garland, but not every month and not for the cover of a magazine. Also, "celebrity" was big back then, but not the massive machine it is today. For that, you need all the help—and clothes, and accessories—you can get. These days, more isn't more. It's industry standard.

# G.I. JOE ZEE

## (AKA THE CEO OF HALLOWEEN)

**I**HATED HALLOWEEN AS A CHILD. I FOUND IT intimidating, to be honest. I mean, I got the point: dress up, look adorable, get free candy. The economics of the day did not escape me; Halloween made sense for kids and definitely for all my friends, but for me, it was different. I was always entirely too self-conscious to really feel like I could dress up as anything convincingly (I even felt the pressure to be a convincing *ghost*). But more, as a Canadian-Asian kid in a Canadian suburb, I didn't see a lot of characters I thought I could be. Who'd ever heard of an Asian Lone Ranger? Or an Asian pirate, for that matter? As a ten-year-old, I assumed my only choices were Bruce Lee or the Karate Kid (though I realize Ralph Macchio is Italian, not Asian). In any case, neither felt appealing.

Another problem: I cared a total of squat about candy, and especially candy of the mass-produced drugstore/bodega variety. If they expected me to eat it, never mind walk around begging strangers for it, someone was going to have to do something about all that brown 1950s packaging and plastic-flavored taste. Halloween needed a serious redesign. And it still does. I mean, I am all for a classic carryall, but how can it be that forty years after I was a reluctant young trick-or-treater myself the choices for candy collection remain a smirking "Made in China" pumpkin and a pillowcase?

But Halloween—people love it. And I don't blame them. And so at some point—I was maybe eight or nine—I figured out a way to muddle through this annual ritual that, it seemed clear, was never going away. Turns out all that was required was a small shift in perspective and, of course, the essential promise of something in it for me. Let's see: If I didn't care about candy or playing pretend, what did I care about? For starters, money and winning. Winning Halloween might make it bearable, I thought. Better yet, what if I could get paid to win Halloween?

With a goal of acquiring more candy than anyone else in my neighborhood had ever before and would ever again, I came up with a high-impact business plan that aimed for maximum profitability with minimum effort. Fun was not a factor; this was strictly business. If I was going to do this intimidating holiday at all, then I was going to do it better than everyone else. The cornerstone of my plan was the fairly genius idea of employing costumes that allowed for instant but distinct variations: the Halloween version of "glittens," the love child of gloves and mittens. Or jackets whose sleeves unzip and detach, turning them into vests. This was obviously an early precursor to my future career plotting endless day-to-night transitions. But back then, a two-in-one costume simply meant I could ring the same door twice, once up the street and then again on the way back, without having to run home to change into an actual second costume, therefore enabling me to collect twice as much candy covering the same amount of territory. After that, I'd sell the high-fructose haul for a profit to all the pathetic, singularly costumed sugar addicts who'd eaten my dust.

One year, mid-Snoopy obsession, I dressed as Charlie Brown. I created Charlie's signature zigzag sweater using a yellow sweatshirt I already owned and some black felt, which I carefully cut and applied while sitting on my bedroom floor. I paired it, as Charlie would do, with some brown pants. I did not shave my head, figuring the poo-colored poly-blend trousers were sacrificial enough. For my candy-collecting alter ego, I added a pair of antennae, black mittens, and a felt eye mask, and presto-chango: bumblebee.

I repeated this Jekyll-and-Hyde routine for hours: Charlie Brown, bee. Charlie Brown, bee. Not a single person caught on, or if anyone did, he or she was too nice to say anything or, more crucially, refuse me more candy, which was pretty much all I cared about anyway. Canadians are famously polite, and I exploited that for all it was worth. So there I was, in alternating costumes, much to the bafflement of my grandmother (and I'm sure some neighbors, too), carrying my two different orange plastic pumpkin carryalls from a local Kmart and a cardboard UNICEF box, scoring more loot (and loose change) than any other kid on the block. I was definitely ahead in this competition of one.

By the time I got home, I was rolling in 3 Musketeers and Baby Ruths and Reese's Peanut Butter Cups (the last being the most appealing candy, if I had to choose, by my standards). With enough mini Tootsie Rolls to derail a suburban middle school's worth of orthodontia, I would make my friends and sibs count their stashes so that I could declare myself the clear chairman and CEO of Halloween. Then I'd start liquidating. From year one, it was clear I'd hit upon something. Everyone wanted to win Halloween, just like me, and so other kids would dig pennies out from between their parents' couch cushions or beg for advances on their allowances just to buy candy from my pile to make their own bigger. Kids were even willing to pay higher than retail value for full-size candy bars because they felt more special than their bite-size counterparts. In the end, I wouldn't earn a lot of money—twenty, maybe thirty bucks—but it was enough to stash away for the latest logo T-shirt, which I would take over bad chocolate any day.

Eventually, my friends stopped wanting to play along, probably because they realized I was getting the far better end of the deal. After that, I boycotted Halloween altogether.

Until I got to New York.

Here's something you need to understand, something I learned very quickly: Fashion people take Halloween very, very seriously. For most of us, Halloween is nothing less than a religious holiday. Everyone becomes completely consumed with excess and dressing up and transforming and putting on an act, which for this crowd is pretty easy given their access to some of the world's best makeup artists, hairdressers, prop stylists, and wardrobes, not to mention their general propensity for putting on acts. For fashion people, Halloween is the one night of revelry—or several nights, in some cases, since there's always parties leading up to the actual night—where you can wear the latest designer clothes with some new hair and statement makeup and declare you're dressed as someone from *The Great Gatsby* or "Jackie O on vacation."

I was first schooled in how the fashion industry does Halloween in 1997, not long after I started working in magazines, when I was invited to my first big glamorous Fashion Halloween party, thrown by Kate Moss and Naomi Campbell. The location was some Gramercy Park venue that I probably wouldn't have gone to on a regular night, but of course, the right people can get the other people to go anywhere, and for these two, and the promise of all the hijinks they brought with them, I would go absolutely anywhere. I assumed, though, that no one would be dressing up. I mean, fashion people were too cool for costumes, weren't they?

Turns out, no. No, they were not.

Or, at least, they were not too cool for *Halloween* costumes—and the more inventive, the better. Unlike the rest of the adult world, which tends to see Halloween as a chance to be as sleazy and underdressed as possible in some utilitarian clothes with an exposed bra (slutty princesses, sexy cops, and the rest of their kind), fashion folks don't rely solely on over-exposed boobs and legs to qualify as a "costume." Like the year I saw lots of '20s flapper girls done up in Galliano, or the '40s gangster molls in Prada, or, my personal favorite, the Tom Ford Pocahontases of 1996. And while there are always the Karl Lagerfelds and the Anna Wintours—what I like to call min/max costumes: minimum effort with maximum results—the easy way out is rare.

As a guy, though, Halloween for me has always been different, especially in those early years when I didn't have identifiable designer clothes to fall back on. When I learned (in advance, thankfully) that costumes would be expected at the supermodel party, I decided that the best way to proceed was with extreme caution—nothing too adventurous, no big risks, but still something that might allow me to showcase my creativity. My first and only stop that year: Uncle Sam's Army Navy.

Uncle Sam's is this musty old place in the West Village where camo goes to die, or maybe stock up on camping gear. The owners buy new and secondhand military gear straight from government surplus warehouses, but also from veterans themselves, so if you're lucky you might find an old love note or, I don't know, a shell casing tucked away in a hidden pocket. You can get anything here in camo print: duffels, sweatbands, water bottles, Band-Aids, you name it. There's also a Soviet-era G4 suit hanging from the ceiling (not for sale), a sometimes-working vintage dog tag machine that can inscribe your name, rank, or quote of choice on stainless steel, and appropriately gruff employees decked out in fatigues and the sort of steel-toed boots you do not want to find your ass on the wrong side of.

For Kate and Naomi's party, I decided that G.I. Joe fit the bill as being just clever enough and just risky enough. And butch enough, in a subtle sort of way: Army looks on guys automatically reek cool without screaming Channing Tatum in *Magic Mike* or, um, Channing Tatum in *G.I. Joe*. Being an actual fictional character absolved me from the criticism of being too lazy to muster up more than just "army guy."

At Uncle Sam's, I assembled a head-to-toe camo ensemble: camo pants, shirt, belt, coat, and hat. At home, for that final authentic touch, I popped open a bottle of wine, had a glass or two, burned the cork over a candle, and then smeared the black residue from the burned end of the cork all over my face to resemble the dirt from sleeping in a ditch all night as wartime camo so I could have even more authenticity. I'm not even sure where I learned that trick, but it works in the best possible way. I'm sure my dermatologist would cringe reading this.

Camo-ed out and half a bottle of cheap wine in, I was starting to get really into it. That old Halloween feeling was coming back to me: *Must. Win. Halloween.* Here comes G.I. Joe Zee.

\* \* \*

# THE SECRET OF THE ARMY-NAVY

Army-navy stores are a great year-round fashion resource. The military look is always current in at least some way, whether we're talking the skinny cargoes of the early 2000s or the now hot lace-up combat boots or the timeless peacoat. Since so many designers time and again have turned to classic military looks for inspiration, why not go right to the source? Most towns have an army-navy store chock-full of grommetted canvas belts, shawl-collared fisherman sweaters, Chuck Taylor sneakers, and very Elizabeth & James army-green fatigue jackets that look super authentic because, well, they are. And let me tell you: The goods are a hell of a lot cheaper when the army boots don't have "Valentino" stamped across the sole.

But you don't have to go all G.I. Joe in everyday life; in fact, please don't. The military look almost always works best in moderation, as in an oversized fatigue jacket over a feminine dress or military boots with a preppy-leaning jeans-and-button-down ensemble. (Shop Uncle Sam's Army Navy online at armynavydeals.com and tell them I sent you!)

**S**UCH SMALL BUT UNDENIABLY KEY DETAILS AS USING a cork to give myself an authentic camouflage face would prove to be the hallmark of my subsequent Halloween costumes. I was the newly minted fashion director of *W* when I was invited to Heidi Klum's first, now annual, Halloween party. I do not know a person so devoted to a holiday as Heidi is to Halloween. She starts to prepare sometime in November the year before. Over the years, the ante for me had been upped and there was no more running to Uncle Sam's for a semi-last-minute costume, no matter how amazing my G.I. Joe costume was. And not when I was now a fashion director. A fashion director didn't just dash out the day before and pick up some cheap duds. This is how my full-on obses-sion with Halloween began. I might not have been able to pull the latest Helmut Lang dress straight off the runway—or, more precisely, pull it off—like my female counterparts could, but I could still be inventive. I developed a very careful, very time-consuming process. It went like this.

Sometime toward the beginning of summer, I would start breaking down pop culture refer-ences and creating a list of potential costumes, rating each according to how fun they'd be to wear and how well I'd be able to wear it. I tried to be brutally realistic: No matter how hard I tried, I probably wouldn't be particularly con-vincing as, say, a *Baywatch*-era David Hasselhoff or even Pamela Anderson. But I could be a cholo gangster from *Carlito's Way*, no problem.

Once I'd made a decision, I'd start gather-ing as much information as I could find, which often included pictures culled from books (pre-Google, you know), screen grabs from rele-vant movies and TV shows, and runway looks that might help inspire the mood. Then I'd create a storyboard, which is a visual outline professional stylists often use to help develop a concept for an upcoming shoot, a road map of sorts. Never mind that as an actual professional stylist—this sort of prep work is something I

( BELOW )

Halloween as a gang member (1999).

never, ever do. I work on instinct and always pull together looks the morning of a shoot.

And yet there I was, gluing pictures on poster board in June and starting to collect pieces of the costume by August so that I wouldn't be rushing last minute, also very unlike me. I did not then nor do I now excel at meeting deadlines, as the editor of this very book well knows. But I knew that last-minute scrambles meant pawing through the dregs of everyone else's costume searches, only to emerge with a half-assed getup that I'd need to explain all night. For whatever reason, Halloween prep was the only thing in my life I've ever been able to do early.

Once I'd assembled all the components, often enough stuff to fill the entire surface of my bed, that's when I'd start trying things on, snapping selfies with a self-timing Polaroid propped up on my jumbotron TV. I'd then spend hours laying out the Polaroids, analyzing them, shifting some pieces around, adding hair and makeup ideas where necessary. When my look was finalized and I felt all the pieces were in place, I bagged everything carefully and hung it like I might a $30,000 couture dress trimmed in crystals, in the way I learned from my first mentor, Polly Mellen. Bottoms were clipped on a hanger, undershirts neatly pressed and hung, and outerwear draped carefully on top. Accessories were individually bagged and stapled to the bottom of the garment bag, and a Polaroid was taped to the front for reference.

This holiday made me anal.

Ultimately, I participated in Halloween in this way for a total of four years before I ran out of the requisite steam, or time (except in 2014, when I revisited the concept again and it was no easy feat). I'm including some of my greatest hits here; feel free to use them as your own inspiration (or not). Wine cork camo not required.

There was the year I was a gangster/Kevin Costner nemesis from *The Untouchables*. This, obviously, required me contacting Warner Bros. movie studios, which rented out costumes for photo shoots. There was no photo shoot, of course, but I had authenticity to think about, and what they didn't know wouldn't hurt them.

The costume arrived, and lo, the '30s-era high-waisted pants they sent gave the illusion I was wearing a diaper. I thought about the endless

# THE POWER OF THE SELFIE

T HERE'S A NAME now for my Halloween Polaroid tradition: "selfie." The Kim Kardashians and tween beauty bloggers of the world think they invented selfies, but fashion people have been using them for years. After years of looking at models and then the photographs of those models, we know that the camera, for the most part, doesn't lie, even when the mirror might. And so we'd rely on self-shot Polaroids of ourselves in order to make any necessary adjustments before heading out to a job interview or going out for the night. On photo shoots, Polaroids (and later iPhone pics) documenting what a model is wearing became fashion currency.

These days, instant outfit selfies are a piece of cake thanks to the smartphone, though purists remain. My friend actress Tracee Ellis Ross told me she still Polaroids every single one of her outfits to see how she looks in it before leaving the house. But while you may no longer require a Polaroid camera, you should rely on the classic techniques in order to get it right. Note: Do not feel compelled to post these photos to social media, though I know you will.

### ✓ ANGLE

For outfit purposes, you'll obviously want to take a full-body shot. Do this using a full-length mirror and hold your phone, pointing at the mirror, as low to the ground as you're able while still getting the entire outfit in the frame. Keep the background as simple as possible: no messy closet, strewn clothes, or cats walking around. You want the clearest possible shot of you only.

### ✓ LIGHTING

Turn on every light you have. The best light comes from in front of you, not behind, or else your outfit will appear too dark.

### ✓ POSE

Look at the camera lens rather than at yourself on the screen or in the mirror. This may seem unimportant if all you want to do is see what you look like in an outfit, but remember that how you look to others is about more than what you're wearing. It's the entire package that matters. Otherwise, you might as well just shoot the individual components spread out on your bed.

{ ABOVE }

Halloween option—
Carnaby Street punk.

{ ABOVE RIGHT }

Halloween 2014.
I'm Liberace; my boy-
friend, Rob, is Scott.

bathroom lines Halloween promised as people already inclined to take longer than necessary in there to do whatever they were doing now had com-
plex costumes to deal with and wondered if I should consider it. The diaper,
that is. Who would know?

But no, gross. Not happening. There were other questions that the folks at
Warner Bros. would not help me answer, such as: On which side should I wear
my holster? What type of gun would be authentic? And should it be a real gun
(unloaded, of course)? Jacket on or off? Fedora tilted back or covering my
eyes? So many decisions, and each one had to be carefully wrought. That's
where the Polaroids came in handy. (Final decisions: Hat tilted back, for practical reasons, plus jacket off, shirts sleeves rolled with a shirt garter—aha! who
knew such a thing existed, but it does!—and gun, fake, of course, on the left.)

Another favorite was the year I dressed as a Carnaby Street punk. My
friends and I were going out as a big group and wanted a single theme that
could enhance the gang mentality while working for both guys and girls. We

also didn't want to have to try too hard (I went along with that ruse, even though I was secretly obsessing). For those reasons, London punk seemed obvious and vague enough that everyone could still have their own individual interpretations.

I knew I wanted to wear a kilt because when else would I ever get the chance? I pulled together some old pics from the days of Vivienne Westwood and Malcolm McLaren, the mom and dad of punk fashion, and went for a layered look, with tartan skinny pants under a matching Black Watch tartan kilt, both of which had been flown over from London under the guise of another photo shoot, though I also had a backup option from Trash and Vaudeville, a famous wannabe punk shop on Manhattan's St. Mark's Place. On top, I wore an old, torn BCBG T-shirt borrowed from a girl from my office beneath a tuxedo jacket I'd scored from a thrift store. I ripped the sleeves off, leaving the exposed shoulder pads. I hit six different hardware stores in search of the perfect padlock and chain to serve as a choker.

{ ABOVE }

Makeup, hair, and faux lip ring for my punk year.

{ ABOVE LEFT }

Halloween DIY for my punk year.

# THE LESSONS OF HALLOWEEN

**T**HE TRUTH IS there's no shame in recycling clothes, even Halloween costumes. That's one trick you can use all year round, and it's one of the secrets of truly stylish people: how to repurpose, reimagine, and reinvent the treasures in their wardrobe, whether for one night's costume party or to get another season's use out of a beloved item. Here, I'll take elements from a few classic costumes and show you how to restyle and recycle them into classic, everyday looks.

## THE CLEOPATRA

**OCTOBER 31:**
Glamour-puss Liz Taylor embodied her, and Angelina Jolie is up next. In fact, I don't think there's a woman out there who doesn't fantasize about being Queen of the Nile—the jewels! Mark Antony!—for one night, at least.

**HOW I'D STYLE IT FOR EVERYDAY:**
This is an easy fix. As Cleo, you might rock a gold pleated maxi skirt. As you, I might suggest shortening the skirt to whatever's the most current skirt length and then pairing it with a simple sweater or top.

## THE PIRATE

**OCTOBER 31:**

You can thank the success of the *Pirates of the Caribbean* franchise for this most ubiquitous getup. As Penélope and Keira have demonstrated, swashbuckling women are fierce yet sexy and camera ready. A peasant blouse is a given for this costume.

**HOW I'D STYLE IT FOR EVERYDAY:**

The other 364 days of the year, I'm not a big fan of the peasant top—it often looks sloppy. And boho chic is so done (and hopefully never coming back). But when it's worn tucked in with a tailored blazer, jeans, and sleek heels, the hippie blouse becomes part of something else altogether: the perfect daytime uniform.

## THE FREDDY KRUEGER

**OCTOBER 31:**

Forgoing the typical "sexy" characters? Yay for you. Channeling the nightmare on Elm Street plays to such trends as menswear and ever-fashionable stripes.

**HOW I'D STYLE IT FOR EVERYDAY:**

What self-respecting woman doesn't adore a staple striped top? Put your black-and-red Freddy stripes into everyday practice by slashing the sleeves to create a tank, then pairing with some slim white denim.

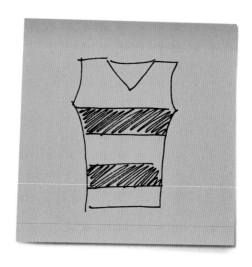

## THE '50S SOCK HOPPER

**OCTOBER 31:**

Olivia Newton-John as Sandy is endlessly chic, if a little cutesy. Vintage wool plaid skirts are as common as sex under the bleachers. Find them at any corner thrift shop.

**HOW I'D STYLE IT FOR EVERYDAY:**

The poodle skirt screams librarian, and not in a good way. Shorten plaids to a mini—or if you're just not that daring, to at least just below the knee—and top with a modern knit for something closer to Upper East Side day school debutante than bespectacled cat lady.

The final touches were as important as ever. Throughout the month of October, I grew out my hair. Day of, I shaved a Mohawk and then stiffened it with a sugar-and-water concoction that I learned about from asking around the East Village. I then sprayed the Mohawk neon orange. A faux lip ring and some eyeliner capped it all off, the cherry on my punk sundae. Of course, the first thing I did the next morning, after about a gallon of water, was to head straight to the barber to remove the Mohawk and resume life as Professional Joe, with a respectable buzz cut.

*Get a load of these!*

{ RIGHT }

Customized Vans for my club kid look.

But one of my absolute favorite costumes might have been the year I went as Michael Alig, the iconic New York club kid famous for killing his sometime roommate, drug dealer Angel Melendez, in the mid-'90s. The year Alig was my muse, Macaulay Culkin was portraying him in the movie *Party Monster*. I'd met Alig during his club kid heyday in the early '90s, at the club Limelight, a deconsecrated Gothic church where he threw a weekly party called Disco 2000 and kids came to do ecstasy and dance.

I remember Michael vividly. He was part of the romance of why I wanted to live in NYC in the late '80s, early '90s. The city was so colorful back then, and club kids ruled the night scene. Even though I was too young to fully embrace the Studio 54 era, over-the-top club kids were my gen. I can still remember an episode of *Geraldo* where all the club kids made an appearance shortly before I moved from Toronto to New York City, and a VHS tape of that episode was one of the only things I brought with me. I played it endlessly until the tape wore out. Michael Alig, among others, was on that episode, and I can still remember every single thing he and the others wore and said.

Dressing up as Macaulay Culkin or as Michael Alig would allow me to wear colorful and ridiculous clothes—what was the club kid look, after all, if not one that made it seem as if you got dressed in the dark? Still, I craved a method to my fashion madness. I had read that fashion designer Richie Rich from the label Heatherette, a former club kid himself, would be doing all the costumes for Macaulay's character, so Richie was my very first call. Since I obviously wouldn't fit into any of wee Macaulay's set costumes, Richie offered to remake one for me in my size, in time for the holiday, as only a fellow Halloween obsessive would.

( ABOVE )

Fitting Polaroid for my club kid costume, Halloween 2003.

The end result was really just a T-shirt and jean shorts, but I made it anything but simple, including, but not limited to, a pair of eight-inch platform rave sneakers I had customized by the same cobbler all the real club kids used, some little old Polish guy in the East Village, and a Versace bomber jacket I conveniently borrowed from a photo shoot that day. Because I scheduled a photo shoot for Halloween, coincidentally or not, I had the genius creative team of makeup artist Dick Page and hairstylist Kevin Ryan on hand to do me up. And do me up they did. By the time I left the studio, I had a

Gisele Bündchen and me at Halloween. She's a sexy nurse (of course), and I'm a club kid. Jacket by Versace.

lopsided, bowl-cut wig glued on my head and makeup that's perhaps best described as Kabuki clown meets Dior. It was only 6 p.m., which meant there were at least four more hours before I'd even be getting in costume. Plus, I had to walk home.

Not that, it turned out, anyone noticed. In New York, where everyone is painfully aloof, you have to really be salacious to get attention, even if you're, like, Tom Cruise or Brad Pitt. Apparently, even tragic runway Kabuki clown didn't warrant me any second glances in this cold, hard town.

# I DON'T DO HAIR

**I** REMEMBER BEING SIXTEEN AND TALKING TO George, a much older friend of mine in Toronto, about wanting to move to New York to do something—what, I wasn't sure—with clothes and fashion and magazines. George was a hairdresser, and so when he told me, "You should be a stylist," I thought he was talking about cutting hair. "No disrespect," I told him. "I like what you do. But I don't think I'd be any good at cutting hair." When he told me that he meant a *wardrobe stylist*, I was confused. That's a job? To pick out clothes? To shop for other people? And they pay you? I didn't get it.

A few months later, George called to ask if I might be interested in styling a "test shoot" he was doing with a photographer, a makeup artist, and a model. This is something creative types often do (when they have the time) in order to experiment, help fill out their portfolios, or just have fun. I said yes right away, though I still had plenty of questions, including: What was it, exactly, I'd be doing again? "You can dress the model however you want," he told me.

Armed with that and little else, I went to all the local department stores, charged armfuls of clothes to my mother's credit card—looking, I'm sure, like a young drag queen getting ready for the show of his life—and then hauled the bags and bags of pretty dresses and coats and shoes and

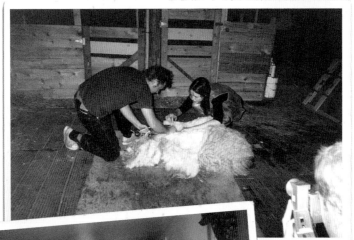

tights to a dirty warehouse in east Toronto. This would mark the beginning of my penchant for overpulling and overprepping for magazine shoots. I might bring ten racks of clothes and some fifty-five pairs of shoes for a one-girl story. The more stuff, the better, because I never know how I'll feel in the moment and the worst is being on some remote set and wishing I'd just packed that one busted skirt everyone despised. A skirt is never so perfect as when it's three thousand miles away. I am sure many other stylists will tell you the same thing.

During the daylong shoot in the Toronto warehouse, I kept all the sales tags attached, was super careful when getting the model dressed, and when the photographer asked me about pinning and taping things to fit the girl (who knew stylists did that?—because, let's face it, I had never done this before), I inwardly *freaked out*. This photographer wanted me to *pierce* these new clothes with a pin? And where exactly was I getting this pin? Yeah, suddenly, in my disorganization, dressing someone seemed a little less fun. Instead I found a piece of masking tape that had been used to tape a shopping bag shut and I carefully pulled that off and used it masterfully to make the shirt look more fitted. Looking back, I realize I MacGyvered my way into this career. When the shoot was done, I returned everything immediately to all the department stores, making absolutely no eye contact with the disapproving saleswomen but secretly feeling so satisfied. I don't even remember much of the in-between, including what the photos looked like, but I will never forget the intoxicating feeling of walking through the mall on a mission to make something of my very own. From that day on, I was a stylist.

* * *

IN THE MID-'90S, I WAS HIRED AS FASHION director of *W* magazine, my first really huge, now-I'm-on-my-own job. I'd been working there for all of what felt like five days when we were scheduled to shoot supermodel Claudia Schiffer for the October cover. I'm pretty sure no one there knew I had never actually done a cover shoot before, school extracurriculars aside. I'd come from *Allure,* where I was market editor. Definitely a real job, but it hadn't included

{ OPPOSITE TOP }

On set for *W,* model Tasha Tilberg and photographer Juergen Teller shearing a sheep.

{ OPPOSITE MIDDLE }

On set with *W,* bringing a few things with us to a photo shoot at a farm in Canada.

{ OPPOSITE BOTTOM }

On set with *W,* behind the scenes at Gisele's house, shooting with Michael Thompson.

much of my own styling. I had spent the better part of my days there assisting other stylists. Now, I was supposed to oversee and execute my own shoot. *Very* different from that day in the Toronto warehouse. For one thing, this time, I would have pins on me and the rest of my "prop kit," as we stylists call it. The contents include, always, a lint roller, binder clips, safety pins, Topstick (double-stick tape), a shoehorn, insoles, underwear, nipple patches, silk scarves (to put over the model's head, so her makeup doesn't get on her clothes when she changes), a hand steamer, and scissors.

Until this point, my solo work experience really consisted of what the industry calls "doing market." Market editors have nothing to do with marketing. Instead, they spend their days shopping, essentially—visiting showrooms, seeing what's out there, determining trends a magazine should cover, calling in clothes—but the only people they dress are themselves. In Europe, the person who holds this position is called the shopping editor, though no one actually *buys* anything. (Confusing, I know. But whoever said that fashion careers were conventional?) And while I'd been an assistant stylist at plenty of photo shoots before I'd gotten promoted to the market job, I'd worked mainly under the unimpeachable Polly Mellen, a woman who most definitely did not need anybody's help. Which meant I had plenty of experience in steaming clothing and running out for afternoon lattes. But could I dress someone for an actual publishable photograph? And a cover on top of that? Unclear.

Actually, that's wrong. I had done two photo shoots by myself while at *Allure*. My boss at the time, *Allure*'s editor in chief Linda Wells, had given me the opportunity to style two very different celebrities, before the era of celebrity magazine takeovers. They were both portraits, and they were both going to run at one page each. Easy enough—but not for a perfectionist kid, and not when you threw in my styling variables. The first pic would be with Roseanne Barr, who was at the height of her career with her sitcom and a movie, *Even Cowgirls Get the Blues*, that had just come out. On top of that, she had just made an appearance at the Isaac Mizrahi show (a hotly attended show during Fashion Week) with her new bestie Sandra Bernhard. And Sandra was BFFs with Madonna, who was the reigning queen, so that made Roseanne a queen-to-be by association. But of course, Roseanne was not a sample size and showing up with runway clothes would neither work nor make the best impression. I only had a few days to make it happen.

Not knowing what to do, I figured my only solution was to call Isaac's showroom. If she could sit front row at his show, surely they could muster up something to fit her? Isaac said that he didn't have the time to design and make something from scratch, but I got on the phone with his head PR person, Dawn, and we figured out that I could actually borrow a few things from the current season in her size. Most notably, a chiffon dressing gown

## "Why would a BIG TV STAR LISTEN TO SOME KID?"

with a fur collar! I loved that! A glamorous Roseanne was the perfect counterpart to her suburban sitcom self. Now I only had to convince her of my vision when I got to the shoot, but I worried: Why would a big TV star listen to some kid? I headed to LA, alone and sweating. And you know what? She didn't even need much convincing.

Roseanne *loved* the idea of being glamorous and sexy, and I remember leaving the shoot thinking, *Okay, this wasn't so bad. I can do this*. A few months later, I got my second break at the magazine for styling another actress, a recent Oscar winner. She was the opposite of Roseanne. She was sample size, sure, and young and conventionally pretty, with long blond hair and delicate features. All the physical challenges I had with Roseanne didn't exist, and I was shooting her in a studio in NYC besides, so if there was a problem, it would be easier to figure out. And, of course, I had hit it big with Roseanne. This one, I thought, should be a home run. I was a huge fan of her work—she had this dry comic delivery that I appreciated in a beautiful woman—and I was unbelievably excited to meet her.

Blondielocks—let's just call her that—turned out to be a total monster, no exaggeration. I was heartbroken, and panicked: I didn't know much, but I did know that a difficult subject is difficult to make look good. I'm not sure Blondielocks looked me in the eye even once—a feat considering we spent at least ten hours together and I changed her in and out of probably fourteen looks. She insisted on moving the lights around herself, thinking she knew more about "dimensionality" than the photographer, and was endlessly demanding and exact about how she looked. She liked *none* of the clothes I pulled for her and there were *tons* of them, so she basically liked nothing designed that season. The shoes weren't "her style" (because she doesn't wear heels or flats or boots?) and she "wasn't feeling the accessories."

This was my first taste of celebrity clothing rejection, and as a kid, on his second big assignment, I wanted to die. During the shoot, she bossed every-one around. "Are we sure that camera angle is the most flattering?" (Yes, this photographer shoots all of our covers. He knows what he's doing.) "That's not my best angle." (You're an Oscar winner. Every angle is a good angle.) "What exactly is this picture saying and conveying?" (That this is a miserable experience and we are working hard to mask that.) It was endless.

Then, after the issue was published, I had to block the entire episode from my memory. To this day, it ranks as my worst celebrity encounter ever. I wasn't sure I was made for this. I didn't think I could ever style celebrities again. Maybe Roseanne was the fluke and Blondielocks was the norm. Or maybe I just needed more experience. But either way, I still feel that pit in my stomach when I think of this shoot.

* * *

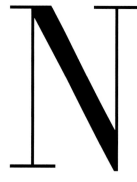OW, THOUGH, ALL THAT WAS BEHIND me. I was *W*'s fashion editor, an admittedly fancy job for a twenty-seven-year-old. I was hired for such a very important job because, well, I was relentless. And outgoing, literally. I went out every single night. A good friend of mine was an editor at *W* at the time, and he and I would attend every last fashion event, which is how I

{ ABOVE }

On set with *W*, getting model Nadja Auermann dressed in Thailand.

met Dennis Freedman, then the creative director of *W* and my future boss. I was such a crazy fashion person. I really would go to the opening of an envelope. But more, it was just amazing fun to go out and talk about nothing else but magazines and editors and photography and fashion, because I loved it. I was inspired by the British movement of *i-D* magazine and *The Face* and that newcomer named Kate Moss and all her pictures shot by Corinne Day and David Sims, and looking back now, people want to call it "grunge" or "heroin chic" but it was neither of those things. It was more like fashion documentary. A study of real life, all the auspices of that '80s supermodel glamour washed away and replaced by our version of "real." Jeans, T-shirts, and Converse sneakers were the new bandage dresses and gladiator heels. Big hair and saturated colorful pictures were slowly moving out for black-and-white portraits with very little makeup and awkward poses. Loving all this naturally made me very knowledgeable about those topics. Meanwhile, I had the stamina of a twenty-seven-year-old because I was a twenty-seven-year-old. These days, if I'm out at 10 p.m., I'm usually wishing I were home in bed instead. The young me would have died hearing this. I was convinced I was going to be super fun and social forever.

Because when you're in your midtwenties, you *know* that you will never change. Well, spoiler here, guys: You change.

For many years, most notably those times during my teen years in Toronto, I'd thought of *W* as a biweekly broadsheet in the style of the *New York Times*—oversized and folded but printed on beautiful glossy paper, and very high society. As a teenager, I would consistently open *W* and see the giant ads (Claude Montana, Byblos, etc.) unfold as a giant poster, which I would use to wallpaper my bedroom, floor to ceiling. So going to work there in my twenties had a completely different nostalgic quality.

"… when you're in your midtwenties, you *know* that you will never change. WELL, SPOILER HERE GUYS: YOU CHANGE."

Under Dennis, *W* had become a traditionally bound magazine but over-sized and big, and still aimed at the Park Avenue who's who but also the crazy fashion photography junkies like me. Almost overnight, people were starting to talk about it. And by "people" I mean those influential tastemak-ers in the fashion industry, aka the people who matter. I didn't realize as much at the time, but when I worked at *W*, it was a real moment for that magazine. I meet with designers today who cite spreads that appeared in mid-'90s *W* as their inspirations—spreads I had styled. Recently, I asked a very prominent young designer about what had inspired his latest collec-tion and he pulled out some photos of this all-American Gwyneth cover I'd styled, the one timed to the release of *Great Expectations*. It made me feel ancient—a fashion dinosaur, as I like to refer to myself—when I realized that I'd become a point of reference. But it also made me feel like I'd done something important. That was my first cover with Gwyneth, and despite the half dozen more I would style later on, this one I remember the most because it was my first with her.

Before I was hired, Dennis and the fashion director, Bridget Foley (who was—and still is—a top critic at *Women's Wear Daily* because she's the one who all the designers want to review their collections), asked that I put together a few concepts for fashion spreads as an edit test of sorts. I assembled an inspiration board, reminiscent of a sixth-grade poster board project, with pictures I'd collected from other magazines and the newspaper—whatever I could find on the latest collections—and xeroxes from books, along with Polaroids of runway looks I made from a slide collection in the office. That was our method in pre-Internet, pre-color-copier days. Slides of entire runway collections would arrive a few weeks after the show, we would sleeve them, alphabetize them in a filing cabinet, and when we had shoots, we would go through them on a light box and then make instant Polaroids of them. Requesting them from a designer required assistants and market editors to xerox the slides and write a short description of color and fabric so that there would be no miscommunication. Then we would messenger over the Polaroid requests and follow up with a discussion over the phone. This was what was considered speedy market work back in those days. If it took three days to get a look from a designer, we were on rocket speed.

So of course I would utilize that method when it came to doing my edit project for Dennis and Bridget. I came up with stories like the one I called "Urban Police," a sexy, military-inspired homage to such '90s staples as Helmut Lang suiting and Calvin Klein separates that represented the sort of uniform a confident city girl might wear. There were others, but I remember "Urban Police" because when I went in for my final interview, Bridget and Dennis made a point of telling me how much they liked it, and I almost cried with relief.

When I got the job and finally started, though, I was being asked to do it for real—no more poster board—with an actual supermodel with whom I'd grown up fairly obsessed. I mean, my first assignment was a *cover*. With *Claudia Schiffer*. *Okay*, I thought. *Sink or swim, I guess, is the motto*

# DRESS FOR YOUR FIRST DAY OF WORK

NEW JOBS ARE great, and also awful: Where's the bathroom? Who am I supposed to eat lunch with? Lunch is key; I could be sixty and starting a new job and still fret about who I'm going to eat lunch with. Or whether people might not like me or laugh at my jokes. Or what if I am terrible at this job and they realize hiring me was the absolute worst mistake in the history of hiring people?

While I actually think a bit of insecurity is a good thing and I hope never to lose it—not being too sure of yourself is a gift that keeps you on your toes—you should never have to worry about what you're wearing. To that end, I'm going to tell you the absolutely perfect, no-fail first-day-of-work essentials achievable at pretty much any price point.

**1. PENCIL SKIRT**

A pencil skirt in a dark color is timeless and almost universally flattering.

**2. A GROWN-UP BLOUSE**

Worn with or without a blazer, a chic blouse in a silk or similarly flowy fabric (skip the men's-style button-down unless it's very fitted) reads professional and feminine.

**3. HEELS**

While flats can be very polished, heels will always be more professional, so go for height—2.5 inches at least.

**4. ACCESSORIES**

Depending on your work environment, choose simple accessories—a pair of stud earrings, a few bangles—or have a little fun with a statement necklace. Since the rest of the outfit is conservative, you can safely take a few chances with your accessories.

*here*. Back as a fashion-loving teen in Toronto, I'd had a dream that I was the president of the Supermodels Fan Club, and in a totally non-stalker-y, noncreepy way, this was really that dream come true. I was going to have real collaborators, too: Sam McKnight on hair, Dick Page on makeup. Major people. Miles Aldridge took the pictures, and while he was also young, maybe only a few years older than I was, he already had this reputation for being very particular, with heady, important pop culture influences and photos that really did tell a thousand words. He was—is—very British; I think John Lennon was actually a family friend of his parents when he was growing up. Anyway, he was not the sort of guy who was going to impress easily.

The shoot with Claudia was at night and needed to be done in a few hours. *W* was still relatively new so we were only granted a few hours, at the end of the day, whereas a bigger magazine might have been given a whole day to shoot. This was 1995, and Claudia was a megastar, very busy, but a pro. We wouldn't have much time per shot, but we didn't necessarily need it, either. That was one of the major upsides of the days when models ruled magazine covers. It was incredibly efficient. You didn't need to waste time teaching them how to pose for the camera or coaxing them out of self-consciousness the way you often need to do with actresses. For the most part, models also checked their egos at the door. They were personalities, and celebrities in their own right, but they were also aware that they made their living as vehicles for clothes.

I tried to project the sense that I knew what I was doing. Inside, though, I was quietly but completely freaking out. I wanted readers to like the end result, and for my new bosses to as well, but what I really wanted was for everyone in the fashion industry to like the work, too. As much as fashion people create things for themselves, they're also creating them for one another, for their competitors and colleagues. It's not a bad thing; I think it's what helps keep us fresh. And I was a kid who'd just left another job to do this. I needed to make an impression, to myself but also to the industry.

Maybe you're still wondering what, exactly, a stylist does. Essentially, an editorial or commercial stylist's job is to create a story's look and feeling. The stylist will choose the clothes and dress the subject on set (which, of course, requires getting all the clothes to the shoot; in my case, this may be many trunks' worth—to be a stylist is to resign yourself to a life of endless baggage). At *Elle*, I styled shoots myself and also worked as creative director. In that case, I'd work with individual stylists to come up with and execute their concepts, but I'd also have control over the photographer, the hairstylist, and the makeup artist.

It's a full-on team effort, though. I don't need the clothes to be center stage; *I* don't need to be center stage. When everybody who is part of the puzzle wants to be the person who makes the statement, then it all just falls

# "…TWO PARTS TO FOUR…

two should be statements and two should step back."

apart. Something has to give. I do a simple math equation I call "two parts to four." So, say, if there's hair, makeup, clothes, and photography, two should be statements and two should step back. If everyone is ringing the bell at ten, there's nothing but a lot of noise. I'm always the first one to check my ego at the door. There's just no time for that.

Aesthetically, when I pull clothing, I tend to like to mix high and low; I like contrasts, but that wasn't the case back then. Sometimes we need to be sure to include certain brands, for business reasons; almost always, you want to incorporate some trend or overarching theme. Since magazines work many months ahead, we'll pull samples directly from showrooms instead of stores. This can be a political process in instances where multiple magazines might be interested in shooting the same designer look at the

# ON LEARNING
# TO LET GO

I FIGURED OUT PRETTY quickly—literally almost overnight—that being a great stylist, especially an editorial stylist, is not about dressing people in the things that appeal to you personally. There are many stylists working today who only work with clothing they'd wear themselves. I question that philosophy, and not just because I'm not a woman but because I think you have to be nimble as a stylist. You have to be able to transform, not just look good for brunch. I realized this early on by studying some great stylists whose work I admired (of course Polly Mellen and Lori Goldstein are included there): While they have their visually stylized signatures, they can also step out of them and amaze. That was always my goal. Of course, when I style guys—I won't lie here—I often dress them the way that I dress or would want to dress. Yeah, a personal double standard, I guess. While it's important to have an aesthetic, and an angle, a stylist's job is to convey an idea and tell a story. I've learned not to get too attached to any one look. Whenever I've tried to force a piece into a story, that's inevitably the photo that we end up cutting.

This is a lesson I have found applies to many other aspects of life beyond fashion styling: Don't take it—no matter what "it" is—personally. Often, what you want and what works are two different things.

# DEFINE YOUR PERSONAL STYLE

I DO A LOT of advising people not to follow trends but to dress according to what works best for their shape and their lives. But what if you're not sure what that means? Easily one of the questions I get asked most often is: "I know I'm supposed to dress to fit my personal style, but how do I know what my personal style is?"

1. First thing to know: You don't have to have one personal style, and you needn't stick to it for life, either. A good first step is to look for a style icon, someone whose fashion sense you admire (or who you just think looks great all the time). My personal style icon is Jessica Biel. I think she looks perfect—she never tries too hard and knows what works for her for both casual and dressy occasions. Two others who get cited often are Sienna Miller and Kate Bosworth. Yours might be a combination of a few different people.

2. Once you've identified a few icons, pick a few words to describe them and their look. Are they classic? Modern? Edgy? Preppy? Choosing a few fitting words will help you clarify and define your look.

3. Next, choose a signature piece. For me, it's always the shoes—a great pair of high-tops, usually, and each season I have two or three pairs of sneakers that I wear to death. An easy way to establish a signature style is to pick one item that remains a constant: your grandfather's big gold watch; an amazing coat; or, like me, your preferred style of shoes. Rely on staples and what makes you happy. Maybe you love stripes and own a closet full of them.

4. Mistakes happen when you try too hard to emulate someone else, so even though you might look to a few icons for inspiration, you should always aim to wear whatever makes you feel like the best version of yourself. Straying too far outside of your comfort zone because you think something is "cool" will only look unnatural and awkward. Same thing goes when putting something on that just doesn't work for your body type. Some women can't wear crop tops or skinny jeans. Forcing the matter won't make you look stylish; it'll just make you look uncomfortable.

5. When an outfit works, write it down (or snap a photo). Figure out what made it such a success and refer to it often as inspiration.

# NEVER GO OUT
# OF STYLE

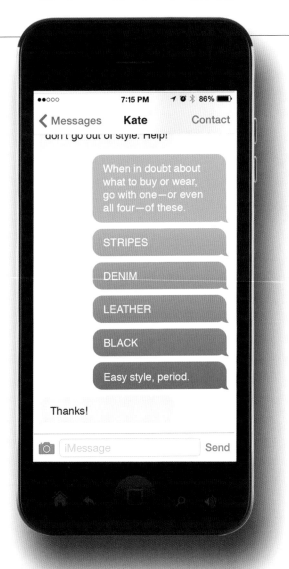

...don't go out of style. Help!

When in doubt about what to buy or wear, go with one—or even all four—of these.

STRIPES

DENIM

LEATHER

BLACK

Easy style, period.

Thanks!

same time, or perhaps a sample might be off at a shoot in Europe on the date you're interested in photographing it. If you think I have a busy travel schedule, you should see the mileage logged by the season's must-have Gucci look. Often, elite magazines, like ours, will request an exclusive on an item, which means we get to shoot it before any of our competitors.

The concept for Claudia's shoot was sporty fall essentials, and the image that made the cover was one of the supermodel in a simple, pale-green-and-white sheath by Dolce & Gabbana. The dress wasn't spectacular, but it's a cover. Believe it or not, sometimes, even on a fashion magazine, I wanted the covers to be about the person and not just the outfit. Of course there are exceptions, always, but if you are going to put Claudia Schiffer or, say, Jennifer Lopez on the cover, then you sure as hell should make it about them. At least that's my theory, and I think that's why I've always worked so well with celebrity covers.

When the cover came out, it was the first time I'd seen my name on an actual story, the first time I had something I could show my parents that said, "This is what I do. I made this." Other people loved it, too. I got great feedback. And that was incredibly, incredibly affirming.

People always say that the key to happiness is not caring what others think. But come on. The reality is, you always want validation and respect from your peers for the work that you do, no matter what industry you work in. And that's not unique to fashion. That's just life.

My first really major—big, big, big (where you know this is for real)—story for *W* was a '70s-inspired, Kate Moss–goes-to–Studio 54 (in Halston!) spread. It was my first important collaboration with photographer Michael Thompson, who became my partner in crime during the ten years I spent at *W* and who is still a very good friend. We got François Nars, the go-to guy for all things risk-taking and glam, to do the makeup. Oribe—a Cuban-born hair god who became one of the first "celebrity hairstylists," highly sought-after by those in publishing and in Hollywood—did the hair, so the team was already beyond stellar. We wanted it to be monumental, great. Would I want people to talk about it? Sure, but that was never an intention or agenda going into anything I did, at least not back then. The viralness of creating a story would come later, in my foray into celebrity covers.

The thing about Kate: She was smaller than the supermodels of the era before her, and so you often had to fit the sample size clothes to her using pins and clamps and tape and whatever else you could pull out of your bag of stylist's tricks. (Though this was common with anyone on every shoot. The perfect fit was always key.) I became a master pinner; I could change the shape of anything with safety pins, binder clamps, straight pins. For this shoot, every pair of pants I put on Kate was pinned meticulously down the back and hemmed with double-sided tape. The bodysuit was pulled in. I might as well have been sewing the clothes right on her.

Nowadays, the availability of retouching makes life so much less stressful. Clothes that fit are still an absolute must. But I can throw a clamp on the back of a coat, and if it shows up in a frame or two, I can wipe it out during the postproduction phase. Life without Photoshop was very limiting and very time-consuming. There were days I'd spend twenty minutes pinning an entire pant leg, only to have the photographer decide to shoot from a different angle. Then I'd have to unpin everything, resteam the pant to take out the creases, and repin on the other side. I don't miss any of that.

That said, you do have to learn to check yourself since it's easy to get a little carried away in "post," as we call it, especially when you want a picture to look perfect. This is how oddly proportioned waist-to-hip ratios happen or, say, Cindy Crawford's belly button goes missing. Photoshop is like plastic surgery. There are moments when it can absolutely go too far, and I think in recent years it's been no secret that publications have taken way too many liberties with it. Do I love Photoshop? Sure, who doesn't, especially when it's a picture of yourself, but the best work is where you don't see the work at all. There are certain aspects of the work we do now

# RETOUCH YOURSELF

E VEN IF YOU'RE not Avedon, you can still retouch your own pictures. Here are some popular apps for retouching your own photos—brighter, sharper, thinner, whatever you want, all in a quick download. Professional graphic designer not required.

that are far more "real" than they were twenty years ago. Photographer Richard Avedon was one of my earliest teachers of stylists' tricks, like stringing up a scarf with fishing wire to create the illusion of wind to create that perfect picture. Those days are long behind us. That kind of precise technical detail rarely exists anymore on photo shoots. So while I miss some of the imperfection that can give a picture personality, I also know that even back then fashion photos were manipulated to serve a purpose and fulfill a vision. In that sense, nothing's changed, technology or no.

Sometime after the Kate Moss story was published, I came home to a message on my home answering machine (yes, ha-ha, there was such a thing). "Um, hi," said a woman's voice, in a thick accent, "I don't know if I've got the right number, this is what the 4-1-1 operator told me, but I'm looking for a Joe Zee." She'd been reading the latest *W*, she said, and, oh my God, she *loved* what I had done with Kate Moss's hair. "And I looked and it said 'styled by Joe Zee,' and so I had to call because I'm getting married next weekend and I said to my fiancé, Ken, I *must* get this hairstylist to do my hair the same way he did that model's. I can't believe I found you. I just hope you're free next weekend. So call me back, please. I'll pay you whatever you want."

I thought about it. But in the end, I spared her whatever tragic '70s beehive I'd have whipped together all in the name of a good story to tell. In the end, I just saved the message for a good year, and replayed it over and over again to whoever came over, or when I needed a pick-me-up smile. At least I wasn't the only one who had originally thought a stylist only did hair. I think if I still had that message today it would be my ringtone.

# WHY I LOVE THE '90S

## (BECAUSE I LIVED IT)

ONCE, FOR A shoot with Juergen Teller (you know him from those muted Marc Jacobs ads starring various celebrities in compromising positions), we went to supermodel Stephanie Seymour's house in Connecticut. She'd married billionaire media mogul Peter Brant a few years earlier, and had invited us to her Greenwich estate to photograph her among her various collections: vintage clothing, art, animal-skin rugs. For three days, we shot all over her house. I had never seen so much wealth. Her basement, the kids' playroom, was the size of an elementary school and filled with enough stuff to entertain a school's worth of kids, too.

But what was most remarkable, and perhaps unheard of today, was the work vibe. We sat around and took pictures. We sat around and didn't take pictures. The resulting story was something like twenty-six pages long. It was work, but it was also fun, and the photos conveyed that sense in a way that photos just don't—just can't—today.

When I was coming up in the business, people used to tell me all the time about the fun they had in the '80s. But the '90s were pretty amazing, too. I haven't done a three-day shoot in I don't know how long. These days, you're in and you're out in one. Budgets are tighter, maybe. There's that. But more, I think it's that we just live in a faster world, where we push ourselves (and other people push us) for more, more, more, faster, faster.

{ ABOVE } In 1990 I moved to New York City and *Beverly Hills, 90210* came on the air. In my fanatic moments, I saved money and got the Dylan doll, which still to this day has moved everywhere with me and remains in the box.

# FASHION WEEK:

## A LOVE/HATE STORY

**HERE'S NO OTHER INDUSTRY RITUAL** that has remained as enduringly fashionable as Fashion Week. It's been around in some form or another for something like seventy years. I remember one of my mentors/bosses at *Women's Wear Daily* telling me about how she would travel to the Paris shows on the *QE2* each season. Back then, in the early '60s, fashion shows were intimate salon affairs narrated by the designer with nary a celebrity or paparazzo in sight. Buyers and editors sat in the front row, and the clothes were the stars. It's so different today. That front row has changed. A lot. Where there used to be the most prominent, and seasoned, fashion editors and editors in chief there to plan their next few months of coverage, there are now twenty-something (or younger) fashion bloggers, pop divas, and reality stars, many of whom are there for no other reason than to be seen.

What's not so different: the endless Fashion Week bitching. (Bitching is the preferred form of cardio among fashion people, followed closely by SoulCycle.) Let me explain: I know Fashion Week *sounds* very glamorous, and in many ways it is—lots of parties with an endless supply of free champagne and tiny (TINY) hors d'oeuvres like vegan pigs-in-blankets and gluten-free mini-quiches and oil-free, dairy-free, nut-free kale buckwheat

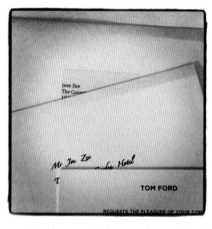

cupcakes, plus celebrities, models, fabulous outfits, and goodie bags overflowing with serums and sprays, accessories, books, protein bars, gum, CDs, branded water bottles, gift cards, and anything else a person, usually a size-2 woman, might find appealing. I've gotten more bunion-prevention products than my non–high heel wearing feet would know what to do with.

But what many people don't realize is that Fashion Week is really Fashion Month—because after New York you've also got London, Milan, and Paris, which means an entire month straight of being on call, being on planes, and generally being on the go. One year, after Fashion Month, I tallied up how much unnecessary swag I'd received. It all ended up on the magazine's giveaway table, eliciting a feeding frenzy among the junior assistants pawing over what was new this time. All magazines have a giveaway table, where editors put items sent or given to them that they don't need or want, though you're more likely to find some bottles of drugstore shampoo or unedited versions of anticipated novels than the latest handbag. Still, when something is free, you'd be surprised how enticing that callus remover or those fishnet socks suddenly look.

"Swag feeding time" was fairly consistent: You knew to check that giveaway table, generally stationed on top of a filing cabinet somewhere near the men's bathroom, a good three times a year—after each show season and around the holidays. Pickings were first come, first served, and you never put anything there you didn't want to get snapped up within minutes, including your Starbucks. I'll never forget the time some poor unsuspecting intern set some merchandise on the counter for an editor to run through before a shoot, only to have it all picked through like a midday carcass when she stepped away to the bathroom. She learned a pricey lesson that day.

Though you might consider Fashion Week one of the more exciting fashion job perks, it is, but it's also a lot of work. Hold on, before you think I'm ungrateful: I love Fashion Week. I love the energy, I love the creativity, I love the community. But after all these years, it can take a toll. I'm very aware that going to glamorous cities, flying business class, and staying in five-star hotels is nothing to bitch about, and I'm not, but after four weeks, I start to become homesick and long for something familiar and a conversation that doesn't exist in my fashion bubble. In fact (please don't tell anyone), there were times when after more than a month on the road traveling, doing nothing but rushing from

# "FASHION WEEK IS REALLY FASHION MONTH

—because after New York you've also got London, Milan, and Paris . . ."

fashion show to fashion show, I just hit the wall with fashion overload. One afternoon in Paris, I actually skipped a fashion show, snuck away, sat in a movie theater on the Champs-Élysées, and watched an American action flick, something mindless. It was the best two hours of my life. After that much creative stimulation, I just needed something to help activate my reset button, you know?

I'm sure outsiders see Fashion Week as a weeklong party, what with all the celebrity inundation and paparazzi photo ops and social media overload. But while Fashion Week can be a lot of fun, and very festive, attending shows is still

{ LEFT }

Carpooling to the Estée Lauder party at the Guggenheim with my muse Hilary Rhoda, Keith Pollack, and Jeff Dickhaus during New York Fashion Week.

work. Twice a year, at least—because that's not even counting resort, pre-fall, couture, and men's fashion week—we editors all abandon our office duties and personal lives to spend entire days on end at shows, presentations, and parties. Yes, parties! Parties can be work, especially if not going would offend someone, make your job more difficult, or give someone else (say, your competitor) the edge. If I RSVP'd to something important but just cannot make it because I suddenly came down with the flu or my dog suddenly came down with the flu or I got sideswiped by a cab en route (this has happened), I always send flowers and an apology note the next day. This goes triple for any party at which the guest list is "exclusive" or "elite." Better safe than snub.

# "SO MUCH OF FASHION IS ART."

The fashion shows and Fashion Week, in particular, have always served a purpose. Traditionally, boutique and department store buyers have used runway shows and designer presentations to think about what they may want to purchase for the upcoming season. Editors use them to cull trends and plan magazine stories. Buyers, meanwhile, will have already bought most of what they need from that particular designer *before* the show (from collections they see ahead of time at an event called the Commercial Collection) and the runway just serves as branding. Big department stores will buy a small portion from the runway, but most of the time, their money has already been spent. So the runway has become our theater. The spectacle, the drama, the theatrics of why we love fashion.

That's not to say shows are irrelevant—not at all. They're just now more about the literal *show* of it all than about selling clothes. For lovers of fashion or those who've chosen to make their living in fashion (sometimes the same people, though not always), it's like the difference between watching a live play and watching a television show on your laptop while sitting on your couch, eating a bowl of cereal. Fashion is an art form and the runway is one of its many stages. Watching models parade down the catwalk in gorgeous clothes can be a thing of great beauty. Some of the runway clothes don't actually even make it into production. They're there just for the drama and the spirit of the collection.

People—people who aren't fashion people, anyway—often ask me whether I think "real women" really can, or even want to, wear those looks that the admittedly freakishly tall, reed-thin models parade down the runways. I think that yes, for the most part, they do, but I think it's also important to remember that so much of fashion is art. Sure, we want most of it to be wearable—that *is* how clothes work—but some looks are more inspirational, or entirely for fun. Is every single look that you see going to be accessible and wearable? No, because that's the fantasy of fashion. The great thing about seeing a designer's interpretation on a runway and in seeing an editor's point of view of it in a magazine is that it allows the reader to take from it what works for them. In the end, though, what you can pull off is ultimately up to what you decide you can pull off. It's a matter of confidence and what you, personally, feel comfortable wearing outside of the house. For some people, that's harem pants, a crop top, and six-inch platform open-toed booties. For others, well, it's maybe something else.

\* \* \*

IT WAS THE EARLY '90S, AND I HAD MOVED TO New York City from Toronto for my fall semester at FIT right at the beginning, it so happened, of Fashion Week. Of course, I was just a student; I was invited to nothing. Fashion Week was something I had romanticized in my head as a Canadian teenager, so being in the same city but not being able to enter was more than I could bear. I didn't care, though. I was determined to work my way in somehow. That's when I snuck into my very first show.

I decided that I would be, for the night, an Extremely Important boutique owner, the sort who can make or break designers with a single buy. I had a legitimate business card to prove it (someone else's, of course), dug out of the bottom of my Filofax. It helped that the boutique owner was someone in Toronto, so people were fuzzy on what that person really looked like. I'm not sure if he was Asian. Or even a guy. Pretty sure on at least the second count, but it was a long time ago.

I spent the entire day planning what I'd wear, and eventually landed on a professional suit, but a *fashion* suit, of course. I had found a Jean Paul Gaultier women's blazer on sale in a discount store from one of his earlier collections: peak lapel and double-breasted, with a pinstripe illusion and the armpits cut out. *Perfect!* I thought. *Fashion—and it fits!* It was respectable, showed I had taste (and designer duds), and had the bonus of being that insider secret handshake that only a true fashion person would know. When I strolled up to the door, there would be that slight tilt of the head and a nod, to signify, yes, he's okay, he's wearing a signature Gaultier. I knew enough to know that no legitimate store-owning professional would show up to a fashion show wearing eight-inch platform rave sneakers, or crazy spiked hair, or all leather. The show was in SoHo, which back then in the early '90s was the cool artsy area of New York. I remember walking up to the building from the subway and seeing it swarmed with clusters of people outside and the requisite clipboard girl diligently guarding the door. *That girl in the minidress is the gatekeeper*, I said to myself, *and I need to get past her. She holds the key for me tonight.*

I took a deep breath, jaywalked across Broadway, and pushed through the crowd, hoping it would part like the Red Sea (it didn't). Once I got to the front, I thrust the business card at the girl and just said, "I'm on the list." In a flash, she grabbed my wrist and very firmly said, "Hang on. I need to check." Sweat was building up under my outfit, and for the first time in my life I was sweating right through my armpit-less lady's blazer. That's when she said, "Okay. You're fine."

OMG. I was in.

# CRASH A FASHION PARTY

IF, IN FACT, you're not looking for a good way out of a fashion party but a good way in, try this plan of attack. Just don't use my name, okay?

### ✓ USE SOCIAL MEDIA.

If you want to be a worldly, cultured person, you should be reading the *New York Times*. But if your goal is to catch a Miley Cyrus sighting, skip the Gray Lady and make social media your main news source. Good feeds to check out are the official Twitter of Mercedes Benz New York Fashion Week (@MBFashionWeek) and those of nightlife know-it-alls like @GuestofaGuest, and, of course, me (@mrjoezee—but much shame on you if you're not following me already). This is how you'll find out what's happening when and where and who's supposed to be there. Pro tip: Designers' parties are always held on the same night as their runway shows.

### ✓ DRESS STRATEGICALLY.

Obvious, right? But this doesn't mean put on your craziest "fashion" outfit. Put on whatever makes you look most fabulous and, more important, sane. Fashion is full of crazy people, but you have to earn the ability to be crazy *and* a VIP. So your job is to look like you belong there without looking like you came from a flash mob at a sample sale. So find something that makes you feel comfortable, confident, and chic, and top it all off with a cool pair of sunglasses. Maybe "comfortable, confident, and chic" is your sequin leisure suit. But it probably isn't. Likely, it's something way less shiny. Way.

### ✗ DON'T BE AN ENTITLED ASS.

Note from your mom, and from me: Once you reach the head of the line, be polite. Please. The girl working the door is not in a good mood, and she doesn't want your shit. Play it like you have every right to be there, but be gracious about it. Give her your name and then give it again (something about saying it twice will give you an air of confidence). Insist you're on the list, but be calm and understanding when she can't find it since, of course, she won't. The most entitled jerks are the ones who don't actually belong at the party. Oh, and another thing Mom and I agree on: Do your homework. Find out of the name of the PR person in charge of the event in advance, and have her number in your phone. Or, better, assign her name to a friend's number and have that friend text you with the following: "You're in, doll! Just tell them I said so. xox."

### ✓ GO IN THE OUT DOOR.

If all else fails, there's always a second entrance. Find it.

# FASHION WEEK CRIB SHEET

**P**ERSONAL PICKS—AT HOME and abroad—from some of my favorite fashion insiders.

**LORI GOLDSTEIN:**

"For shopping in Paris, Printemps and Le Bon Marché both have great overall viewing of new and upcoming designers. L'Eclaireur is a favorite, too! Each shop is so unique, truly the best edit in Paris. I love the delicious buckwheat crepes at Breizh Café in the Marais. A warning: It's closed on Monday and Tuesday. For hotels, I love to stay at the Le Bristol Paris. It's elegant perfection with great room service and the best mechanical pencils!"

**EVA CHEN:**

"Ladurée may get the lion share of fashion buzz—who wouldn't love their collaborations with artists like Will Cotton and pop culture mainstays like Hello Kitty!—but when in Paris, I actually prefer the macarons from Pierre Hermé. They have a location just off Rue Saint-Honoré and I can't pass by without a chocolate macaron. The boutique Scarlett is an under-the-radar cornucopia of vintage Chanel and Yves Saint Laurent. I love L'Avenue, the Cheers of Paris, a lovely, luxurious bistro where you can't stop in without seeing at least a few fashionable friends. I find the best Japanese noodles in Paris at Kunitoraya. It's the perfect food for when I'm homesick for NYC's ramen bars."

**ASHLEY MADEKWE:**

"When in London, stay at Hazlitt's. It's right in the heart of Soho but tucked away and private. It only has thirty rooms so you can get away from the Fashion Week crowds. Go for tea and cakes at Maison Bertaux on Greek Street in Soho. It's London's oldest (and best!) patisserie. Opened in 1871 and still serving the yummiest cakes. Dover Street Market is one of my top shopping spots. It always has the best bits from all my favorite designers."

**COCO ROCHA:**

"Corso Como in Milan is a great one-two punch. You can sit and eat and then peruse the art gallery, clothing shop, and bookstore, all while under one very fashionably chic roof. The Magna Pars in Milan is a great place to stay. It's like your own apartment with modern finishes and superior service and dining. Trussardi

Café is a really beautiful restaurant, with so much greenery that you feel like you're out in the wild. In Paris, one of my favorite spots for a group dinner is the private room at Chez Julien. It's a restaurant within a restaurant and a chance to have a moment with your friends and still have the superior cuisine and service of the Costes group. I love to stay at the Westin when I'm in Paris, for the priceless view it offers over the Louvre gardens and the Eiffel Tower. That view always brings a smile to my face, and the manager is always so kind to give me and my husband the most beautiful suite whenever we stay there."

{ ABOVE } Coco Rocha and me at a fashion event I had just hosted.
Hours before, I had had a root canal.

That was the Spring '93 Marc Jacobs for Perry Ellis show, which eventually became legendary for announcing the glamorization of grunge. Of course I didn't know it at the time, but it was a show that would literally go down in history. Now, each time someone brings it up, I can say I was there. I didn't have a seat so I stood, crowded into a corner against a pillar the whole time—but it was thrilling: Big-name models of the day like Christy Turlington and Claudia Schiffer starred in a romantic, punky show featuring crocheted vests, Doc Martens, slouchy knit caps, and lots of flannel, reinterpreted in silk, of course. It was revolutionary.

But fashion brands don't always appreciate revolutionary, especially when the business types have a say, which they did. The collection was critically beloved—Marc won a CFDA award for it—but Perry Ellis fired him not long after. Things turned out pretty okay for him, though, I'd say.

Fashion shows are also most definitely about commerce: the bottom line. As bloggers have risen to power among the fashion elite, designers—many of whom are after the youth audience, dubbed the millennials—cater ever more to them, putting them in the front-row seats formerly reserved for longtime print editors with major credentials. And while Man Repeller hasn't exactly replaced Anna Wintour in the front row, she's certainly part of an important new guard, given that an Instagram of her favorite runway look will reach hundreds of thousands of followers in, well, an instant. (Meanwhile, some things don't change and shows really do wait to start until Anna has arrived and settled into her seat, at which point the lights seem to dim almost immediately.)

But the undeniable primary focus of runway shows is, these days, personal branding. Fashion Week has become a see-and-be-seen sort of event. Not too long ago, the most influential designers—Ralph Lauren, Marc Jacobs—might invite a celebrity pal or two, someone very special to the designer or the brand, to attend the show. Nowadays, though, legitimate fashion editors are sharing the front row with Justin Bieber and the cast of *Mob Wives*. Celebrities have become staples at designer shows of all calibers. For newer or struggling designers, a celebrity presence can generate important, crucial attention and cachet. If you're an emerging designer, Fashion Week can make you, or it can leave you broke. A well-done show can help raise a brand's profile, create buzz, or project a certain image, which is one reason designers, or their backers, are willing to spend upward of $250,000 to produce what amounts to a ten-minute presentation.

The celebrity-designer Fashion Week love fest is entirely mutual. After all, most stars looove a stage. Celebrities (especially CW stars and just-signed female rappers) attend shows to be seen, to show support for a designer they admire, or because they get paid to be there by the designer or the show producer either as part of a contractual obligation or in exchange for a one-off appearance fee. Yep, another fun thing celebs get paid to do: look at models in pretty clothes. An actress can get paid anywhere from $50,000 (I'm thinking style stars and TV stars) to $250,000 (Oscar winners here) to attend a show, and that's not including first-class airfare, hotels, hair and makeup teams, free clothes, and per diem spending money and expenses for her and her entourage. It's always eyebrow raising when I bring this up, but designers aren't stupid people. They would not be laying out this type of cash if they weren't getting a return on their investment, so suffice it to say that a pic of an Oscar winner sitting at your show will circulate worldwide and garner more publicity for that one designer than any other way. It can literally turn that designer into a household name. And for that celebrity, they get a fun, free vacation where they are only inconvenienced for that hour of the day. Win-win.

This has given rise to celebrity booking as a career: people who make a living securing celebrity presence at events. These people, as you might suspect, are in very high demand. Magazines also have celebrity bookers, often on staff and almost always born master negotiators. My friend Jen has been booking *Elle*'s celebrity covers for nearly twenty years and my other friend Andrea has been booking celebrities for *Details* and *Wall Street Journal Magazine*, and after witnessing some of the most cutthroat negotiations they have had to undergo all in the name of granting the magazine the privilege to put an in-demand movie star on the cover, I feel confident that they would be overqualified to negotiate peace in the White House.

# BELLES OF THE FUR BALL

SOME OF MY favorite fashion personalities are furry and four legged. I'm talking about pets! Pets have firmly established themselves on Instagram as certified celebrities. Whenever I share photos of my Chihuahuas, Porkchop and Cornelius, on Instagram, people go crazy (but I'm biased, and I don't care). Of course they do. Those two are totally adorable (follow them at instagram.com/porkchopadventures).

If you think I'm silly for creating social media accounts for my animals, I hope you know I'm hardly alone. Here are some of my (and Porkchop's) favorites.

### CHOUPETTE LAGERFELD
KARL'S SIAMESE CAT
Models for Shu Uemura, no kidding.
instagram.com/choupettesdiary

### CECIL DELEVINGNE
CARA'S BUNNY
Has his own nanny, who probably makes
more money than I do.
instagram.com/cecildelevingne

### NEVILLE JACOBS
MARC JACOBS'S BULL TERRIER
Looks amazing in a suit!
instagram.com/nevillejacobs

### TANK AND BAMBI
NICOLA FORMICHETTI'S
POMERANIANS
These two look better with a buzz cut.
instagram.com/tanknbambi

### BERT
LARA STONE'S BORDER TERRIER
Loves cheese.
instagram.com/lara_stone

### BLU AND LUPO
ROBERTO CAVALLI'S PARROT
AND GERMAN SHEPHERD
Just two of an entire zoo of animals
owned by one of fashion's most
outrageous designers.
instagram.com/rc_lupo

# THE CATTY-WALK

**F COURSE, EDITORS AND BUYERS** want prominent positions at shows, because where you sit says everything about your standing in the industry. It's the unofficial status quo.

Where you sit says everything about you. At least in my world.

I was a fashion assistant at *Allure* when I received my first very own invitation, for a Todd Oldham show (row 7, not terrible, but not good, either). To this day, I can remember the weight of that invitation in my hand (as I was the one in charge of opening and distributing the mail). I'd been to a few shows before, but always with another, more senior editor's discarded invite, so getting one actually addressed to me, with my name spelled right and everything, was beyond thrilling. I remember pulling the envelope out of the mail cart the Condé Nast mail guy had dropped off. *For me?* I thought, looking around and quickly stuffing it in my pocket so that I could run off and rip it open in private.

But the *real* moment when I knew I'd really, truly made it came the day I called—yes, on the *telephone*—to RSVP to a show for Jeanette Kastenberg, a designer who was big in the '90s with her spandex, marabou feathers, and tight jeans, and was given my seat assignment by some overworked assistant who obviously had no idea what a pivotal career moment this would be for me, fodder for my future memoirs: "One A," she said, lamely. "Don't forget to write it down." Then *click*. I'd made it to the front row, baby!

This is what you need to know about the front row: It's a big damn deal. Fashion people might pretend that it isn't—that seating is all about currying favors or repaying grudges and they're "above all that" and "besides, it's the clothes that matter and those look just the same from back in row 3 as they do in row 1" and "it's easier to avoid all those annoying crowds in standing room only so I prefer it" (lies, all)—but it is. It's a big deal. This is why those same fashion people love to do what they can to secure a better seat. "I need to see the details/accessories/makeup," they tell whoever it is tasked with seat assignments, or "I can't guarantee we'll be able to cover if I can't get any closer." It's true that we fashion editors and stylists could all do our jobs just the same if we were sitting in row 3. The real reason everyone wants to sit up front is less about the work than about what your seat says about you. If you show up in the front row and people don't already know who you are, believe me, they will by the time

## "This is what you need to know about the front row: IT'S A BIG DAMN DEAL."

you leave that seat. And if you're a Someone who used to be in the front row but is now a few back, well, you might just be on your way out. Consider that a warning.

*Me-ow*, right? So you can see why Fashion Week isn't just a happy, carefree time of celebrating clothes and swilling champagne cocktails with your colleagues. But my biggest beef with Fashion Week is that it's just endless, and every year even more so. Last count I think there were something like 350 shows over nine days. Less than a third of those shows these days actually take place in the organized tents, instead being held at galleries, warehouses, or studios around the city, which means you spend most of your day either in or trying to hail a taxi. And because you can't be seen as playing favorites, there's pressure to get to as many as you can. I can't show up at Michael Kors's show but then skip Ralph's. And I also want to see the new rising stars. I want to see everything. That was something I learned working for Polly Mellen. She was relentless when it came to covering new design

# SPOT A FASHION EDITOR

Y OU'D THINK FASHION editors would be the masters of sartorial experi-
mentation, given that their job is dressing other people and that they're constantly exposed to what's new. But most fashion editors actually subscribe to
uniform dressing because (a) they know what works for them, because that's their
job, and (b) they spend their entire day dressing other people, so when it comes to
themselves, it's easier to just wear a go-to look. With a few exceptions (hello, Anna
Dello Russo), fashion editors tend to be the most understated dressers in the row, or
the room. In the last few years, certain street style bloggers have gotten all gussied
up in "take my picture" outfits. Don't get me wrong: Those fashion bloggers look
amazing, but it's just a different attitude toward personal style.

My former boss at *Elle*, Robbie, one of the most stylish women in the world, had a
definite uniform. It was black, it was sleek, and it was Prada. And most fashion editors
are the same. Telltale pieces of flair might include a pair of statement earrings or a
few chunky rings, some chic sunglasses, and, of course, an amazing bag, but beyond
that, their outfits, their style, and perhaps especially their haircut don't vary too much
from day to day or even year to year.

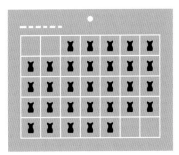
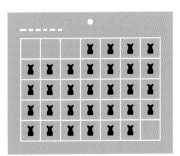
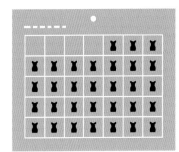

talent. There wasn't anyone she was above seeing, and she would squeal with delight every time something fantastic came out. She didn't live by label alone. If she liked it, she *liked* it, and the whole office—and industry—knew about it. I was there with Polly when she championed new designers like Helmut Lang, Alexander McQueen, and Martin Margiela at their first shows. She always knew the potential in people, sometimes even before they knew it themselves. Maybe myself included.

But I wouldn't say I'm now old and jaded. And at the end of the day, I'm super thankful for my job and I love every second of it. I often go to ten shows a day, but each one of those designers worked on his or her show for six months, so I always pay attention. I never, ever want to be rude or seem disengaged. People in fashion love to complain, as I've just spent a few hundred words detailing, and it's hard not to get swept up in the collective attitude. At my most exhausted, I often remind myself that I'm not lifting heavy loads or doing hard-core labor. I'm running around a beautiful city, being driven from fashion show to fashion show in a nice car, and afterward I'll have a great dinner and go to sleep in a nice hotel room and someone will make my bed for me the next day.

## DEATH BY FASHION

AS MENTIONED, "FASHION WEEK" IS A misnomer. It's Fashion Month, or Fashion Just About Five Weeks. After New York Fashion Week, you've got London, Milan, and Paris, with little to no break in between. It takes a long time for my body to figure out what time zone it's in after so much travel!

On top of all of that, other cities that want to get in on the branding power of fashion have launched their own fashion weeks, too, including LA, Sydney, Stockholm, and many more. I think even Boston has a fashion week, and I picture a week of cable-knit sweaters and belts with whales on them and people complaining about the cold, but I could be wrong.

Still, even with all the self-reminders that my job is the best, by the time I get to Paris in early October or early March—Paris, one of the most beautiful and glamorous and romantic cities in the world, a place I know so many dream about—the train is pretty much out of steam. All I want to do is be home on my couch with my boyfriend and our Chihuahuas and a grilled cheese and fries from the diner downstairs. For so many people, the best part of traveling is everything that's new and different. For me, though, I've learned how to make even the most exotic places as comforting as watching reality TV in my sweats.

## Starters

| | |
|---|---|
| Fresh carrot and ginger juice *Jus frais carottes gingembre* | 8 |
| Seasonal vegetable soup *Soupe de légumes de saison* | 11 |
| French onion soup *Gratinée à l'oignon* | 11 |
| 6 Burgundy snails *6 escargots de Bourgogne* | 18 |
| Crispy goat cheese, mesclun salad *Croustillant de chèvre* | 13 |
| Endive salad, poached egg, smoked salmon *Endives* | 19 |
| Parisien salad *La Parisienne* | 17 |
| Niçoise salad *Salade Niçoise* | 17 |
| Chicken Caesar salad *Chicken Caesar salad* | 17 |
| Lentil salad and poached egg *Salade de lentilles* | 13 |
| Fresh green beans and sliced mushrooms *Haricots verts* | 12 |
| Home-made duck foie gras *Foie gras de canard maison* | 21 |
| Iberico bellota "Maison Da Rosa" *Ibérico Bellotta* | 24 |
| Deep fried chicken spring rolls "Frères Tang" *Petits nems* | 16 |
| Scottish smoked salmon "Maison Kaspia" *Saumon fumé* | 25 |
| Caviar Osciètre 30g "Maison Kaspia" *Caviar Osciètre* | 150 |
| 6 Special oysters Gillardeau N°2 *Huitres* | 28 |

## Main Courses

| | |
|---|---|
| Grilled rib eye steak 300g, béarnaise sauce *Noix d'entrecôte grillée 300g, sauce béarnaise* | 27 |
| Casti Burger or Bacon Casti Burger, French fries *Le Casti Burger ou Bacon Burger* | 24 |
| Steak tartare (raw) with toasted "Poilâne" bread *Steak tartare, pain Poilâne grillé* | 21 |
| Chicken tajine with vegetables and mild spices *Tajine de volaille aux épices douces* | 24 |
| Veal milanese and penne pasta *Escalope milanaise* | 26 |
| Rack of lamb and green beans *Carré d'agneau* | 35 |
| Beef filet, pepper sauce *Filet de bœuf, sauce poivre* | 33 |
| Organic steamed salmon *Saumon bio vapeur* | 29 |
| Sole meuniere and crushed potatoes *Sole meunière* | 42 |
| Prawn risotto *Risotto de gambas* | 31 |
| Grilled cod and crushed potatoes *Dos de cabillaud* | 29 |

### SIDE DISHES

| | |
|---|---|
| Crushed potatoes *Ecrasée* / French fries *Frites* | 7 |
| Basmati rice *Riz* / Fresh green beans *Haricots verts* | 7 |
| Lettuce heart *Laitue* / Wilted spinach *Epinards* | 7 |

## A Little Hungry

| | |
|---|---|
| Beef carpaccio, arugula salad, parmesan cheese *Carpaccio de bœuf, roquette et parmesan* | 19 |
| Club sandwich with chicken and potato crisps *Club sandwich au poulet, chips* | 18 |
| Club sandwich with smoked salmon, potato crisps *Club sandwich au saumon fumé, chips* | 22 |
| Penne pasta with tomato and basil *Penne tomate & basilic* | 17 |
| Black truffle risotto *Petit risotto à la truffe noire* | 29 |
| Omelette of your choice (organic eggs) *Omelette de votre choix, aux oeufs bio* | 11 |

## Cheeses

| | |
|---|---|
| Low fat fresh soft cheese, honey or red berry coulis *Fromage blanc 0% nature ou au miel* | 8 |
| Raw milk Camembert *Camembert au lait cru* | 6 |
| Brebis d'Iraty (sheep cheese) and black cherry jam *Brebis d'Iraty & sa confiture de cerise noire* | 9 |
| St-Marcellin de la Mère Richard *Saint-Marcellin* | 11 |

## Desserts

| | |
|---|---|
| Rum Baba *Baba au "rhum agricole"* | 11 |
| Thin apple tart, vanilla ice cream *Tarte fine* | 11 |
| Chocolate fondant and vanilla ice ceam *Moelleux* | 11 |
| Vanilla flavoured crème brûlée *Crème brûlée* | 10 |
| Lemon tartlet *Tartelette au citron* | 10 |
| Caramel pudding *Crème caramel* | 10 |
| Fresh fruit salad *Salade de fruits frais* | 11 |
| Sorbet: raspberry, mango or passion fruit *Sorbets : framboise, mangue, fruit de la passion (with liquor 5€)* | 4 |
| Ice cream: vanilla, coffee, chocolate, toffee *Glaces : vanille, café, chocolat, caramel beurre salé* | 4 |
| Café Gourmand | 9 |

www.lecastiglione.com

# PARIS SWEET HOME

WHEN I'M IN Paris, I miss my friends. I miss my dogs. I even miss my doorman, which I think makes perfect sense. Other than my coworkers and my boyfriend, he's the guy I see every single day. He's always there to greet me coming home, most times with a smile. For many, many years, I've combatted Fashion Month homesickness with a burger from Le Castiglione, a café in Paris's Place Vendôme. It's basically the equivalent of a New York City diner but just so much more chic simply because it's in Paris (this is also why the burger costs $24, fries not even included). In fact, the burger's so amazing that I now make it at home, too, to remind me of Paris.

My take on the Castiglione cheeseburger is, of course, not the same as eating the real thing while sitting at the Paris café, where you might also down a bottle of good French red wine, but it's still worth a try. The secret to this burger is in the sauce and the excess of ooey-gooey cheese. This is not a burger that needs to be disguised with lettuce, tomatoes, or pickles. It's pure burger: just meat, cheese, and sauce.

## JOE'S CAFÉ CASTIGLIONE
## CHEESEBURGER

*Makes 4 burgers*

1 pound ground sirloin

Salt, pepper, and onion powder to taste

¼ cup finely minced shallots

½ cup finely minced onions

¼ cup finely chopped cornichons

1 cup mayonnaise

¼ cup ketchup

2 tablespoons sriracha

1 hard-boiled egg

4 large sesame buns

16 slices organic American cheese

{ OPPOSITE } This is the burger that always makes me feel a little less homesick, but after my fat era, I started eating the steamed salmon there.

1. Loosely pack four meat patties so they are roughly ¼ pound each. Sprinkle generously on top and bottom with salt, pepper, and onion powder. Set aside.

2. In a medium bowl, whisk together the shallots, onions, cornichons, mayonnaise, ketchup, and sriracha. Finely mince the boiled egg—try pushing it through a sieve—and whisk it into the mixture. Season with salt and pepper to taste. Once all the ingredients are fully combined, let chill in refrigerator.

3. Lightly toast the buns and set aside.

4. Place the patties on a very hot grill or cast-iron skillet. Let sear for 2 to 4 minutes on each side, depending on how rare or well done you prefer your burger. Halfway through, place two slices of American cheese on top of each patty and cover with a domed lid (a metal mixing bowl works perfectly) for 1 minute, to allow cheese to steam-melt perfectly.

5. While the burgers cook, spread a generous layer of the sauce on both cut sides of the buns. Add two more slices of cheese to the bottom of the bun. When the burgers are cooked to perfection, assemble the burgers. When you see the sauce run out the sides, you'll know you've got the perfect Castiglione burger.

CHAPTER

# THE ISLAND OF
# MISFIT TOYS

I F YOU'VE WATCHED *THE DEVIL WEARS PRADA*
or *Ugly Betty* or even, yes, *The City*, I would not blame you
for thinking that the people who work at fashion magazines
are a bunch of label-obsessed, food-averse, backstabbing
masthead climbers with perfect hair and the unfailing ability to chase down a cab while wearing ridiculous heels. But a fashion magazine office is just like any other: Some people fit the prevailing stereotype,
whatever it may be, while others do not. Certain magazines might have an

overarching "type" that dominates—like the *Vogue*
girls with their multihyphenated, pedigreed names,
or the downtown punk *Nylon* editors who juxtapose
their Céline messenger bags with a stripe of blue
hair. And since we're generalizing, I'll say that *Elle*
editors tend to be well read in both literature and
designer labels, but are just as likely to sit around in
the morning meeting deconstructing last night's episode of *Mad Men* while wearing dresses they got at
Target paired with Miu Miu heels definitely *not* from
Target. Fashion-wise, *Elle* is about celebrating personal style, and the girls in my office really embodied

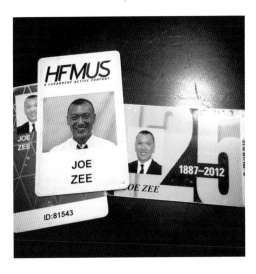

that philosophy. They definitely had fun with getting dressed, and they rebelled a bit, but they didn't obsess over every last detail or feel the need to interpret the runway head to toe. Now that I'm at Yahoo, I work with more men than I've worked with before at any office, and with the majority of employees being under thirty, let's just say casual looks cool in the office again.

{ ABOVE }

Me and Snooki, my birthday twin, at *Elle* (2009).

My favorite place to see magazine-girl stereotypes in action has long been the magazine cafeteria. These aren't anything like the old high school cafeterias (though the cliques will be familiar). Condé Nast, parent company of *Vogue* and *Allure*, was famous for their Frank Gehry cafeteria at 4 Times Square that was so chic that even Anna Wintour regularly ate there, though she had a specially designated table that no one else was allowed to sit at, although it wasn't actually labeled as such—it was just information passed along from one employee to the next. It's not exactly the sort of information that comes in the HR packet, but it was still one of the first things you learned when you started working there. Hearst, which has owned *Elle* since 2011 and also owns *Marie Claire*, *Esquire*, and *O, The Oprah Magazine*, also has an amazing cafeteria. I used to live for it—for the sushi bar first and the people watching second. I might stay in some of the world's best hotels and eat in some of the greatest restaurants, but I still think of the office cafeteria as one of my biggest job perks as creative director at *Elle*. It's also an amazing place to study the complicated species known as Fashion Girl, from the *Oprah* editors in jeans and Converse delicately picking their tomatoes out of the salad bar to the stiletto-clad *Harper's Bazaar* staffers walking away from the pizza station with a few slices, then going back afterward for chocolate pudding. That's the thing about Fashion Girls. They defy classification. The cafeteria at Yahoo in Silicon Valley, on the other hand, is the size of a football field with every possible cuisine you can think of, from juice bar to Indian food to barbecue, and it's all good, and it's all free. People even tell me that the engineers have two lunches a day, which I tell you, no fashion girl ever did.

It might seem, from movies or TV, that fashion is made up of popular girls all grown up, but I don't necessarily see it that way. In my opinion, there aren't more mean girls in fashion than there are in any other creative industry. As I see it, beneath the shiny surface, the fashion industry is a sort of island of misfit toys, including me, composed of all those kids you knew back in high school who were shy, a bit different, but who now have found their home in an industry where individuality and uniqueness can be celebrated. But for all our successes, we are still those same old insecure kids inside, still trying to figure where to sit, and who to sit with, in the cafeteria.

Before Hearst bought *Elle*, the magazine spent most of its existence at 1633 Broadway, a mostly glamour-free building on the edge of the Theater District. Downstairs there was a touristy theme park of a restaurant whose employees dressed up as aliens and paced around outside, stalking tourists and me. "I'm just trying to get to work," I'd say, pushing by whatever silver-suited man was pawing at me as I walked by with my deli coffee.

Inside, we had a great view of New York outside—you can see a lot from forty-four floors up—but the actual offices were less than glamorous. There were no pristine white walls, lacquer desks, or bouquets of hydrangeas. That was strictly the stuff of TV fantasy. I regularly had to steal chairs for my guests from someone else's empty office, and they certainly weren't ergonomic. There were stains (unidentified brown ones) on the carpeting and the walls, one of which had caught on fire and remained black, charred, and unexplained for years until we moved out. There were boxes and enormous trash bins out in the hallways for weeks on end. If I told you that I worked at an insurance company, you might have believed me. Before MTV arrived to film *The City*, the network paid to have the reception

# THE HANDSHAKE
# VS. THE HUG

I N FASHION, THINGS are less formal than in other industries, so it's not uncommon to meet someone for the first time and have him or her bypass the introductory handshake and reach out to give you a big, awkward hug. The hug, in fact, has become something of the default greeting in my world. Normally, I'm all for affection—I'm a pretty friendly guy—but I also like my personal space, especially if I do not really know you or where you've just come from (hugs, above all else, are an excellent method of germ distribution). At the same time, I also hate confrontation, so I'm not especially likely to tell you flat out that no, I'd really rather you not take me in your arms, as it were. So I thought I'd make my declarations here. Hug me if:

You've met me at least twice in person (and I'm likely to remember).

We've gotten tipsy together.

You're Heidi Klum.

We used to ride bikes/ do algebra/ stalk Boy George together, or you otherwise knew and liked me when I was an awkward young teenager.

You love chihuahuas, or specifically, my Chihuahuas.

I've had you over for dinner.

You can commit, even if I'm a little stand-offish. Maybe I'm not expecting it. But if you go in for the hug, you need to go all the way because the only thing worse than an unwanted hug is an unwanted half hug.

area, my office, and a few choice pieces of hallway near my office newly painted. Literally, the walls outside my office door were bright white, but a few feet out, you'd see the white dissolve into a dingy grayish cream where they'd just let the paint strokes fade out. And my favorite part, which still puzzles me to this day, was the narrow hallway right outside my office back then, where the windowless walls were lined with every *Elle* cover from the first issue back in 1985 until present day, framed and sun-bleached. How was that possible, I loved to wonder, in a corridor that never saw sunlight? Can fluorescent light bleach pictures? Can that *happen*?

We liked to say that we saved all the glamour for inside the magazine, but in truth, we all knew we didn't need the surface to produce good work. And in fact, I loved those scrappy moments where you could just roll up your sleeves and get the job done. Sure, I would have loved to have Le Corbusier chairs in my office, but I would rather have a smart, beautiful magazine.

Needless to say, there was no fancy cafeteria then.

As creative director at *Elle*, I was responsible for all the visuals in the magazine, cover to cover, so the fashion editors and on-staff stylists all reported to me. My first major change upon arriving at the magazine was to change the roster of photographers and stylists we used because for a very long time the same photographer shot *Elle*'s covers and most of its big shoots were styled by the same editor. And they were good, but they had not changed in more than fifteen years. That's a long time, especially in fashion, when everything else changes so quickly.

People—men, mainly—regularly asked me about how amazing it must be to work in a place where I would see beautiful models coming into the office day in and day out. Or where the hallways smell of Chanel No. 5. I got a lot of "oh my God, I want to come see your office!" or "oh my God, how hot are the girls you work with?" But let me be real with you: Models do not just parade freely through the office at any given moment like you see on TV.

That's not to say there were no scantily clad women, not exactly. One day, when the air-conditioning broke, one staffer removed all of her clothes and sat in her office in her bra and underwear, her leg up on her desk, fanning herself. So if that counts as model behavior in your book, come on by. "I can't look at you right now," I told her as I walked by her office, shielding my eyes.

A few weeks later, a few of us were holding a meeting in another office when I heard a loud bump. I looked around; no one else had seemed to hear it. Then, again: *thud*. "What is that?" I said. "Did anyone else hear that bumping sound?"

"Don't worry about it," my colleague said, waving me away and going on about how she planned to write about yet another crop top comeback in the next issue. Then she stopped suddenly and spoke, it seemed, to the floor beneath her desk. "Okay," I demanded. "What is going on?" Turns out there was a petite manicurist squeezed in the space at her feet and the bump was the sound of the poor woman hitting her head on the desk above her. She was getting a pedicure in the middle of our meeting. "Okay," I said again, "I'm going to go."

She didn't understand what my problem was. "I have an event tonight and I have literally no other time to get this done!" she said. "Don't worry about her. Come on, let's finish."

Though most people don't get into journalism or publishing for the promise of big bucks, you'd be shocked if you knew how little fashion assistants are actually paid. For such a glittering industry, the salaries, at least for those starting out, are alarmingly close to poverty levels, especially for living in New York City. Fashion might be big business, but magazine publishing typically is not. A typical starting salary at *Elle* for an assistant (who is often right out of college but sometimes not) is in the mid-20s, though she'll also get overtime on top of that, which helps, especially since the hours are pretty damn long. When I started as an assistant in 1992, I was paid $21,000 a year plus overtime and I was told that I was on the "higher" side of the pay scale since I was older and had some experience. What did a novice make then? Eighteen thousand dollars a year. I considered myself very lucky. And hungry (in more ways than one). That said, assistants generally receive overtime. As an assistant you not only rely on it, you *exist* because of it. Without overtime, I would have been a street urchin; with it, I could actually have pizza once or twice a week.

As an assistant, you're almost always on call, even if you work for the most kind and reasonable boss (a rarity in fashion, I have to admit). A typical day might start in the office at 9 or 10 a.m. (fashion editors never get in before 10, but as an assistant, you've got to beat the boss) and end at 8 or 9 p.m., and that's not counting after-work dinners, parties, openings, or other events that are as much about networking as they are about recreation.

# PLAY A FASHION EDITOR IN REAL LIFE,

## EVEN IF YOU'RE NOT ONE

THE FASHION INDUSTRY plays by a different set of rules than most other lines of work. For example, you could legitimately wear your grandmother's fur stole to work over a plain white tee, jeans, and a great pair of heels. Or a cocktail dress to a 9 a.m. meeting. Heel heights keep getting taller and taller, to the point where, as a sneaker-wearing dude, I was often the shortest person in the office. That said, there are some basic rules to live by if you want to look like (or be) a fashion editor.

### 1. YOU CAN NEVER HAVE TOO MANY LBDS.

The little black dress is a year-round industry staple. It is also known as the FPU (Fashion Person Uniform). That said, don't feel married to the B. Your LBD could be navy, for example, or hunter green—dark and solid is what's key here. But there's a very good reason something is always the new black. Black never goes out of style, and you will always look chic and flawless in it.

### 2. SHORT AND TIGHT— KEEP IT TO NIGHT.

The hemlines in my office rise and fall as the seasons change, but I've noticed that

when they creep up, they really creep up. Sometimes this is simply about efficiency: There's no time, they claim, to go home and change before an evening event or Friday night party. ("Why not just bring a second dress to work?" I ask. "Oh, Joe!" they reply, rolling their eyes, as if I'm just having a little fun with them and am not totally, completely serious.) Luckily there's an easy fix: Just combat the 9-to-5-showgirl look by pairing the dress with a great blazer and flats.

### 3. THAT SAID, KEEP THE FLATS FASHIONY.

In other words, lose the *Working Girl* sneakers, already. I get that your walk

home is your daily cardio, or that those Valentino Rockstuds don't exactly make for great subway wear, but there are too many comfortable and stylish options for you to rock the dingy trainers for your commute home. If you must leave the office in shoes other than the ones you wear around the office, go all the way and change into your gym clothes, too. Don't mix and match.

## 4. DON'T UNDERESTIMATE OUTERWEAR.

A great coat can be pricey, but it's always with you, like your hair. So make it great. Opt for a bold statement piece—a colored fur, for example, or a unique silhouette—or a version of a classic, like a peacoat or trench. The classic may last you a few more seasons, but you really can't go wrong with either.

{ ABOVE } Me dressed as Rachel Zoe for Halloween, though I think it came out more Faye Dunaway . . .

You will work weekends. I like to joke that no one in fashion has a real life outside of work. We're like doctors; we're always on call. Everything feels like a fashion emergency. If I call my assistant at 7 a.m. or at midnight, I pretty much need her to answer, and if she doesn't, I worry about her like an overprotective parent. Is she okay? Does she need my help?

The low salaries are one reason the fashion industry remains largely populated by people of at least some privilege. Three weeks of pay might barely cover a month's rent in an apartment shared with three other kids, someone's ex-boyfriend, and a mishmash of hand-me-down furniture. It's like the magazine industry's form of hazing: How bad do you *really* want to work here? Bad enough that you'll live in a railroad apartment in a questionable neighborhood with four roommates? Because success—or a bigger paycheck—won't happen right away. And in an industry where you'll work demanding hours and juggle multiple, often tedious tasks, you do have to want it, and bad. I certainly know many very successful editors who broke into the business and climbed the ranks without any sort of pedigree or connection or "in" whatsoever, myself included. There are so many times I remember struggling so much financially, I would literally hold back tears in bed at night, not sure I could keep going. There just wasn't any way to live on my salary. But I would wake up, the day would be new and I'd be excited again about what was ahead, and I knew I was supposed to be here, creating in the fashion world and making my mark. So what if I did it broke? *If I love it*, I told myself, *I can do it*. And I did. When I was first starting out, my roommate, Carter, and I were so broke that taking the subway to work was considered a splurge. Walking, after all, was free. We'd steal fashion magazines from the supermarket, where we'd buy our weekly cans of Slimfast. I wasn't dieting, but at only 85 cents a can it was an unbeatable lunch bargain. If we didn't waver for a whole week we'd treat ourselves to dollar slices on Fridays. Every weekend, we'd pool our loose change from the week and treat ourselves to an ice cream sundae—one sundae, which we'd split. How tragic is that! A single sundae. But you know, those were the most delicious and gratifying sundaes of my entire life, and somehow Carter and I didn't mind being so cash-strapped. We knew we were working toward a much bigger goal. We knew that sharing sundaes wouldn't be forever.

# SPEAK FASHION

Fashion People Have their own language. Some key phrases to help you get to know the locals.

## for reals

**No, seriously.**

*"After this fifth glass of champagne, I'm going home to crash. For reals."*

## major

**Important. Alt. usage: "maje" (pronounced "mage").**

*"These furs are so maje."*

## genius

**Innovative.**

*"Alexander Wang's debut for Balenciaga was genius."*

## too street style

**Wannabe.**

*"In head-to-toe Lagerfeld, she was far too street style."*

## turn the plane around!

**Get me that look—no matter what.**

*"Turn the plane around: Prabal Gurung's look 14 is a game changer!"*

## baesics

**Essential wardrobe pieces such as sweaters, jeans, and T-shirts borrowed from you bae.**

*"This Opening Ceremony LBD is one of my favorite baesics."*

## PR-gument

**A fight with a fashion publicist.**

*"I got into such a PR-gument with the girl doing the seating at that fashion show. Can you believe she sat me next to that Housewife again?"*

# SEASONAL ESSENTIALS

## THE ONE ITEM YOU NEED FOR EACH SEASON

EVERY SEASON BRINGS another round of "wardrobe must-haves," and it's easy to overbuy (and overspend). I always get the question: "If I purchase just *one thing* this season, what should it be?" While I can't necessarily tell you which *trend* to follow, I can give you my advice for the absolute, single most important *item* in your closet each season. This item should always be something you love, and if you choose only one thing to splurge on, this is the one.

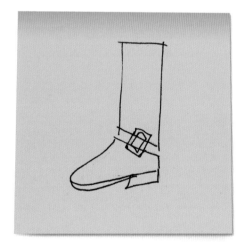

### WINTER: BOOTS

Find the one pair that fits seamlessly into your existing wardrobe—not the sort of statement boots that you need to build an outfit around. I always suggest a decent pair of motorcycle-style boots. They work as well with tights and dresses as they do over jeans, and they're sturdy enough to handle most winter weather (and chicer than most snow boots). Plus, a well-made pair will only get better looking with age.

### SPRING: DENIM

Jeans don't have to be expensive, but a pair that you look and feel great in will always be worth the splurge. The styles may change—skinny, high-waisted, etc.—but denim is here to stay, and it's a piece of clothing you can easily wear a few times each week, dressed up or down, throughout the spring: out to dinner, shopping, maybe to work if your workplace is casual.

### SUMMER: BAG

You're wearing fewer clothes in the summer, but you've still got plenty of stuff to carry around. A summer bag should be hardworking but light and fun, something you can throw over your shoulder or toss into a backseat but which will glam up a sundress or jeans and a tee. During the season of easy dressing, your bag is what will give your outfit polish.

### FALL: COAT

Whether yours is leather, fur, long, or short, a great coat will be fall's most essential item. Classic cuts and colors like black and navy will often last you a number of seasons, though I'm always a fan of a big pop-of-color coat to take you through the long slog of winter. Personally, I want all the help I can get.

Plus, once you're at work, how much money you do or don't have and who you parents are matters less. Everyone works hard, whether he or she was born rich or not. If you don't, there's an eager replacement right around the corner perfectly willing to answer phones and fetch dry cleaning and schlep to Starbucks eight times a day for grande soy skinny vanilla lattes for just over minimum wage. And be damn happy about it, too.

In fact, the reason the salaries have remained so low in magazine publishing may be because the jobs are in such high demand. For an entry-level opening, *Elle*—or any magazine for that matter—will get hundreds of résumés, and many of these kids are extremely well qualified, if not also well connected. Everyone's done an internship or edited his college paper or run a fashion blog since she was 11, or all three. Some of these kids come to work already more famous than me, and here they are, ready and eager to sit in the fashion closet all day color-coding shoes. And I will gladly let them do that.

Not that working in magazines is exactly like working in a sweatshop. Pay may be meager, but there are plenty of perks to help make up for the low pay, which is how an assistant might be able to tote around a Céline bag likely worth more than her entire apartment. Such perks include, but are not limited to, discounted or free clothes and access to sample sales, press trips or other on-the-job travel to exotic destinations, free bottles of wine, tickets to concerts and shows and movie premieres, exclusive invites, not to mention an endless assortment of hair and skin care products, especially if you're nice to the girls in the beauty department. I literally have not bought a bottle of shampoo in twenty years.

# LIFE WITH THE A-LIST

FOR ITS APRIL 2006 ISSUE, *VANITY FAIR* had put together a story on Teri Hatcher, star of the then super hot TV show *Desperate Housewives*. It was meant to be a small feature, nothing major. But in the interview with writer Leslie Bennetts, Teri had revealed, for the first time ever, that as a child she'd been sexually abused by an uncle. And, of course, *that* was major. The magazine's editors had decided to scrap their previous cover plans and put Teri in the slot instead.

The story had already been styled and shot, but the photos that had worked for a feature story wouldn't work for the cover: too much background, maybe, or not enough white space for the all-important cover lines. I was freelancing regularly for *Vanity Fair* at that time, but happened to be in Las Vegas on another job—Celine Dion's new fragrance campaign—when the decision was made. I got an urgent call from the photo director summoning me and photographer Michael Thompson to LA immediately to work on the new Teri cover. Because of Teri's *Desperate Housewives* schedule, the only time a shoot could possibly happen was the following morning in LA, starting at 6 a.m.—and she only had two hours to give us. We had two hours to pull off a *Vanity Fair* cover.

*Game on*, I thought. Except for one thing. It was already 8 p.m. in Vegas and I had no clothes to put her in.

The showrooms on both coasts were already closed for the night. All I had on hand for clothing options were the things I'd pulled for Celine, a mass of sequins, leather, and general glittery slinkiness—nothing at all appropriate for such a serious-sounding story. And most of that was already en route back to NYC besides. I had to think quick.

"No matter how close the call,
or last minute the emergency,

# IT ALWAYS
# WORKS OUT.

I never remember this."

Thankfully—and for this I bow to the shopping karma gods—Las Vegas is a city that never turns off the lights (or says no to a sale), which is how I found myself racing up and down the Vegas Strip at 10 p.m. on a Thursday night, where all the stores were still open. There I was (completely sober, unlike everyone else) with my assistant, tearing through the town, buying whatever I could find that wasn't hot pink or made of latex: $50,000 worth of Chanel, eight pairs of Manolo Blahniks. It was like my own personal, super deluxe version of *Supermarket Sweep*, grabbing things at Gucci and Armani like they were going out of season, praying that the stores would let me return everything later even after it had been worn. (Most editorial shoots feature clothing samples pulled from showrooms and not retail stores, so while you never want to ruin a dress, it's not life ending if you get a little self-tanner on it. Retail stores don't have such a forgiving policy.)

Running around buying clothes in Las Vegas for a photo shoot, knowing I would return them later, made me feel like I was in school again.

That night, I *was* Pretty Woman. By the time we finished up, just a little past midnight, the last flight back to LA had already taken off. My assistant and I rode to LA in a chauffeured town car, making it to the studio at 5 a.m. with just enough time to mainline coffee and set up before Teri arrived looking fresh-faced and rested.

The take that made the cover featured Teri with a white sweater in a simple, sexy look beneath the provocative cover line "Teri Hatcher's Desperate Secret." The photo was flawless, she looked gorgeous, and the issue was one of the year's best sellers. My boss was pleased; everyone at Condé Nast was pleased. In the end, it worked out. Of course it did. No matter how close the call or last minute the emergency, it always works out. I never remember this.

\* \* \*

IT'S HARD TO IMAGINE, SORT OF LIKE THINKING about life before color TV or gluten-free cookies, but once upon a time, magazine covers were reserved for models. Our lives these days are so consumed by celebrities—the clothes they wear, the movies they make or songs they sing, the people they sleep with—that I can barely believe it myself, that there was once a time when a supermodel cover was the norm and not the exception and we weren't all clamoring to know what famous person walks her dog exactly like we do. Though I am one of the biggest and earliest embracers of celebrity culture—I came out of the womb a total TV nut—the pre-celebrity magazine world was, in many ways, so much easier.

If also a lot less interesting. (Depending on who the model was, of course. I could always count on the supers to bring their fair share of drama and intrigue.)

At *Elle*, and every other magazine, for that matter, the cover girl is always the most important, and most time-consuming, decision to make for any given issue. She is the billboard, the poster, the singular message that says, "Hey, I am a personification of this issue." She has to be the right balance between megastar and mysterious; it's important that she looks great in clothes, especially if she is covering a fashion magazine, but also that she has something to say (and has something to promote) and that the audience would be interested in reading about her. She needs to be news. At *Elle*, the editor in chief, entertainment director, design director, and I would often spend months going back and forth about a cover, sending endless emails debating the pros and cons of the women on our wish list, often planning slots up to a year in advance. Who's the most *"Elle"* girl? Who would create the most buzz? Who'll look amazing in couture and have the most interesting things to say? And, since we compete with dozens of other magazines for the same women, what will it take to get her?

In most cases, the entertainment director at any magazine will propose a list of celebrities who seem right and possibly available, and we'll prioritize as a team, knowing that our first choice might not necessarily be the one we land. There's always the "wish list," the dream choices, versus the "pitched list," the choices most likely to say yes. The competition to book celebrities for magazine covers is often fierce, especially when we're talking about the super A-list actresses with highly anticipated projects or exclusive stories to tell, and, very often, that process can start more than a year in advance. If we know there's a major project, movie, or album being released by a certain A-lister, we will be stalking her publicist to try and secure her for that elusive and exclusive cover. One of my last covers at *Elle* magazine, I was wooing Angelina Jolie for a cover to promote *Maleficent* for more than eighteen months. Everyone wants the same few girls at the exact same time, me included (yes, even at *Yahoo Style*, I'm shooting original covers with celebrities). Because the celebrities don't get paid for being on the cover, they get the ultimate say on which magazines they want to do.

The first celebrity I ever photographed for a magazine cover was Liv Tyler, for *W*, in the summer of 1998. It was also the first celebrity *W* had ever featured on its cover. Liv was starring in *Armageddon*, a major summer blockbuster, which was a Disney movie, and, coincidentally, Disney also owned *W* at the time.

I love Liv. The late nineties was a new era and the early beginnings of celebrity covers, and while I loved them, it was an adjustment for all us editors and stylists to go from the supermodel mind-set where we would *create* an image with them to shooting an actress who already had an established image. But to this day, I am glad I popped my celebrity-cover cherry with Liv, who is as sweet to this day as she was back then. I still don't know if I ever told her she was my first.

How times have changed. Though there is hardly a magazine out there today that doesn't feature, or aim to feature, a celebrity on its cover (in recent years, even nonfashion magazines like *Wired* and *Fast Company* and *Bon Appétit* have gotten in on the celebrity game) or a fashion designer who doesn't partner with at least one celebrity "muse," the Hollywood-fashion partnership is just part of the business now. You either embrace celebrities because you have to, or you rebel and decide that you can do without them. Most of us embrace celebrity. Are we all chasing celebs? I think we are a little bit. Is our world oversaturated with celebrity? It is sometimes, but I don't see the celebrity fascination letting up anytime soon. Like it or not, celebrities—and I mean celebrities, not just movie stars or pop stars—are a part of the culture we live in. They account for a big part of the business of fashion. Something worn by a famous woman can translate into huge sales. Award shows have become red carpets. The Oscar preshow is more interesting than the ceremony—and I don't say that just because I'm a red carpet commentator. But honestly, most people care more about what someone looks like on Oscar night than they do about who wins the prize for Best Actress. I'm not saying that's right. It's just the way it is.

When it comes to magazines, the biggest difference between dressing actresses and dressing models is that actresses usually come to you with a style they've worked hard to define, either on their own or with a personal stylist. But supermodels make a living being photographed wearing clothes. They have opinions, too, of course—they know what looks good and what doesn't look good—but they're usually far more amenable to direction and in general more interested in pushing the boundaries and being "first" and "different" because their job is to sell the clothes. A celebrity, on the other hand, is just getting *styled* in clothes, but their first goal is to promote their project. By nature, actresses are not always that adventurous, but I don't blame them. They're scrutinized and judged on a level we could never understand, and in the end, they want to be safe and wear what they're comfortable in. With a celebrity, you have to factor in "who she is" in a way that doesn't really ever apply to models. A supermodel wants to take it to the next level all the time.

My first major, major movie star cover was Gwyneth Paltrow for *W* in the fall of 1998. This was when Gwyneth was at her true prime as a fashion icon—though let's be honest: She's never gone out of style. It took a year for us to negotiate that cover, and when it finally came through, we had something like twenty-four hours' notice to pull it all together.

I got the call from our entertainment editor at 5 p.m.: "We're a go for Gwyneth," she said. *Amazing!* I thought. I had been mulling this whole all-American angle for her. Maybe I'd pay a visit to Donna Karan later that week, or . . . Then: "She's giving us four hours, tomorrow night between 6 and 10."

Oh.

The clock was already ticking. I had approximately twenty-four hours to pull together enough outfits to create a fourteen-page fashion spread featuring one of the world's biggest—and, when it came to fashion, most knowledgeable—movie stars. Less than that, really, if you consider that for fourteen or so hours the showrooms and stores would be closed and everyone—besides me, of course—would be sleeping. Michael Thompson would be shooting, and he and I decided to move forward with dressing Gwyneth exclusively in clothing by American designers. This not only suited her personal aesthetic and professional Girl Next Door image, but there also was no way in hell I was going to get anything flown over from Europe in time. So, all-American it was.

I called in all my favors, and had my assistants call in all their favors, and together we pulled together about forty looks in eight hours with the idea that we'd photograph Gwynnie in one look from each designer: Ralph Lauren, Michael Kors, Calvin Klein, etc. She appeared on the cover in a white sheath with a deep-V neckline, smiling wide and looking fresh-faced and not at all like we'd pulled the whole thing off in less than twenty-four hours. But then, I guess that's why she's Gwyneth Paltrow. And that year she won her first Oscar. I'm just going to say our cover was a lucky charm.

\* \* \*

JOE ZEE
EDITOR-IN-CHIEF
TELEPHONE **212.630.3539** FAX 212 630 4120
JOE ZEE@FAIRCHILDPUB COM
7 WEST 34TH STREET NEW YORK, NY 10001-8191
FAIRCHILD PUBLICATIONS, INC

{ ABOVE }

My first business card
as editor in chief of the
magazine I created and
founded for Fairchild
Publications. 2004–2006.

FTER ALMOST TEN YEARS AT *W*, I LEFT
the magazine in 2004 to launch *Vitals* magazine,
as founding editor in chief, for Fairchild, the publishing company that also owned *W*. *Vitals* was a
general interest magazine born out of a section of
the men's magazine *Details*, which I'd worked on
for a time. Part of what I always loved about magazines and what made me want to be a part of the
industry was having an idea and then being able to see that idea come to life.
There is nothing more personally satisfying than when an idea that was fer-
tilized in my head makes it onto an actual printed page. Reading magazines
became not only an enjoyment and release for me but also a game of "How
would I do it differently if I were in charge?"

A few years before the *Vitals* gig even came up, I began toying with the
idea of pitching myself to run a magazine. I knew I had the ideas; I knew
I had the vision. Now I just needed an outlet. My passion then was (and
probably still is, to some extent) the teen market. As my close friends can
attest, there will always be a thirteen-year-old girl trapped inside me. So
when I read in the trades that Primedia, the company that owned *Seventeen*
magazine (as well as *New York* magazine), was looking to sell *Seventeen* and
that Fairchild might buy it, I quickly dialed an art director friend of mine,

Carl Byrd (who I knew loved that market as much as I), and I said, let's do it. Let's put together a pitch to show that we can do something new, different, innovative, and great. That *we* should take over *Seventeen* magazine. It wouldn't be precious, and it *would* be cool, and of course, in my mind I already knew how it could stand out. So we got to work.

I sent Carl a bunch of celebrity photos I had styled along with swipes (a term for "found art," or photos pulled to use in a mockup that will not be published, so no permission is needed), and he toyed around with a few layouts. We sent them back and forth to each other until we knew we'd hit on a winning version, when we hit the aha.

The aha for me, as an editor, is that indefinable moment when I just know something is right. "It" can be an idea, concept, layout, story pitch,

{ ABOVE }

Me and Sarah
Jessica Parker.

feature, anything. Just something that really strikes me at a gut level. By the time Carl and I were done with a few sample spreads and some cover options, I knew we had something. It was "poppy"—we wanted the covers to look like billboards—and had a tinge of MTV energy and brought in some of the fun elements of a Japanese shopping magazine. We came up with ideas for how to incorporate the "Internet," a relatively new frontier for fashion folks at the time, and how it could encourage readers to get involved and feel like a part of the *Seventeen* community. We wanted to make the magazine much more interactive. While I worked, I thought a lot about how dumbfounded I was the first time I saw my name in print—which is to say, if my life were a cartoon, I would have had those stars and exclamation points circling my head while I was passed out on the sidewalk—and how I might give *Seventeen* readers that same feeling. I knew that if I could actually involve those teenage readers in the making of the magazine, the magazine itself would become their best friend, their confidante, the cool girl at school. That, I thought, was a great way to build loyalty.

When I was done with my project, I set out to pitch it to my boss, Patrick McCarthy, the editorial director of Fairchild Publications, and to Mary Berner, the president of Fairchild Publications, who would decide the viability and potential of my idea. I had no idea where it would lead me, but it didn't matter. I was still the fashion director at *W* and the magazine was at an all-time high, so I had nothing to lose.

In the end, Fairchild never bought *Seventeen*, but Patrick and Mary really liked my concept. More, though, they started to see me as more than just a fashion guy. I suddenly became a magazine guy. And that was the beginning of *Vitals*.

When *Vitals* was a section within *Details* magazine, it was in the center of the book. In magazines, the center of the book, generally speaking, often feels like a stand-alone magazine, with a separate cover, separate ideas, etc. "A magazine within a magazine" is how I explain it to those not in the industry. It is often reserved strictly for product (rows of denim jackets)

## "The magazine itself would become THEIR BEST FRIEND, THEIR CONFIDANTE, THE COOL GIRL AT SCHOOL."

and service (finding the right jeans for you). When Fairchild execs first decided that *Vitals* might make for a great magazine spin-off, I think they imagined it as a special supplement that would be mailed out to top subscribers. But the "shopping" magazine was a huge craze at the time, led by the success of *Lucky*, and *Vitals* was Fairchild's way to get in on it.

While *Lucky* and the soon-to-be launched *Cargo*—the *Lucky* for guys— both targeted the general population, *Vitals* was meant to tap into just a small group of top spenders, a group we referred to as "the top of the pyramid." These people were easily singled out by going through the current list of *Details* subscribers as well as purchasing—yes, purchasing—additional lists from credit card companies. This is a common practice among companies looking to target a specific audience.

Knowing that I was targeting top spenders, I sat down to create editorial for that market and define what the magazine would be. I knew I wanted to combine service with shopping. I really believed that men didn't just shop; they not only wanted to browse, but they also wanted to *know*. Men, I believed, were happy to spend $5,000 on a coat if they knew specifically how and why the coat costs that much. So when I was finally given the job as editor in chief, I officially left *W*, moved into a cubicle upstairs, and went about putting together a concept and hiring a staff.

# "WE WERE A CRAZY FAMILY.

## We fought, we hung out, we all slept over . . . and most of all, we loved the project."

The first person I called was Paul Ritter, who would become our creative director and with whom I would ultimately work for almost ten years—at *Elle* after *Vitals*. Paul's background was *Life* magazine and record labels, and I loved that. I was inspired by creative people who didn't come from the world of fashion; I figured their unique perspective would help us be different in a sea of magazines. Paul came to work that first day at *Vitals*, and we sat down and figured out what the magazine was going to look like and whom it was for. I have always been a foodie and was particularly inspired by the food world. I wondered: *How can I translate that world into fashion, when to most, they seemed like polar opposites?* Paul and I both mentioned a cult cooking magazine called *Cook's Illustrated* that was, for the most part, made up of dense recipe pages with boxes of service and line illustrations. It was packed with information that was easy to understand, but sophisticated enough to not feel "mass." It was the PBS of magazines.

Paul and I both knew that concept would be a good springboard for how we created *Vitals*.

In the two weeks that followed, we tore pages and sections out of any and every magazine we loved, from *National Geographic* to British *Vogue* to *Forbes*. We didn't want to confine ourselves to just what the fashion world was doing. Even though Fairchild had largely been interested in *Vitals*'s potential in a category filled with magazines like *Lucky*, *Cargo*, *Domino*, and *Shop Etc.*, I never wanted *Vitals* to be just a shopping magazine or a "maga-logue" as people often called them. Instead of sneaking in service—the sort of how-to/where-to stuff that magazines like *Good Housekeeping* and *O* special-ized in but that "luxury" magazines tended to shy away from—we decided to highlight it. Let's put it in a box, like *Cook's Illustrated*, and tag everything as a how-to. Let's be unapologetic about it! And that's how *Vitals* was born.

The magazine was a great concept that was probably a bit ahead of its time: a fashion and lifestyle magazine that could act as your most knowledge-able friend or a trusted hotel concierge. And we delved deep: We didn't just tell readers the best hotel in Morocco or the best airline to take you there, but which room you should ask for and how you could score an upgrade. This was how my brain worked already. I always wanted the best, and that didn't nec-essarily mean the most expensive. In many cases, it was the opposite. I wanted the best inside knowledge. *Vitals* was going to give readers exactly that.

We launched *Vitals Man* in September of that year with Matt Damon on the cover. A female counterpart, *Vitals Woman*, followed in February, and featured Hilary Swank. And, as we intended, everything was super functional. An eleven-page story about Matt Damon, for example, might have included six pages of fashion photos, two pages of text, and three pages of Matt's personal recommendations about fashion, food, travel des-tinations, and where to sit at Fenway Park—real insider access that you couldn't get anywhere else.

I led a small, but brilliant, staff of very committed editors who con-stantly amazed me with their different ways of thinking. I loved my *Vitals* staff. We were a crazy family. We fought, we hung out, we all slept over sometimes (not kidding), we went to the movies together at midday, and most of all, we loved the project. None of us were paid handsomely, but the income came in the pride in what we would produce. And we produced some great issues, featuring covers with celebrities like Adrien Brody, Heidi Klum, and Jake Gyllenhaal. We would begin to see our small magazine influence other, bigger publications. Even though we were annoyed, we were also secretly flattered. I know Fairchild probably didn't intend on it being the magazine it became (Julia Roberts was on the cover of the last issue exclusively, choosing to do it over *Vogue* or *Vanity Fair!*), but the company restructured and the shopping magazine bubble burst, and in the end, *Vitals* folded in 2005, after less than a year and only seven issues.

I remember that morning when my bosses, Patrick and Mary, asked to speak with me. During the entire two-year *Vitals* process, they had pretty much left me alone, but I could tell that this meeting wasn't going to be good. Once I sat down, they told me that we'd published the final issue and that there would be no more because, business-wise, they couldn't sustain it. I just sat there in shock. I nodded. What could I say? Hysterics wouldn't have changed anything and this was a decision that was beyond them. Fairchild was merging with Condé Nast that same week and the business structure was changing. These changes were here to stay. I was disappointed, obviously, and looking back I still don't believe the company gave us enough time to really get our groove, but of course I'm biased. To this day, I see the influence of *Vitals* in other magazines that use smart, clever ways to deliver readers super useful information, and I still get the occasional message about missing *Vitals*. I'm glad I had *Vitals*. I never thought I would have ever been an editor in chief, much less create something strictly from the depths of my brain. This was already far more than any fashion-obsessed Canadian kid could ask for.

But now what? Life goes on, and it wasn't as if I was out on the streets. Condé Nast offered me a contract to stay on at the company as a contributing editor for *W* and *House & Garden*, complete with my own office, even if it *was* on the floor with the accounting department. The week I received news that my magazine was closing, I got a call to work with designer-director Tom Ford on *Vanity Fair*'s Hollywood issue. This was 2006, a few years after Tom had left Gucci to develop his own ready-to-wear line and direct movies, and he was having a real Hollywood moment. Apparently (and this is what I read—I wasn't there) over martinis one night with Graydon Carter, he'd criticized the annual portfolio as having gotten dull, dull, dull. And so Graydon agreed to let Tom run the thing as "artistic director," selecting subjects and overseeing photo shoots. And by "overseeing photo shoots," I mean Tom had the final word on everything from location, lighting, and clothes to how an actress parted her hair or where she placed her hand. In Tom's case, that "where" was almost always a little subversive.

Elizabeth Saltzman, who was the fashion director of *VF*, called me about working on the main portfolio, a twenty-plus-page feature, plus the cover, which was a mammoth project. I can remember answering the phone

# "SCARY EXPERIENCES
are the ones you need to go after . . ."

and listening to her describe the project to me, and being excited yet hesitant. I told myself that I had to try to find another editor's position—versus just go back to styling—but to be honest, I think I was intimidated about working with Tom and *Vanity Fair* and legendary photographer Annie Leibovitz and what it would mean to take on such an enormous project. I certainly knew Tom from the fashion industry and having covered him in various capacities while I was at *W*, and many of my best friends were good friends with him or had worked for him, so he was anything but a stranger, but he was still *Tom Ford*. And styling for him is scary because he is *Tom Ford*. But, as I've learned so often in life, the scary experiences are the ones you need to go after, so I closed my eyes, jumped in the deep end, and said yes. And through that job I got the chance to work with a variety of photographers I hadn't worked with before, and have some of the most memorable, if slightly insane, experiences of my career.

* * *

THE HOLLYWOOD ISSUE WAS ANCHORED BY A more than twenty-page portfolio plus the cover, a mammoth project. Tom had very strong opinions about the clothes, the setup, the locations, and yet my most memorable styling moments from that project have more to do with the clothes I was taking *off* celebrities, not putting on.

The cover concept, for example, was to shoot a trio of seminaked starlets: Scarlett Johansson, Kiera Knightley, and one more actress, who I won't name. Tom wanted to re-create a sort of Renaissance painting feel—all flesh and white-skinned curves—and Annie loved the idea of delicate French lingerie as the unifying clothing element in this cover. The fashion department was tasked with pulling just about every single piece of lingerie that existed in New York, Milan, and Paris, because in Tom's (and Annie's) world, you can never have too much silk charmeuse and lace trimming. And I very quickly learned that the *Vanity Fair* fashion department was well trained in this, as I didn't have much to explain in terms of canvasing the market as they knew to call *everyone* around the world for their best lingerie.

The photographer was Annie Leibovitz, and of course she had no shortage of opinions, either. Annie was quite used to doing things a certain way. You don't get to become Annie Leibovitz by being mild-mannered and indecisive. She's ultra efficient and organized, and a real stickler about position, often calling in body doubles for days before a shoot to set up lighting and establish the ideal positioning, so that when the actual shoot day arrives, all the VIP needed to do was step into the scene and Annie could snap a few frames and be done in ten minutes. This is a pretty genius way to work with celebrities, who generally do not have the sort of stamina models have, but it's a process that requires great patience, as well as a big budget, since you're essentially assembling an entire crew for an extra day.

Richard Avedon had worked that way, too. I was an assistant at *Allure* when super famous makeup artist Kevyn Aucoin, whom I'd met on a few shoots with Polly and around the offices of *Allure* where he was a regular columnist during those early days, recommended me to Dick Avedon, one of the most important fashion and beauty photographers of the twentieth century. Somehow, I had made a good impression on Kevyn, and he'd taken me under his wing, so to speak. Kevin had a line of cosmetics with Shiseido, and he and Dick were about to shoot an ad campaign for it with model-then-actress Milla Jovovich. Kevyn, after getting permission from Linda Wells, asked me to style it. I nearly died. I was twenty-four, maybe twenty-five.

The way Avedon worked was very methodical and meant for efficiency. The day before the shoot, Dick, his many photo assistants and lighting techs, and I spent the day in the studio, where I dressed the body double (who was a real model, approximately the same size and height as Milla) and moved her around into different positions, changing lighting as needed and snapping Polaroids of every setup for Dick to review later. The picture was to resemble Milla sitting in the backseat of a car, but the way that Dick worked, it required precision and exact lighting and posture. The studio was big and white and vast. I arrived (with my in-awe eyes, of course) to find a car had been completely cut in half with only the back part, seat intact, propped and meticulously lit against the studio's white cyc (aka a white wall that's curved and sloped at the bottom, instead of being perpendicular to the floor, in order to create a seamless background). The assistants fussed with the lighting all day, while we tested different colors from the clothes in the picture. They would snap a ton of Polaroids (the days before digital!), readjusting, re-evaluating. There would be more lights being moved, the body double shifting, the clothes being swapped out. And that was the day. When we thought we'd landed on the perfect setup, we left everything the way it was. The next day, Milla arrived at 9 a.m. and went into hair and makeup until about 10:30. I put her in the outfit that Dick and Kevyn had decided on, based on the Polaroids, and she was dressed and in position by 11. Because all the lighting was done the day before, Dick took a few test shots, moved her around a little bit, and then took the real photos. We were done by 11:30. Lunch hadn't even arrived yet.

Ironically, for that *Vanity Fair* Tom Ford Hollywood cover, we actually shot at Dick's old studio on Seventy-Ninth Street, which is the ground floor of his old brownstone and incredibly narrow. We had rows and rows of lingerie, more lingerie than you can imagine existing—new, vintage, cheap, extravagant—hanging on racks along every wall and overflowing out the door into the hallway. I would say there was probably close to five hundred pieces of lingerie (though very possibly more). You had to have everything, just in case someone felt something in the moment. People at photo shoots are always feeling *something in the moment*, including me. That's why I never, ever do a run through in advance. I basically just pull as much as I can manage, and then decide in the moment what feels right.

"... fashion people see a
# SENSUALITY AND ARTISTRY
## TO THE HUMAN BODY
... that's why we make clothes: as an artistic expression for the body."

The women showed up in great spirits and, surprisingly, without the large entourage you would expect. The sight of all that lingerie was a little frightening, I'm sure. At least, that's how I would feel. I started trying bras and camis on these women, these famous women naked in front of me, with all their handlers barking various things, "she won't wear that, no way, love that," all these voices coming at me like I was slowly going mad. I'd just about gotten Keira, the last girl, into a lacy pink, mostly appropriate lingerie set that Tom and I agreed coordinated with the other two when it happened. Everyone was feeling something on set, and the concept was changing.

Maybe the Renaissance painting idea might be better interpreted if there was no lingerie. It wasn't about nudity in an exploitive sense but more nudity in an artistic sense. This has always been a gray area in the world of fashion, when people argue whether nudity is tasteful or tasteless, and like many artists before them, fashion people see a sensuality and artistry to the human body. If you think about it, that's why we make clothes: as an artistic expression for the body. And having fashion credits brings the art to reality and makes the statement into something else.

So of course, now my job was to get everyone in position, as we'd plotted the day before. There was just one hitch. One of the actresses was okay with the lingerie in a tasteful manner but nudity was a different issue; meanwhile, Scarlett and Keira were up for anything. I tried to take a confiding approach with the other actress, and I really did feel bad. The direction had changed, and she wasn't on board.

And she left.

Which is how the cover of Tom Ford's Hollywood issue got even crazier, and even more Tom Ford. "Well," Annie said, unfazed. "Tom, why don't you pop in? You're our third cover subject." And since he was always impeccably dressed, he didn't even need an outfit change (Tom, somehow, got to keep all his clothes on).

In the end, the cover made perfect sense: the gorgeous Tom Ford lounging over two naked ingenues. You just don't get much more Hollywood than that. As Tom got into his pose, I readied Scarlett and Keira, getting them into Annie's desired positions, very carefully unhooking each of their bras and nervously showing them where they should put their arms. On the bottom, they were wearing tiny little G-strings, the ones that we stylists all carried in our prop kits. (Generally those nude G-strings of choice were Calvin Klein or Only Hearts.) Once Tom was in place and Keira and Scarlett were positioned, I snipped their underwear on both sides and slid the bits of fabric out from under them. I remember at that moment, with no less than twenty-five people staring at me, wanting me to hurry so we can get the shot, I was thinking: *This is what my job has been reduced to. Cutting thongs and carefully sliding them out from underneath A-list movie stars.*

Many years later, I photographed that actress who left for the cover of *Elle*. I remember bringing up the Hollywood-gone-naked episode, and she smiled. I respected her for standing her ground, and for saying no to us. It's very easy in fashion, and in Hollywood, to doubt your own convictions and let yourself be swayed. But this actress made the decision that was right for her at that time, and I admire her for doing so.

\* \* \*

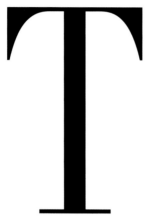HE SAME ISSUE OF *VANITY FAIR* also had me talking actor Eric Bana out of his shirt. Terry Richardson was the photographer, and if you are familiar with Terry Richardson, you know he is pretty famous for bringing a certain level of sexuality into his pictures. He's not just about shock, though; he's immensely talented, and his photographs have this raw quality, like the most intimate personal snapshots. I loved Terry's pictures because, yes, they were raw, but more so, he got celebs to do things for him that they generally wouldn't do for anyone else, and you have to respect that. I love someone who can coax a new picture out of someone whose picture has been taken a thousand times.

Eric Bana, though, was this fairly proper Aussie, but as the new heart-throb—I think he held the title in that spread of "The Man's Man"—Tom wanted him to be the sex and the sizzle of the Hollywood portfolio. And he was all lean and muscly, having just filmed *Hulk* and Steven Spielberg's film *Munich*. Everyone knew from the beginning that the goal was to get Eric Bana's clothes off.

Everyone, of course, but Eric Bana.

There are some celebrities who don't need much smooth talking before they're gamely pulling their sweaters over their heads. I'm not saying they get naked easily; they're just less inhibited. We all have friends like them (or maybe *you're* the friend like that). In any case, a guy like Eric Bana is not that kind of celebrity. He would need convincing. *Munich* was a huge movie, and Eric wanted to be respectful to Spielberg. He didn't want to always be portrayed as the hunk, never mind naked. He didn't even want to be shirtless. He wanted to be a serious actor, and that I completely respect. I think when it comes to young actors, it's so easy to immediately say, let's take that picture with your shirt off, but I can see how that just reduces anyone to being "hot" and not necessarily talented. Today, a picture can live forever, so in ten years when you win your Oscar, it'll be your shirtless picture that everyone will see.

Tom was a true art director. He really believed in the artistic importance of getting the shot just as he'd imagined it in his head: sexy, provocative, cheeky, and, at the end of the day, very Tom Ford.

We were shooting at a beautiful house in the San Fernando Valley, in the middle of the dry-as-dust desert. We started shooting Eric dressed in an

## "Everyone knew...the goal was to
# GET ERIC BANA'S
# CLOTHES OFF.
## Everyone, of course, but Eric Bana."

Armani suit, but it was the Valley, and over a hundred degrees that day. I was wearing shorts and a T-shirt and sweating through. Tom Ford, meanwhile, always maintained his cool composure in his three-piece navy suit and French blue shirt. BLUE SHIRT! All without a single drop of sweat.

Terry and Tom suggested Eric get into the pool. "You'll be more comfortable," said Tom, "and, of course, it's sexy, a man wearing a suit in a pool," like it's the sort of thing you see all the time. Though I do admit, that's a photo idea I have resorted to many times. There's something about being fully dressed—in black tie, no less—submerged in a pool that makes the fashion all the more enticing.

Eric, fully submerged but still fully clothed, waded around the pool, his Armani suit sleeves floating around him. He pulled himself up on an inflatable lounge chair. After a few takes, Tom turned to me and said, "Joe. We've just got to get him sexier. I know you can do it."

"What should I do?" What *could* I do?

"Just do what you do, Joe!" Tom said. "You can make it happen. I believe you can."

Ugh.

I climbed in the pool in my shorts and T-shirt—because I was not about to strip down in front of Tom Ford—to try to sweet-talk the Incredible Hulk out of his clothes. "We got the suit pictures," I said to Eric, as charmingly as I could, as I bobbed alongside his floatie. "They look great, really amazing. But maybe, hmm, what do you think? Would you consider letting us try something more swim appropriate?"

"Sure," he said, smiling. "But I don't want to wear a swimsuit." Let's see. What was swim appropriate if not a swimsuit?

I suggested a compromise: He'd wear a swimsuit, but with a bathrobe on top. "That way, it still feels appropriate in the pool," I said, "but you'll be covered up."

We changed into the bathing suit, a turquoise-blue Speedo with a big, plush white robe on top, and I accessorized with '70s sunglasses and a gold watch—I told Eric as getting into character, "Very *Scarface* meets Versace model." Now I had to get Eric onto the raft in the pool without him getting wet, one of the more glamorous aspects of my job. Naturally, the floatie had floated away, as they do, and I had to wade into the pool to go after it and bring it back for Eric, and then very strategically get him on the thing without a drop of water getting on the bathrobe or Speedo. Then I moved out of the frame as Terry began to shoot.

Between each shot, I moved in to adjust the robe, showing a little more leg, a little bit more abs, and a little bit more chest. There I was, a sopping wet grown man trying to pry open Eric Bana's bathrobe. Each time I showed more skin, he pulled it back a little bit.

Because it's Terry, he of course got the perfect iconic shot—there's leg, abs, and only a peek of Speedo. To this day, I think Eric would agree it's a really good picture. And it's one of my favorites ever.

What I learned that day was that when it comes to celebrities, you *are* a negotiator. A photo shoot is a big group of people with a vision, and everyone's got to be traveling at the same speed, in the same lane, with the same destination. It's the job of the person in charge to get everybody aligned with that vision. If one person is off course, the whole thing falls apart. So you're a negotiator, a director, a therapist. You're whomever they need you to be to get the photo. This would come in handy later as I worked with more and more celebrities. One of my most memorable shoots was with a starlet who loved to take things home with her from shoots, without asking—as in, steal them. I knew this when I would go shoot her because many designers would not lend us clothes because they assumed they'd never get them back. But I thought, clearly they must be exaggerating. How bad could one person be? I can handle this tiny girl.

Couldn't I?

I remember this one particular shoot with this girl (let's call her Miss Five Fingers). She had spent the better part of the day fawning over the jewelry she had borrowed. "I love Cartier," Miss Five Fingers would say. And then she would go on to tell me that the jewelry company would be fine with her "borrowing" it for an extended period of time.

"That's great," I said, trying to hide my horror. "Let me just call them and let them know." My assistant called, and, shocking no one, Cartier said not to give it to her.

Twenty minutes later, I went to go get one of the bracelets to put on her for the photo and it was gone. And I knew exactly where it was. I didn't want to accuse her to her face. I also wanted to make sure we got the photo shoot done, so I needed to keep the peace. So—good judgment or not—while we were taking the photos, I just had my assistant go into Miss Five Fingers' handbag and take the bracelet out and put it back on the jewelry tray.

Half an hour later, the bracelet was gone again. *This is comedy*, I thought. "Go get it back out of her bag again," I directed my assistant. Things went on like this for a few rounds—she'd steal the piece, we'd steal it back—while the photo shoot was going on, and not a single one of us, her nor I, would acknowledge any of this insanity—until finally I had my assistant call Cartier and asked them to send over a security guard, who stood there for the rest of the shoot as Miss Five Fingers scowled. A good stylist, I realized, also knows when it's time to call in the backup.

# GET INTO
# ERIC BANA'S ROBE

## (AND OTHER LESSONS IN GETTING YOUR WAY)

I'VE SPENT YEARS cajoling and coaxing celebrities to wear things they're not that into or, in some cases, to not wear things at all. I've actually gotten quite good at it—and have found that those skills of persuasion have applications in other areas of life. Here are a few things styling has taught me about getting your way.

✓ **BE THE COCONSPIRATOR.**
Look him in the eyes. Tell him you're on his side. Maybe grab a shoulder. And blame someone else, if you can.

✓ **SHOW RESPECT.**
You will never convince anybody of anything if you're not respectful.

✗ **DON'T LIE.**
Or make promises you can't keep. 'Cause you'll get busted later.

✓ **PRACTICE ACTIVE LISTENING.**
Nod your head. Say you get it. Repeat back to him what he's just said. Respond to his concerns.

✗ **BUT DON'T BACK DOWN.**
Show you're willing to listen, but that your beliefs are firm.

✓ **GIVE CREDIT.**
And here's the real trick: If you can manage to convince the other person that what you want was actually her idea first, you're golden.

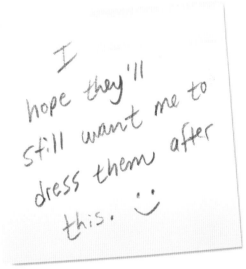

*I hope they'll still want me to dress them after this. :)*

{ OPPOSITE } Eric Bana for the *Vanity Fair* Hollywood portfolio, photographed by Terry Richardson. I'm the one who had to take his clothes off.

# ANNIE LEIBOVITZ, 1; AL GORE, O

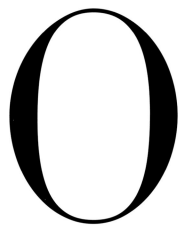

**O**NE OF MY FAVORITE COVERS of *Vanity Fair* that I styled was the first-ever "Green" issue in 2006, featuring Julia Roberts, George Clooney, Robert Kennedy, and Al Gore. Annie planned to shoot each person separately, because of their schedules, and then assemble the photograph in postproduction because coordinating four major news-making celebrities would require military precision and with the technology we have today, we have the opportunity to shoot them separately.

We photographed Julia Roberts first. Thanks to the theme, I was tasked with finding the perfect green (obvi) gown, which took forever because there is no such thing as the perfect green gown, especially when you're looking for it. The Stylist's Rule says that when you're looking for something, it doesn't exist until the shoot's over, at which point you will see fifty of them.

A great fashion department really knows how to dig things up. But there are limits, and green eveningwear is one of them. Ultimately, I had to have the gown specially made, by designer Richard Tyler. Like always, we set up the shot with a body double, and when Julia arrived, she popped in for twenty minutes and we shot that picture. Then we shot George, then Robert Kennedy in the same manner. Minus the green gown, of course.

The last person to be photographed was Al Gore. By then, of course, the picture was three-quarters done, and completely done in Annie's head. All Al needed to do was sit in his designated position, inspired by an old Penn portrait. I hadn't met our former vice president before, but I didn't expect anything other than perfect professionalism. I was ready for him the minute he arrived, Secret Service and all. In fact, I had been prepped earlier by his aides that he wanted suits from Big and Tall. True story. But when he arrived, he headed straight for Annie, who showed him how the other three had

{ OPPOSITE }

Thank-you notes. My favorite thing. Getting them and giving them.

{ FOLLOWING SPREAD }

If there's one thing you can say about fashion people, it is that they are polite.

come together and what the whole thing would look like. Al was meant to be in front, seated, so that you could see all of him but not miss an inch of Julia's green dress and because that's just how Annie had pictured it happening.

"I'm not sitting on the floor" is all Al said. He wanted to stand. Which, of course, would have been a completely different picture. This discussion was one I stayed out of, leaving the room to go find some clothes that needed to be steamed.

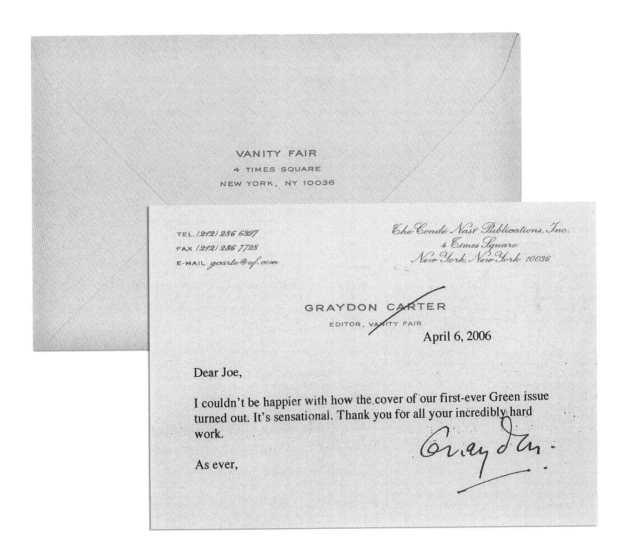

VANITY FAIR
4 TIMES SQUARE
NEW YORK, NY 10036

TEL. (212) 286 6397
FAX (212) 286 7728
E-MAIL goarte@vf.com

The Condé Nast Publications, Inc.
4 Times Square
New York, New York 10036

GRAYDON CARTER
EDITOR, VANITY FAIR
April 6, 2006

Dear Joe,

I couldn't be happier with how the cover of our first-ever Green issue turned out. It's sensational. Thank you for all your incredibly hard work.

As ever,

Graydon

Julien Macdonald

To
Joe
Thank you So Much. I

DONATELLA

Dear Joe,
Rihanna Rod...
AND glamour...
...

ALEX WANG

Yves Saint Laurent

October 2009

Dear Joe —
Wow! The Jule
...cover.

Joe —
THANK YOU FOR THE
PHOT OF 6n...

VICTORIA BECKHAM

Dear Joe,
thank you so much for
beautiful cover!
XVB

MARIA GRAZIA CHIURI
PIER PAOLO PICCIOLI

Dear Joe,
Thanks to have thoug
tino for your est...
The pieces are eme
Hope to see you again
Kind regards,
VALENTINO

ALLISON WILLIAMS

Joe —
I cannot express how fun today's shoot
fun shooti...
You made...
before!
faith in...
wait t...

DONATELLA VERSACE

Dear Joe,
As always, VERSACE & VERSUS
look incredible in your stories!
Love,
Donatella Versace

RICCARDO

Dear

Dear Joe,
That jumpsuit...
AMAZING in your shoot!
Thankyou so much! X Stella

...25 m...
gorgeous cover 4...
Sincerely

RALPH LAUREN

Dear Joe,

Congrat...

new ...

for ma...

os...

---

MICHAEL KORS

DEAR JOE,
WOW! THE GWEN
COVER LOOKS SO CHIC.
LOV...

---

TOMAS MAIER

JOE –

YOU SO MUCH...

OF "EHE...

---

NICOLAS GHESQUIERE

Dear Joe,

ome TO PARIS AND MANY
...ULATIONS
TO ...
...AS VERY
...oined

---

L'WREN SCOTT

Dear Joe,

Thank you so much fa...

London
11.11.10

---

Dear Joe, Thank you
for having me at E! Event
and for making me one of
your Covers. I had a wonderful
evening, and look forward
to working with you in
the future soon.
Best, Elizabeth Olsen

---

...STOPHER KANE

'I..A wanted
...hank you
...t the pic
...my sweater.

...the most
...u support-
...much love...

---

JOE

SJP LOOKS SICK'..
lOVED THE IMAGES, & ENJOY
THE PINEAPPLE BUNS : )

xo ALEX

ALEXANDER WANG

After a lot of heated discussion between the former vice president of the United States and one determined, convincing, and very famous photographer, guess who won?

It wasn't about power, though, at least not for Annie. It was about fulfilling the vision she had in her head. When your vision is so strong, executing it becomes an almost physical need. It needs to live somewhere outside your head. That's how some artists work, and definitely how Annie works. I mean, she sees what she sees. That's why she's so amazing.

# THE PHOTOSHOOT AS
# THE AMAZING RACE

I CONSIDER AN AHA MOMENT TO BE ONE OF those times when you realize, with some real self-awareness, exactly what sort of person you are—and, sometimes more important, are not. I had my first aha moment in the sixth grade. Early in the year, our teacher, Mrs. Benaroia, assigned us a long-term project, the sixth-grade version of the grad school dissertation. Its completion would mean we were ready to "graduate"—to junior high. The project was to put together a full-scale, in-depth, multimedia report on a country of our choosing. It would include a written analysis, a 3-D model, and a final oral-visual presentation in front of the class. It was an exercise in complete immersion in a single topic as well as an undeniable study in time management.

Which I failed, and miserably.

Not the project part, of course. My final grade was an A. But the rest of it . . . Well, call it a precursor to an adult life spent in perpetual last-minute panic. Eight months was an excessively long time to work on even an extensive project, I thought—painfully drawn out and unnecessary besides. Surely, I could get this thing done in one.

I gave myself three—days, that is. On the Tuesday before the final Friday presentation, I packed my backpack and had my mom drop me off at the library to begin my research on the great country of Brazil. I'd chosen Brazil because it's the fifth-largest country in the world and I was nothing if not ambitious. Pulling it off was a seventy-two-hour whirlwind of stats and graphs and plaster molds, and I did not sleep at all that very last night (but hey, I figured, if someone with the energy of a twelve-year-old—i.e., an actual twelve-year-old—can't pull an all-nighter, who can?). On Friday, I walked into school with a hand-painted 3-D relief map of Brazil, complete with tiny plaster monkeys dotting the Amazon; a forty-eight-page report on the country, its industries, and its economic system; and an oral presentation that included a samba demo. I'd like to say I got a standing ovation, but I'm sure I'd just be glamorizing it a bit in memory.

# "I THRIVE ON CHAOS, AND I LOVE BEING SCRAPPY.

I want to sit on the floor, roll up my sleeves, and be as literally hands-on as I can be."

Afterward, I collapsed into my seat, exhausted. But also completely exhilarated. At one point during that seventy-two-hour push, I'd wondered: What would my report, and my experience of doing it, have been like if I'd actually started in September? Or even April? If I hadn't left myself no choice but to crash in this project at an insane, possibly unhealthy pace? My project was going to be flawless, I knew—I was a procrastinator, but I was also a perfectionist—but could it have been *exceptional*?

But then I realized: This is just who I am. There's no sense in dwelling on the what-ifs, since there's no scenario where I'd have done it any differently—as cemented by the adrenaline rush I felt in the wake of completing the presentation with such bleary-eyed success. I was sure I wouldn't have felt so thoroughly, so physically, satisfied with myself if I hadn't been forced to pull off the near impossible. And that was a feeling I wanted to repeat. The harder it is, I thought, the better it feels.

And, of course, this is how I still approach most projects today. While it's true that creatively, I prefer to be able to be spontaneous—to feel "in the moment," as we fashion types refer to it, and allow for the possibility of changing course without warning, whether it's during a photo shoot or a live TV appearance—I'm also just a die-hard last-minute person. After all, it wasn't a desire to feel in the moment that made the twelve-year-old me wait until practically the night before to start a fifty-page report. It's just who I am and always have been, and it's never going to change. This book you now hold in your hands? It was meant to come out a year and a half ago. Truth be told, the number-one rule for being a slashie is to prioritize. And prioritizing for me meant doing in the immediate moment the project that was due.

My ability, and almost necessity, to work under the gun, has come in handy over the course of my career. I live for a challenge. And maybe sometimes I treat my job like a game show—you could win, you could lose; it's anybody's guess—but some of the most satisfying shoots I've put together are the ones that were completely on the fly. I call them "panic-mode shoots," characterized by the fear that this time, I've met my match: *There's no way*, I tell myself, *you're going to be able to pull this one off. This is the job that will surely get you fired.*

When I was styling projects for *Vanity Fair*, photo shoots were big-budget, highly planned labors—true labors—of love. I didn't complain; there was a great luxury in having so much time and money to pull off a certain project. But something was missing. There was no running around. There was no panic. And so there was no adrenaline. What's more, the stakes weren't as high because if the photo didn't come out well, there was often the option of simply not running it. There was always a backup, and a backup to the backup.

But I thrive on chaos, and I love being scrappy. I want to sit on the floor, roll up my sleeves, and be as literally hands-on as I can be. Magazines like *W* and *Elle* have sizable budgets, comparatively, but every year they seem to shrink. At *Elle*, if a story was planned, we always ran it. If you shot Lea

Michele for the cover, there was no backup. So it had to work, whether you were given one hour or eight, a generous budget or a not-so-generous one. But that was fine by me. I can have four hours or I can have twelve hours. I find that if you know how to manage the time you have—and you know what you're doing—the results will be the same.

This is also why I have never turned away any celebrity or subject because of time constraints. For *Elle*'s September 2013 issue, we featured Karlie Kloss in a six-page fashion story. It was the first time we'd ever featured Karlie in *Elle*, and I was super excited. "She'll be at the Soho House hotel giving a presentation," her rep told me. "She can give you thirty minutes during one of her breaks." *Thirty minutes*, I thought. *Really?*

But what came out of my mouth was: "No problem." And I meant it. When the day arrived, my assistant booked a room in the hotel. We removed all the furniture and had the photographer set up a white seamless backdrop along one wall. I put the entire crew on standby. A freelance stylist and I assembled potential outfits, knowing we'd have mere seconds to choose between them; the photo assistants were ready to rearrange lighting at a moment's notice. "When she comes up," I told everyone, "we have to move like lightning." And that we did. During one of her breaks, Karlie rushed up to our room. I changed her into the first look as the hair and makeup people she'd brought along with her touched her up, then put her in front of the backdrop as our photographer, Bruno Staub, began snapping. Our crew of fifteen lined the edge of the room, ready to jump in but out of the way until then, as Bruno's digital tech and I sat on the bed—which had been shoved into a corner—looking at the images as they came through Bruno's camera. I'd hover behind the tech, my eyes fixed on his computer monitor, where each frame would appear in the seconds after it was taken, and yell "Next!" as soon as one came in that hit the mark. We got everything we needed in thirty minutes. Karlie blew everyone air kisses as she rushed off back downstairs.

"Well, that was fun!" I announced to the crew. We put the room back together and headed downstairs for lunch.

\* \* \*

{ OPPOSITE }

A fitting Polaroid with Jessica Biel for her first *Elle* cover (2006).

A T THE END OF 2012, I TOOK JESSICA Biel to Paris for a rare big-production shoot for *Elle*. She was to be featured on the cover. Inside, we'd planned to photograph her alongside eight different designers, dressed in something of their creation and choosing, Jessica acting as their "muse." I had done something similar with Jennifer Lopez in 2008, shooting her in Milan and New York City alongside Domenico Dolce, Oscar de la Renta, and Donatella Versace, and it was a big hit. Lots of work, but with a huge payoff: You had the star power not only of J.Lo but of the individual designers as well. I'd always wanted to try to revisit the idea.

For Jessica, we had two days in Paris to get everything done. Just to give you some context, most of my cover shoots were usually done in four to five hours. But here there were eight different designers on board: Giambattista Valli, Olivier Rousteing, Martin Margiela, Christian Louboutin, Azzedine Alaïa, Jean Paul Gaultier, and Valentino creative directors Maria Chiuri and Pierpaolo Piccioli. Each photograph required a unique location that made sense both for the designer and for the story as a whole. Because they would appear in a single fashion spread, all the photos needed to be linked somehow, to flow from one to the next. At the same time, each picture needed to be able to stand on its own. The absolute worst thing I can possibly imagine of someone reading *Elle*, or any other magazine I've worked for, is of them going "Flip, flip, flip, flip," and not even stopping. If I can get you to stop, even for a moment, and look at that picture, I've done my job. That is the entire point of all this effort.

Because these were major label designers with very strong opinions—not to mention massive PR machines handling their every move—each design house needed to approve the photo shoot's location and concept. They obviously already had a say in what Jessica wore, given that they were

{ RIGHT }

Jessica Biel presenting me
an award in 2013.

choosing, or creating, something for her. But there were many time restric-
tions—no one had enough time.

Which is why this story would not have happened with a celebrity less
agreeable than Jessica, who wanted it to work out as much as I did, or a
photographer less game than Thomas Whiteside. Thomas is a photographer I've worked with since he first started taking pictures—he was a skilled
photo retoucher and used to be a makeup artist as well. He'd been shooting
for *Elle* since 2007, when I brought him on to shoot the opening page of the
front of the book section in *Elle* called "First Look." He graduated to taking
pictures for my column and then fashion stories in the well, which is a magazine term for the second half of the magazine where there are no ads. But
this would be his first cover. You might say it was his Avedon moment: a big
break, but one he also had worked incredibly hard to achieve.

Jessica, meanwhile, is a truly special person, and I mean that in both
the personal and physical sense. If you think she looks good in photos, or in
movies, you haven't even seen the half of it. In real life, she is truly stunning,

mesmerizingly beautiful, with a supermodel quality about her. I like to say, if Cindy Crawford and Christy Turlington had a baby, she would look like Jessica. But the best part is that she's just so damn easy. I hate the word "real," but she's that. She's real. She's like your sister, only a thousand times hotter (and probably nicer to you, too).

Jessica was the first cover I shot when I arrived at *Elle* in 2007, and coincidentally Jessica was also the first cover I shot when we launched *Yahoo Style,* my digital magazine. But at *Elle,* the photographer who shot her first cover with me was Gilles Bensimon, and I could not get over the fact that Jessica just looked good in every single thing we put on her. There was just nothing she couldn't pull off. I remember the first time I introduced Jessica to my boyfriend, Rob. It was at the Fashion Media Awards in New York and Jessica was presenting me with the award for Creative Director of the Year (yay!). "She's so beautiful," Rob said to me afterward, all flustered. "I couldn't stop staring at her. Was I staring? I was staring." She's so breathtakingly beautiful that she glows. She just has that thing. Actresses, too, more than models, become characters in front of the camera. So while she has the beauty of a supermodel, she has the depth and intensity and adaptability of an actress. Don't get me wrong: A model like Karlie Kloss can come in and get the job done perfectly in as few as five frames. But with an actress, it's almost like making a movie.

For two days, I dragged Thomas, Jessica, and our entire twelve-person crew all around Paris. It was early October, and the city was at its worst: cold, rainy, miserable. Jessica was flying in from LA and so we met in Paris—but what I did not know was that she'd recently visited this same city for a final fitting for her wedding dress. She would be getting married two weeks later to her then fiancé, Justin Timberlake, but of course I didn't know that at the time. I also didn't know who would be designing her dress—though I was dying to find out.

I did have my suspicions. But she didn't spill, and I didn't push. It's because we're friends that I knew that if she were interested in sharing the details with me, she would have. I thought perhaps one of our shoots might confirm my hunch: One of our featured designers was Giambattista Valli, one of Jessica's dearest friends. I was prepared to do some sleuthing.

PRADA

BOB MACKIE

GIOIA NECKLACE

LOUIS VUITTON CAPE + BOOTS

PASSION BAIT PANTIES

GIVENCHY

BILL BLASS

PERRY ELLIS by MARC JACOBS

DOC MARTEN'S BOOTS

COURTESY OF GABE DOPPELT

YSL

COVER

GIORGIO ARMANI

F. LEIGHTON NECK & EARS

GUCCI

MARC JACOBS
JP TODS SHOES

yohji yamamoto

STEPHEN SPROUSE (DRESS EAR
ELSE ANITA SHOES

GISELE / DETAILS

NARCISO
VICTORIA'S SECRET

CALVIN KLEIN
JIMMY CHOO SHOES

From CALVIN KLEIN ARCHIVES

CHRISTIAN DIOR
Adrienne Landau
Necklace - KJL RINGS - KUO

RALPH LAUREN
RALPH LAUREN ARCHIVES

VALENTINO

**JUST LIKE US!**

*DRESSING LIKE A CELEBRITY, EVEN IF YOU'RE NOT*

THE REALITY IS, most women do not walk around every day with a glam squad of hair, makeup, and stylist, but I refuse to believe that you still can't look equally as flawless and chic. Here are some rules I learned along the way.

### ✓ KNOW WHO YOU ARE—AND DRESS ACCORDINGLY.

It's not just about knowing your body type, or what's flattering, but knowing what sort of style persona you can realistically pull off. When you try too hard, you end up looking like . . . you're trying too hard. Actresses tend to play it fairly safe for a reason.

### ✓ CONFIDENCE IS THE BEST ACCESSORY.

Actresses are constantly criticized on the Internet and in tabloid magazines. An everyday woman may not have to go through the same scrutiny, but there are times where you may question what you put on. My rule of thumb here is if you love it, do it. And screw the haters. How many times have you looked at a picture of a celebrity and thought to yourself, "Oh, I would never wear *that*, but she looks really great in it"? Because what you see is her confidence, not her clothes, and that's the key.

### ✓ FIND INSPIRATION IN UNLIKELY PLACES.

I know from talking with her that Jessica is endlessly influenced by the characters she plays and the movie sets she's on. You can find similar inspiration in your own life, from people in your town or travels you go on.

( ABOVE )

Jessica Biel and designer
Giambattista Valli,
photographed one
month before she got
married in his dress,
and I had no idea.

(Courtesy of Thomas
Whiteside-Trunk Archive)

But when Giambattista showed up to her room at the Plaza Athénée for our shoot, it was like no big deal. They hugged as if they hadn't seen each other in months. We ordered room service and everyone chitchatted. As we started taking pictures of the two sitting together on the plush bed like a couple of teenagers, I remember thinking: *Maybe?* But everyone was so poker-faced that I thought, *Nah. No way.*

He always wears a strand of pearls—that's his calling card—and in the photograph she's reaching out and delicately examining them while wearing his macramé short shorts and tweed jacket. It was a very big, but very intimate and easy, moment. And yet their body language revealed nothing. At the very least, I thought, there'd be a coy smile exchanged. A side-eye, perhaps. But nothing. Zip. Not a single whisper. When he left, there was no hint of a "call you later." I was convinced that the rumors were true. "It's not Giambattista making her wedding dress," I told an editor friend back home. "It's Oscar de la Renta. It's got to be."

Dear Joe,
I was so thrilled
to see the beautiful
photo of me & Jessica in Elle —
the photo captures the
great relationship we hope—
many thanks again
Happy Holidays—
Best,
Gianbattista

{ ABOVE }

Giambattista Valli's thank-you note for the Jessica Biel *Elle* photo.

Some designers for this story weren't even confirmed until I was already in Paris—that's how on the fly this particular project really was. Back in New York, Joann Pailey, *Elle*'s market director, was placing hourly calls to the press team over at Azzedine Alaïa, whom we'd been hoping to include. Mr. Alaïa, though, is notoriously press shy. "I don't know," his press team kept saying. "He just nevvvverrrrr does these things." What's more, he's very discerning about which celebrities wear his clothes. Jessica had never worn Alaïa to an event. I was sure the photo with him was going to be a bust, but I wasn't going to stop asking until we got a firm no. Jessica is gorgeous, sexy, and statuesque, and I was convinced: If anyone should be wearing Alaïa, it's Jessica.

Mr. Alaïa typically avoids Paris Fashion Week, instead opting to show his latest collection to a small group of editors on his own timetable. That year, this show was scheduled during our Paris trip. Joann called with an idea: "Is there any way you can bring Jessica to the show, and maybe he'll do it after?" There was no guarantee he'd say yes, of course, and then we'd have spent the day at a fashion show for nothing.

It was a risk. But how amazing, I thought, if it actually worked?

I asked Jessica what she thought and we decided to roll the dice. At the very least, we decided, we could say we'd been to an Azzedine Alaïa show, itself an exclusive event. So we went. The final model was barely off the runway when I bolted out of my seat and rushed up to Mr. Alaïa's press director.

"Yes," she said, with a coy smile. "Mr. Alaïa will take a picture with you."

There was no time to get excited. He told us to pick out something for Jessica to wear.

"Can I get the python bra top with long knit skirt?" I asked, referring to a look that had just moments ago paraded down the runway. A few minutes later, the outfit having quite literally been ripped off a model backstage, I started getting Jessica dressed, pouring her into the snakeskin top as Thomas set up the shot in Mr. Alaïa's dressing room. Mr. Alaïa, we were told, was five minutes behind us.

When he arrived, he was incredibly gracious and sweet—and almost in awe of Jessica, which I found so intriguing given his firm opinions on celebrities—but stayed for only three frames. Thomas, bless him, needed no more than that. The resulting photo has Mr. Alaïa standing in Jessica's shadow, peeking out from behind her, his hands on her hips, her long hair au naturel—because we had no time for anything else—and framing her face. Standing at least a foot taller than Mr. Alaïa, she looks like an '80s glamazon and he like the reserved designer he is, content to let people wear his clothes but not seeking the spotlight himself. The entire shoot probably occupied a tenth of the time of his runway show. But it didn't matter. All we needed was one good picture, and we got it.

And, in fact, I don't think it could have been any more perfect. That one picture completely encapsulates Mr. Alaïa's personality, which, of course, was the entire point.

# IT'S A SHOE THING

I DON'T HAVE TO explain this to fans of Christian Louboutin, but in my opinion, the shoes are the most important aspect of whatever you're wearing. A great pair of shoes can make an outfit, while a bad pair can unmake it. Often, in fact, I remember shoes better than I remember names or faces. There's one fashion publicist whose name I just can't keep in my brain, but every time I see her I remember the Chloé booties she wore the first time we met. Similarly, every time one of my girlfriends complains that she has "nothing to wear," I give her a very simple rule: Start with your feet.

It's not even just about looking good. The perfect pair of shoes can transform your entire attitude. When I shoot a magazine cover, I might pull a hundred shoe options even though you'll very rarely see feet in the final shot since the cover photo is almost always shown from the waist up, if not closer. But I need my subject to feel a certain way, and for that you really do need the right shoes. The right shoe changes absolutely everything about the way you look. It changes the way you stand. It changes your attitude. It changes the way you project yourself. Those things are important in a photo shoot, and they're important in real life, too. A friend of mine even chose her wedding dress based on a pair of heels she'd fallen in love with, and I don't think that's strange at all.

The bottom line: Take the time to pick out the right shoes, and keep them updated, too. If you can't spend a ton on both clothes and shoes, put more cash into what goes on your feet. From flats to mega-heels, here are my favorite can't-go-wrong shoes and what to wear them with.

### BROGUES.

Not just for the boys, brogues add a bit of edge to feminine looks. Try a pair with an A-line dress, cropped pants, or cutoff shorts.

### SNEAKERS.

The trainer genre is more fashionable than ever. Wear a pair of Vans with a miniskirt and cropped jacket, or tuck your skinny denim into a pair of bright high-tops.

### CLASSIC PUMP.

You can never go wrong with a classic pump in a midsize (two- to three-inch) heel, which adds polish to denim and a button-down, a jumpsuit, or a simple dress.

### THE WEDGE.

These miracle shoes elongate the calf, making legs of all types look thinner, and they're easier to walk around in besides. They tend to pair best with casual looks, like day dresses or denim, and can also be worn through the fall and winter with opaque tights.

### ANKLE-STRAP HEELS.

Chic with pencil skirts and ultrafeminine dresses. The strap lets you play around with super high heights while not having to worry about losing a shoe when running to catch a cab.

Sometimes, the most satisfying moments—in fashion and in life—are the ones you let happen. Had I insisted on controlling the situation or not been willing or able to shift gears—had I been more of a control freak or dictator about how things went down or how much time I needed—this photograph never would have happened. You have to be nimble, I realized, if you want things to work out. For me, being agreeable and amenable is the most effective professional (and personal) strategy. That's not to say you don't stick up for yourself when needed, but I think so many people, especially in fashion, are ultrastructured and so set in their ways. They have a plan and They. Must. Stick. With. It. For me, it's always been better to roll with the punches.

"So many people . . . are ultrastructured and so set in their ways. They have a plan and THEY. MUST. STICK. WITH. IT. For me, it's always been better to roll with the punches."

On the complete opposite end of the spectrum, but requiring a similar willingness to just go with it, we photographed Jean Paul Gaultier, who is bubbly, gregarious, and all about having fun. He's just as pressed for time as everyone else, and yet he'd have you sit there all day and night, telling stories about everything from Madonna to his recent trip to Bangkok. And he thrives on spontaneity, as we found out.

Jean Paul's atelier is located in an old building on Rue Saint-Martin. It's gorgeous inside: baroque moldings and mirrored walls—the perfect setting for a photograph. Instead, he said: "Let's go shoot on the roof!" It was pouring rain.

And yet who were we to doubt the vision of Jean Paul Gaultier? To get to the roof—which, I learned later, no one ever goes to, and for good reason—we had to climb through two offices and then brave a truly death-defying fire escape accessed through a trap door. Should there be a fire in that building, I can't imagine anyone would be getting out alive. Since it was raining, it was wet and slippery, too.

We dressed Jessica in a menswear-inspired getup: pinstripe blazer, trousers, cotton poplin shirt, and tie, with leather pumps. It was very Madonna Blond Ambition tour. That season's collection had been inspired, Jean Paul told us, by musical icons that included David Bowie, Annie Lennox, Grace Jones, and Boy George. "Give her an umbrella," he directed someone on his staff, who provided Jessica with a black-and-white-striped parasol. To complete the scene, he had male model-dancers on hand to don very Gaultier-esque bondage-type gear: leather pants, stiletto booties, cage corsets, and black leather versions of the classic Gaultier bustier. As they danced and kicked and posed precariously on the slick edges of that roof, Thomas snapped away. Sitting in a chair beside Jessica, Jean Paul was getting soaked. He looked as if he couldn't imagine a better afternoon.

* * *

LATER THAT DAY, WE PHOTOGRAPHED Christian Louboutin at the Musée d'Orsay, one of the most breathtaking, but proper, museums in all of Paris. Museums in general are notoriously impossible to stage photo shoots in, and this one even more so. But Christian is on the board and was set to attend a black-tie event there that evening. He put in the request for us to shoot there, and we were given the okay to get it done in the hour before his event.

Upstairs, museum staffers were setting up for the gala as we had Jessica climb onto a giant clock in front of a window in the Salon de l'Horloge, the twilit Paris skyline in the background, wearing a wool knit dress by Azzedine Alaïa and patent leather T-strap pumps by, of course, Christian Louboutin. Though you can't really tell in the final photo, the clock is suspended high above the ground. Jessica is lying on its beamed edge as Christian hovers behind her—which he could do because he's a trapeze artist. That's right: The most famous shoe designer in the world swings trapeze for fun and exercise, and he's really very good at it. So his balance is impeccable.

But he's not Spider-Man. We couldn't have him hovering there forever—plus, the man had a party to go to. We got the shot in twenty minutes, after which Christian hopped off the clock and went off to his event. "Au revoir," he said. "Thank you for playing with me."

It was an amazingly fitting conclusion to a tornado of a fashion shoot that had us racing against the clock at every turn. And I mean at every turn: Two weeks later, back in my office as the story was about to close, the news broke. Jessica had become Mrs. Justin Timberlake in a small ceremony that had taken place in southern Italy. She had walked the aisle, of course, in a big pink dress made by none other than Giambattista Valli. "I can't believe you kept that a secret!!!" I said the next time I saw her. "You two were cooking that up throughout our entire photo shoot!" There was an accompanying story about Jessica, and she emailed the writer from her honeymoon—later revealed to be in Tanzania—to give us a quick quote to include in our story, revealing only as much as she was ready for but sounding about as happy as I knew she must be. "Honeymooning is the best thing about being a newlywed," she wrote. "I wish I could honeymoon forever."

{ FOLLOWING SPREAD }

One of my last photo shoots for *Elle* magazine with the legendary (and all-around nice guy) photographer Arthur Elgort. I dressed all those superheroes.

(Copyright © Arthur Elgort)

# DASHING
# THROUGH PARIS

TOUR THROUGH SOME of my favorite places in Paris that I visit when I'm there, including during this Jessica Biel photo shoot.

### ✳ PLAZA ATHÉNÉE
25 Avenue Montaigne, 75008,
plaza-athenee-paris.com

### ✳ AZZEDINE ALAÏA
18 Rue de la Verrerie, 75004,
palaisgalliera.paris.fr/fr/expositions/alaia

### ✳ JEAN PAUL GAULTIER'S ATELIER
325 Rue Saint-Martin, 75003,
jeanpaulgaultier.com

### ✳ MUSÉE D'ORSAY
1 Rue de la Légion d'Honneur, 75007,
musee-orsay.fr

### ✳ HÔTEL COSTES
239-241 Rue Saint-Honoré, 75001,
hotelcostes.com
I stop in here for a late-night meal and a to-go candle featuring the hotel's signature scent, created in 2001 by famed French perfumer Olivia Giacobetti.

### ✳ ROBERT ET LOUISE
64 Rue Vieille du Temple, 75003,
robertetlouise.com
Some say rustic, some say hole-in-the-wall, but either way, most Sunday nights in Paris when I'm in town you will find me at this steak-and-salad spot, drinking wine out of cups and, at the end of the night after the kitchen closes, perhaps dancing on a table.

### ✳ COLETTE
213 Rue Saint-Honoré, 75001,
colette.fr
Sure, it's on absolutely everyone's Paris hit list, but there's a reason for that. I like to pick up little gadgets, books, and candles.

### ✳ STUDIO HARMONIC
5 Passage des Taillandiers, 75011,
studioharmonic.fr
Where I get my exercise in Paris, featuring classes by French choreographer Yanis Marshall, known for being one of the few men in France to offer classes taught in heels!

### ✳ BOB'S KITCHEN
74 Rue des Gravilliers, 75003,
bobsjuicebar.com
To counter the late-night meat and wine indulgences, I spend my breakfasts and lunches at this vegetarian spot owned by the brother (whose name isn't even Bob) of American designer and retailer Steven Alan.

# THE FAME GAME

## OR, BLAME IT ON THE MOVIE STAR

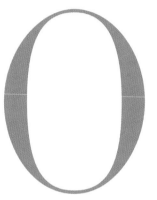

**O**NE CHILLY FRIDAY NIGHT SOMETIME in 2012, I found myself outside on a street corner—instead of comfortably inside Balthazar, eating steak frites with the rest of my friends—on the phone with Barbra Streisand, who had many requirements for our upcoming *Elle* shoot. This was but the first of five such lengthy conversations, during which I called her Ms. Streisand (until the fourth, when, hallelujah, at last she said, "Please, call me Barbra"). We had never before met, and she wanted to know how I might describe my aesthetic, the angle for the shoot, and what I was planning to bring.

I sat on a metal parking structure as tourists whizzed by, happily enjoying the start of their weekends, and I told her. And then I listened. And listened. Ms. Streisand told me about her extensive vintage collection. She asked: Should she wear glasses? Or no. Should she not wear glasses? She wanted me to know that there were certain colors, designers, and fabrics she wouldn't wear. Also, she might be late, and would that be a problem? She hoped not.

Eventually, she called me while getting a manicure in the salon in her house, putting me on speakerphone as her nails were buffed to basically tell me that she had decided that she wanted to look like herself in the picture.

Then, once the magazine was out, Ms. Streisand called one last time, wondering if it might be possible to get the post office to move the mailing label on any issues yet to be delivered. Turns out the label was covering her shoes.

\* \* \*

WHEN YOU WORK AT A FASHION magazine, there are those pop culture, in-the-news celebrities you expect to work with at some point. Then, sometimes, you're surprised by celebrities you don't expect. This is how I might categorize how I ended up on the phone one Saturday night for almost two hours with Faye Dunaway. We wanted to shoot her for the *Elle* Women in Hollywood issue, and so my entertainment director, Jen Weisel, and I got on the phone with her to discuss the concept. Midway through the conversation discussing how the photos would look, Faye wanted to talk about the interview portion of the spread and her clear disdain of *Mommie Dearest*. Jen and I just sat quietly on the phone and listened to Faye talk about not being happy with her performance in the movie, which she had talked about in other interviews before. But when Faye Dunaway is telling you personally on the phone, it takes on a whole new meaning.

Like Barbra, Faye was old-school Hollywood and wanted to talk personally about what the photo shoot would be like, what she'd be wearing, who the woman would be in the picture, and what character she would be playing. It's generally unusual for a cover celebrity to call me to talk about what her cover is going to look like, so you have to give some respect to someone like Faye.

\* \* \*

I WAS ALWAYS COMFORTABLE WITH STYLING CELEBRITIES for a cover, so when I was asked to style them for the red carpet, I thought, well, how hard could it be? It turned out to be a lot harder than I thought.

I mostly got into personal celebrity styling and the occasional red carpet moment because actresses that I had longstanding relationships with asked me, and honestly, it's hard for me to say no. I've always loved and felt very inspired by these women, and so dressing them for the red carpet seemed to be a natural side gig. Fifteen years ago, a personal stylist was rare. Now, celebrities enlist stylists for their everyday life, not just for the red carpet. All those pictures you see in tabloid magazines of young starlets running in and out of Starbucks? They were most likely styled. But it wasn't like that not too long ago, even on the red carpet. I remember watching the 1990 Academy Awards show from the thrift store couch of my first New

"Today, getting dressed for the red carpet is a

# STRATEGIC, PLOTTED EVENT

... that memorable look, good or bad, will be forever immortalized on the World Wide Web."

York apartment when Kim Basinger waltzed along the red carpet wearing a one-sleeved ball gown that, she proudly announced, she'd made herself, bless her, or even when Sharon Stone showed up wearing a Vera Wang skirt with a Gap white cotton button-down she had pulled from her closet at the last minute. Those days are gone. Today, getting dressed for the red carpet is a strategic, plotted event, and for good reason. There are so many moving parts that have to be taken into account to score that winning look—from the right dress that doesn't look like anyone else's to the perfect hair and makeup—because that memorable look, good or bad, will be forever immortalized on the World Wide Web.

For years, I'd been asked over and again whether I might dress so-and-so for a red carpet event, especially so-and-sos who'd loved how I'd made them look in magazines. Though it sounded exciting and glamorous and lucrative, I was always nervous about saying yes. I was worried that I'd be tremendously bad at it, and then what? What would that mean? Again, that creative insecurity came up. I didn't want to be the person who avoided risks out of fear of failure, though I was exactly that person. In many ways I still am. I like knowing, before I start something new, that I'm going to be good at it. Would celebrity styling be my undoing?

When Hilary Swank and her publicist came calling in 2002, for the 2003 Oscars, I stopped saying no. Hilary Swank is lovely and sweet and gorgeous—and just not a person you say no to.

I'd become friendly with Hilary and her publicist, Troy, through some shoots we'd done together for *W*. They'd always been pleased with my sensibility—a little bolder, I'd say, than Hilary typically gravitated toward. But the Oscar she'd won a few years earlier, in 2000, for her performance in *Boys Don't Cry*—and the fact that she wasn't up for any awards this particular year, though she was presenting—afforded her the freedom to take a few chances. Hilary and Troy wanted something different.

That's why they came to me.

Hilary seemed like a sure bet, and a great way to ease into this new world. I felt confident that plenty of designers would kill to dress her, and that people would be excited to see what she was wearing, so I'd have no problem pulling plenty of options or even getting something custom-made. Designers are extremely opinionated when it comes to which celebrities wear their clothes—on the red carpet as well as in magazines—which means stylists are at their constant, if unpredictable, mercy. It's not enough to simply be famous. Top designers often care more about "the message" and whether a girl is "right for the brand" than about exposure. They have to be *feeling* her, and that can mean just about anything. This is how to explain why someone like a reality star, even a Real Housewife, might have a tough time getting designers to dress her. She may be beautiful, and have one trillion followers across various social media platforms, but does she have the right vibe? Fashion is not an especially welcoming industry, even for those

# LEARNING TO SAY NO

### (TIPS FROM A MAN WHO CAN'T SAY NO)

H OW DO YOU know when a trend isn't for you? When it feels like you're trying too hard. If you're not a miniskirt type of girl, don't force it. A good editor always follows his or her instincts. Harem pants are not for everyone; neither are high-top wedges. What works for you? How do you know? Easy. It's instinct. Everyone tells you to step out of your comfort zone, but I stay step back in. Embrace your comfort zone—elevate it, sure, but embrace it, just like how we know what we want to eat and what we don't want to eat. If you like broccoli, have the best-prepared version of broccoli. Don't start eating red meat just because everyone else is.

who help move product. Let's use Kim Kardashian, as an example. Designer Roland Mouret once noted that he's more likely to get orders on a dress that Kim has worn than Kate Middleton.

Hilary, though—beautiful, smart, classy, A-list Hilary—was pretty uncontroversial. She had the body, she had the face, and she was smart and talented, too. Piece of cake.

We had plenty of time, months, to prep. She'd worn American designer Randolph Duke to collect her Oscar, so I was in a European state of mind this time around. Hilary and I talked, and decided that we wanted John Galliano, then at Dior, to custom-design something special for her.

Now: A person doesn't just pick up the phone and give John Galliano a ring. Designers have celebrity liaisons who act as the communications middle men so that the *creatives* can be *creative* and all that. At the time, this job at Dior was held by the VIP handler Alexis Roche. Alexis has a great sense of American celebrities and their personal styles, so I wasn't worried about how negotiations might go.

While I was in Paris for Fashion Week, I met with Alexis and discussed our vision for something feminine but not "gowny." Alexis went back to Galliano, who produced a stunning sketch of the dress he wanted to make for Hilary: pink ombré with layers of tulle, a cloud of chic cotton candy. It was not red carpet predictable, which is what I loved most about it, and it was incredibly beautiful. There was, just, that odd taffeta sort of underlay . . . but I didn't question it, or him. I mean, this was John Galliano. "It's perfect," I told Alexis. "Let's do it."

I later found out there's a reason red carpet dresses are often predictable. Predictable is good, safe.

Predictable is generally not fodder for the year's worst-dressed lists.

When the Dior couture dress arrived from Paris the day before the Oscars in a beautifully packaged crate, it was like seeing the illustration come to life. There's something really magical about a couture dress, because you can see every stitch that was done by hand by skilled seamstresses in the atelier. There were layers and layers and layers of delicate tulle that looked like it had literally been hand-painted. It was not your typical, slinky, strapless gown. It was like a cloud of sugary confection, and that's what I loved about it.

{ ABOVE }

A beautiful
thank-you
note from
John Galliano.

The next morning, I set off for Hilary's hotel room, where she tried on the Dior dress for the first time, and we all loved it, but it was different. I had brought backup dresses with me, because every good stylist knows he has to bring backup dresses even if the dress has been chosen, because in the world of fashion emergencies, anything can happen.

But in the case of Hilary, she felt good in the Dior, so I left her and her team to finish getting ready. I was busy piling my tiny convertible rental with all of the extra gowns (and a clothing rack that refused to fold up) when my phone rang. On the other end was a very good friend of mine, who was a makeup artist. She was with Cameron Diaz—also getting ready for the Oscars—and they were having a fashion emergency (See, I'm not kidding? This stuff does happen!). There wasn't much time left until celebs were expected on the red carpet, but Cameron was hating the dress she'd originally picked out. She wanted something new, my friend said, and could I help? Considering the $600,000 worth of dresses shoved into my back seat, I could! And I could be there in twenty.

One thing about me: I thrive under pressure and I'm excellent in an emergency, particularly a fashion one. As I maneuvered my way through LA traffic toward Cameron's house in West Hollywood, I made some quick calls and ended up stopping by the Calvin Klein and Prada boutiques on Rodeo Drive to pick up some more backup dresses, keeping with my mantra of "there's no such thing as too much" when it comes to styling.

Cameron's house then was at the top of a hill behind the posh Chateau Marmont hotel. An hour before she was meant to leave for the ceremony, I zipped up the street in my little convertible. I was in sight of Cameron's house when I heard a siren. The cops were pulling me over.

I was panicked. These Beverly Hills cops had no idea what was happening. Didn't they know *who I was* (going to see)? I lowered my window, dutifully handed over my license, and tried to remain calm as the officer proceeded to tell me I had made an illegal left-hand turn and I was speeding (*Obviously not fast enough*, I thought) when I blurted out, "But I have to dress Cameron Diaz for the Oscars! Cameron Diaz is leaving *now*!"

He looked at me sternly; then his expression softened. He leaned in conspiratorially. "Does Cameron really live on this street?" I said yes and pointed to her assistant, now visible at the top of the hill in the middle of the deserted road, waving like a maniac. "Good luck," he said, chuckling, as he handed back my license, but not before studying it, "*Joe Zee*."

Lesson no. 1: Dropping a celebrity name (even in LA) will probably get you out of a traffic ticket, so long as it is your first and you are not Lindsay Lohan.

I eventually made it to Cameron, of course, and she chose a stunning black chiffon-and-gauze dress by Prada that, thankfully, wasn't similar to one anyone else was wearing, a minor miracle given that it was chosen so hastily. To my delight, the dress even landed her on multiple best-dressed lists. See? Procrastination, it's my jam.

I was not so lucky with Hilary. In the end, as much as we all liked how different the dress was, it was not a hit with the fashion press. They likened it to a "ballerina costume" and "that time when I was a bridesmaid in the '80s." If you missed the red carpet that year, don't worry, because remember what I told you about the Internet? My styling on Hilary that year still reigns on such lists as "Worst Oscar Looks of All Time" and "The Craziest Dresses from the Last Decade" and "This Decade's Top Five Celebrity Fashion Disasters on the Oscars Red Carpet," right up there with Björk's famous swan frock. I guided Hilary poorly, and I still feel bad.

## THE SINGLE MOST IMPORTANT

# TIP FOR LOOKING GOOD IN PHOTOS

I N OUR INSTA-HAPPY times, everyone's a paparazzo. Good news: You can learn to be photogenic, even without the help of retouching. It's all about learning which angles, poses, and facial expressions work best for you (no to the duck face, the sparrow face, or, for that matter, any "face" that has a name). To do this, pre-Polaroid your outfit. As old school (and maybe vain) as it sounds, an outfit selfie will always be the most reliable predictor of how your clothing will photograph. Resist the urge to actually post it on social media, though. The only one who should be voting on what you wear out of the house is you.

Lesson no. 2: Certain looks work best in editorial and are probably not right for the red carpet.

When I was a kid, I loved this '60s movie called *It's A Mad, Mad, Mad, Mad World*, about a motley group of people on a crazy scavenger hunt for the same bag of gold. They all had the same clues and resources, and they were all battling for the same fortune at the end. It was basically *The Amazing Race*, starring Ethel Merman.

I came to the realization that red-carpet styling is a lot like that: a sport that requires a plotted game plan, expert maneuvering, and smart manipulation. It's a scavenger hunt with a big payoff. To play the game well, you need to plot some serious game, and how well you do that is the difference between being a good celebrity stylist and a great one. There is only one "best dress," there's only one great clutch, there are only so many great

# "RED CARPET STYLING
## . . . It's a scavenger hunt with a big payoff."

shoes. And a good diamond necklace? There's only one in the whole world. So every time, it's about who gets to it first.

I remember once when I was styling a big movie executive for the Oscars and I was trying to find her the perfect clutch. I drove from Jimmy Choo to Judith Leiber to Christian Louboutin, and every time I got to that showroom, someone had beat me there and everything was gone. *I'm never going to win at this game*, I thought.

Editorial stylists are a whole different breed. I don't think we understand this world.

Here's the difference: An editorial stylist worries about the picture. And pictures can be manipulated, tweaked, discarded, and redone. An outfit can look drastically different depending on lighting, attitude, pose, and accessories. Our goal is to fulfill a fantasy and create a beautiful photo.

A red carpet stylist, on the other hand, worries about the person. And unlike a photo, people can't be altered; they are who they are. An outfit needs to make sense for the personality wearing it, and it needs to be as unregrettable as possible because it will live forever in the fashion hell known as the Internet. One wrong pile of tulle, and you will go down in "who wore it worst" infamy.

But fitting a dress to a personality isn't the only reason red carpet dressing is far more restrictive. For events where you're not having something custom-made, you have to eliminate dresses worn by other celebs as well as *anything* vaguely similar. What's left is fought over by every stylist on both coasts, and designers have the ultimate say. My mistake was in thinking that because I dress celebrities for magazine covers, naturally I could dress them for the red carpet. But it's a totally different skill set that I'm not perfectly suited for.

\* \* \*

FOR A CELEBRITY, WORKING WITH A personal stylist isn't just about having someone get you on best-dressed lists or do your shopping for you. And it's also not always about looking good for one particular event. Many celebs turn to stylists to help them get a new look. And for many, wardrobe-driven rebranding is nothing short of reinvention. And it works.

This can be especially true for musicians, who often tend to use new personas—and corresponding wardrobes—to launch new albums or usher in new phases of their careers. I have styled my fair share of musicians, and they are a whole breed unto themselves. Because when it comes to music, image goes hand in hand. You can't think of Cyndi Lauper, Michael Jackson, or even the Rolling Stones and not also think about what they wore, so I understand why they care so much about it. Once, I was shooting Nicki Minaj, who was extremely adamant about looking at every single—and I mean Every. Single.—picture and making the photographer delete the ones she didn't like.

Madonna has reinvented herself many times over the course of her career, and indeed when you look back, her fashion probably defines her different life phases as much as her songs do: the virgin, the dominatrix, the yogi. Pop stars today, including Rihanna, Lady Gaga, and even Taylor Swift, have followed suit in recent years.

So has Justin Timberlake. Justin is one of pop culture's most stylish celebrities. I worked with Justin for many years, even before I got into red carpet styling, and saw him through some of his earlier transformations. I first worked with Justin in the late '90s when he was transitioning out of *NSYNC, which was coincidentally my favorite band at the time. I styled Justin for the cover of *Details* magazine, influenced by old pictures of Steve McQueen. That was the beginning of our career working together. Years later, for the Kids' Choice Awards, I styled Justin and Britney, separately, after they had broken up.

In the dressing room, Britney would burst into tears every time a sad song came on, so I spent more time fretting over how to prevent her from getting mascara on her borrowed dress than anything else.

I have always been a fan of Justin's, and giving him a look was an inspiring styling job. I loved that we were able to move between athletic hip-hop gear to something more sleek, and of course the evolution came even more so with his second solo album, *FutureSex/LoveSounds*. For that album, I was very inspired by "Rat Packers (like Dean Martin, Sammy Davis Jr., and Frank Sinatra) meets Quentin Tarantino," so that the look didn't feel too retro. I have a men's look that I always turn to, what I called the *Reservoirs Dogs* look. A black suit, a white shirt, a black tie. Because there's not one single guy out there who doesn't look cool in that look. But we would throw in touches of the Rat Pack, like a three-piece suit or a classic waistcoat. I remember being in Spain on another photo shoot when I called Justin and his team to talk about this inspiration, and ironically, they were feeling the same thing. And that's my point about musicians. When it comes to their image and the *right* image, they of all people know exactly what's going to work.

And really, that's what fashion is all about.

# SHOP EBAY

BACK IN HIGH school, when I had no money, thrift stores like Goodwill and the Salvation Army were my go-tos for ways to mimic the current trends. A no-lapel mustard jacket with shoulder pads could be Thierry Mugler! A Sears King's Road pinstripe vest: Byblos! I forgot about how satisfying this way of shopping was—the hunt with the big payoff—until I got to *Elle*, where I noticed the fashion assistants were particularly skilled at assembling killer looks on what I knew were very modest salaries by buying used and vintage looks on eBay. Did the new girl just parade by my office door wearing vintage Alaïa? She did.

Of course, with the glut of stuff on eBay—never mind the competition—it's absolutely key to approach online thrifting with a well-plotted strategy. Are you looking for knockoffs of a current designer item? Or a one-of-a-kind, long-extinct piece that you couldn't get—or couldn't afford—the first time around? I drilled the fashion assistants in my office for their latest tips on besting the competition and finding the perfect score. Here's what they came up with.

### SEARCH CONSTANTLY.

Use keywords to help improve your search. It's easy to find something with a designer's name, but try looking by style, genre, celebrity style icon, or fabric: "SJP," "glitter," "Kate Moss," "tribal." Search not for what you want but for how you want to look. Try adding the word "vintage" or "used" for different results.

### DIG INTO THE ARCHIVES.

eBay hunting isn't just about searching for this season's must-have pieces. It's also about looking for pieces from classic labels that are newly desirable—Céline, Balmain, and Kenzo are some current examples—because very often the present-day designer will look into the archives for inspiration.

### GET CREATIVE (OR DUMB).

Deliberately misspelling any proper name can often lead you to an undiscovered item. Yves Saint Laurent might be listed under "Eves Saint Laurent," for example, or Lanvin could be "Lanven," entered by someone who either is not so careful or doesn't know any better. Their silly mistake is your goldmine.

### ADD A PENNY.

When setting your maximum bid, always add an extra cent. Your $60.01, for instance, will beat out the person whose max bid was $60. Similarly, most bidders bid in even amounts, so an odd bid will increase your chances of walking away with the win—by a small margin, but still. Every bit counts.

### HIRE A SNIPER.

For a small fee (usually 1 percent of the final auction price) you can assign an "automatic sniper" to bid on an item for you in its final minutes. These snipers are both at the ready and quick on the draw. (Ezsniper.com and auctionsniper.com are two good ones.)

### BUILD A RELATIONSHIP WITH YOUR SELLER.

If you go back to the same vendor repeatedly, email that person and ask to preview items before they land online.

### BE PREPARED TO ALTER.

Even many of the best finds will need a bit of love: a new lining, a shortened hemline, narrower sleeves. Most local dry cleaners have tailors capable of making simple, high-impact adjustments, but be sure to factor in the potential cost of alterations before emptying your life savings on that "well-loved" Chanel tweed jacket or the black Givenchy maxi dress described as "extra large."

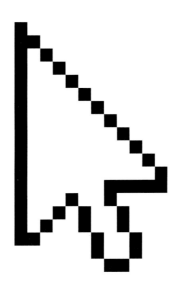

# MY FAVORITE SPOTS FOR VINTAGE

**F**OR ALL THE different musicians I've styled, they're the one group where I always had to look for the most unique things. So I turned to vintage, and, at times, even scoured eBay. And in hunting for those treasures, I've mastered a lot of tricks on how to score the best one-of-a-kind things along the way.

### 1STDIBS
A vast assortment of dresses, outerwear, and accessories from the 1920s onward. *1stdibs.com*

### NASTY GAL
Founder Sophia Amoruso started out rummaging through her local thrift shops for vintage items to sell through her eBay store; now the site offers new looks as well, but the vintage selection remains deep: as many as two hundred Chanel pieces at any given time. *nastygal.com*

### VETTA VINTAGE
Romantic, feminine, and one-of-a-kind items like cinched-waist dresses and animal-print coats. *vettavintage.com*

### COVET + LOU
A tightly curated selection of pristine vintage picks with an androgynous edge—plus vintage home goods to go with. *covetandlou.com*

{ ABOVE } RuPaul and me behind the scenes at *The Face*.

# THE
# BELLY
# WHISPERER

I**T WAS JULY 1991, AND I'D STAYED IN NEW YORK** to take classes throughout the summer. One afternoon, I wandered into the FIT bookstore for my weekly magazine binge, hoping for the new Italian *Vogue* (thank goodness for fashion school booksellers). Instead, I saw sweet Molly Jensen from *Ghost* staring blankly at me from the cover of the new issue of *Vanity Fair*, buck naked and big as sin.

"Demi Moore, that is a *crazy* idea," I said out loud, to no one at all. I was alone in the magazine section. I was confused that Demi, just off a major box office hit and at the height of her career, was posing naked and very pregnant on the cover of such a popular magazine.

And also, where was the *fashion*?

What I loved most about the cover was that it was shot by Annie Leibovitz and styled by Lori Goldstein, one of my icons, who I would go on to assist the following year. But what we couldn't stop talking about was the nudity. In the days following, my conversations with everyone at school were all Demi Moore. I talked about that cover endlessly—with my roommate, Carter, with our friends, with my newspaper staff. It was so shocking, it was all we could talk about. Nothing is shocking anymore. Everyone from twenty-one to seventy-one is baring it all on the pages of every magazine. But back then, a little bit of belly would make me blush.

How ironic, then, that eight years after that groundbreaking *Vanity Fair* cover, when I was at *W*, I would revisit the belly in person?

Cindy Crawford, photographed by Michael Thompson, was to be our next cover, and it was a huge get for the magazine: At the time of our shoot, Cindy would be seven months pregnant with her first child, and she had done very little press. The story was big: She was the first of her generation of supermodels—the first models to be supermodels, really—to get preg-

> "For a long time,
> # GETTING PREGNANT
> had been considered the death knell
> for a working model."

nant, and people wondered what it might mean for her, whether it would end her career or whether it would open up new doors. For a long time, getting pregnant had been considered the death knell for a working model.

We'd be catching Cindy on her last day in New York before she headed back to California, semipermanently, for the no-fly zone of her final trimester, which meant, I assumed, that she must be very, very big. I'd never before, at least not knowingly, dressed a pregnant woman—never mind a pregnant supermodel!—and I pulled a million body-conscious looks designed to highlight, and most definitely not hide, the fact that she was expecting. I'll be honest here: I really did not know how to style a pregnant woman, and I was just winging it.

Now, Cindy Crawford was and is one of the most breathtakingly gorgeous women in the world. She showed up at the photo studio that day

wearing jeans and a very cute—surprisingly tiny, I remember thinking—sweater, looking as flawless as ever.

"You don't look very big for seven months!" I said as I embraced her, and I meant it. Her belly looked no bigger than my own had often looked after a festive night out at my favorite Mexican place.

I won't pretend to imagine what it must be like to carry a child. My intent here isn't to downplay Cindy's, or any other woman's, experience. I think being pregnant is probably one of the best experiences any woman can have, and I wanted to capture that glow on our cover. But of course, she had to look pregnant to get that message across.

What could I do? I put Cindy in a fitted T-shirt and a pair of jeans. Michael took a few Polaroids to check the lighting and get a preview of how she might appear on film (this was routine back in the days before photographers worked in digital). He shook his head, called me over, and said, "Should we try a different outfit?" What came through on these Polaroids was not quite cover material yet.

I tried her in a dress. Still not happening.

From certain angles, Cindy did not appear pregnant at all. From others, she simply looked as if she'd had a beer too many.

"I don't think this is working," I told Michael. "She doesn't look like a mom-to-be. She just looks . . . bloated." We showed Cindy the Polaroids, and she agreed. "Should we try to make me look more pregnant or should we just shoot a close-up?" she asked. "Like a really close-up?" In my mind, while a close-up of Cindy Crawford is a win-win no brainer, I had to deliver a pregnant cover to my bosses. In the end, Michael, Cindy, and I powwowed and decided to try it nude. Michael has always been so successful as a photographer with his incredible eye but even more so his demeanor in working with celebrities. He was incredibly apt at making everyone feel so at ease.

Michael explained to Cindy how he could do it beautifully and tastefully—respectfully. He talked about how his own mentor, Irving Penn, was a master of shooting nudes and how much Michael had learned from him.

Months earlier, when she first announced her pregnancy, Cindy had declared in interviews that while she would continue working throughout her pregnancy, she would not be photographed naked, even though she had posed for *Playboy* the year before and liked the way she looked. But being pregnant was different.

But when Michael and I worked together, we had a way of inspiring trust. And Cindy was a professional. She, of all people, understood the desire to make an iconic picture, and the work we would have to do to get it. This photo was important not just for us but for her as well.

I promise you: Not one of us had walked in that day thinking we'd be re-creating a version of the Demi Moore cover, or anything like it. But the first few Polaroids confirmed it: This was the way to go. Whether it was going to be a giant hit or a giant flop—and I truly didn't know until the issue was out which one it would be—this was going to be an extraordinary, memorable cover. "How exciting for your baby," I said. "You'll always be able to tell your child that this was their first published picture. And it was the cover of a major fashion magazine."

In the end, some thought Cindy's cover was even more provocative than Demi's, and it didn't seem derivative in the slightest: Though her belly wasn't quite as large, Cindy was completely naked, except for a tiny Chanel necklace, and the picture was cropped just above her knee. She was, in the end, even more naked than Demi. And the cover in black-and-white gave it a next-level element.

Readers loved it. They were intrigued, and they were fascinated, and the issue completely sold out. Unlike today, supermodels back then just didn't make appearances while pregnant. Their brands were built on their bodies, after all; if they had babies, they sort of went away quietly to have them. Sometimes they came back. Often, they didn't.

Months later, long after she'd given birth to her son, Presley, Cindy and I bumped into each other. "The day after we shot that cover, my belly totally popped," she told me. We'd been quite literally a day early. But you know, as they say, timing is everything.

For the cover of our first (and, well, only) September issue at *Vitals Woman*, we booked Heidi Klum. She was about to have her second baby, and we planned an entire feature story on motherhood and parenting, highlighting cool celebrity moms plus advice and how-tos for shopping for mom

# WHAT TO EXPECT (TO WEAR) WHEN YOU'RE EXPECTING

N OW FOR A few words from Jessica Simpson. Jessica, a two-time mom, was gracious enough to share with me a bit about the experience of being pregnant in the terms I care about most: fashion and beauty!

*First of all, I tell people to be proud of your bump and show it off as much as you can. Love your body and all of the changes you are going through. You are a part of creating a miracle—embrace it! That said, be comfortable. I lived in leggings. I actually had a pretty hard time finding the perfect pair so I added them to my Jessica Simpson Collection maternity line, and I have heard from so many women that they are a wardrobe staple. I got to wear them in my second pregnancy, too. Drinking gallons and gallons of water a day also helped a lot. I actually found my skin to be better than ever as a result! I would love to bathe in almond oil, too, and I used Epicuren pro-collagen on my belly.*

*— J.S.*

and baby, beauty and fitness, etc. Heidi made perfect sense—there just is no cooler mother on the planet.

I had no intention of photographing Heidi naked, none at all. I was thinking versatile fashion, some forgiving A-line dresses. But there was *no way* I was going to do a naked, pregnant cover.

We did shoot many photos of Heidi wearing beautiful clothes. But, I'll be honest, I went there. Oops, I did it again. Michael was on board. I was on board. Heidi was on board. For the fashion story that would run inside the magazine, we photographed her in various states of dress—and undress: on her knees, naked; lying on her back, pretty much naked. But not for the cover. *Vitals* was a new magazine, and a shopping magazine besides. Did a naked celebrity on the cover make sense? Not really. And I was still wary of repeating myself. I wanted the cover to feel new and fresh. So for that shot, I put her in a very ethereal white dress by Yves Saint Laurent— which I made sheer by removing the lining— and, having remembered the Cindy incident, got a wind machine for the explicit purpose of blowing the dress flush against Heidi's stomach. I wanted the photo to show, in no uncertain terms, that this woman was pregnant.

{ ABOVE }

Heidi Klum and me doing our best duck faces (2014).

And even still, we needed to position Heidi—lunging forward, back arched—in such a way that her belly was emphasized. Heidi had the curvaceous figure, but her baby bump was still pretty modest. Supermodels are in a category of their own. Heidi, you might recall, famously returned to the Victoria's Secret catwalk just five weeks after giving birth to her fourth child. I also once ran into a supermodel at a party who told me she had given birth the night before. Literally, last night. At the party, she was wearing a skintight minidress. "All these other women seem so shocked about it," she complained to me. I was like, *Maybe because you gave birth twenty-four hours ago and damn, girl, look at you.*

I just think there's something so incredibly beautiful and sensuous about a pregnant, naked woman. And special: a real moment in time.

Once my shoot with Heidi was over and she was out the door, I turned to Michael. "No more pregnant covers," I said. After I moment, I added, "For a while, at least."

My resolution didn't last very long. Because soon, it's 2011 and Jessica Simpson has agreed to be on the cover of *Elle*. And she is pregnant, and very. I knew I'd be up to my old tricks again.

Because Jessica was so very pregnant—and I hated how the tabloid media had been such bullies to her throughout her pregnancy—I felt a special motivation to make her look gorgeous. That's the irony with the tabloids, and the readers of them: They bash celebs when they're too skinny and they bash them when they're less so, even when the weight gain is because they're carrying a damn baby. Just look at Kim Kardashian: She received constant negative press throughout her pregnancy for her weight gain, even though most other times she's heralded for not conforming to the "Hollywood ideal." What do you people want?

I knew that Jessica had struggled to find clothes that made her feel comfortable, while at the same time trying very hard to embrace her pregnancy—lumps, bumps, morning sickness, and all. When I started looking at collections from which I could pull flattering clothes, I realized: *Don't fight it, Joe.* I even commissioned my fashion designer boyfriend, Rob—I like to call him my "in-house designer"—to create two custom dresses for Jessica to wear. One she wore in the shoot, and the other she wore in the behind-the-scenes video that ran on elle.com. Both she took home.

And yet: Naked was best. It just was.

Seriously, though: You just can't top the nude pregnant lady. Clothes, for me as a stylist, are too risky. They can make it seem like you're trying to hide the woman's pregnancy—as in a recent *Vogue* story featuring a pregnant Kate Winslet shrouded in layers of thick fabric—or they could make it seem like you're trying to ignore it, sticking her in a tight dress and pretending the bumps aren't there. I did once photograph Nicole Kidman while she was eight months pregnant, but we had to hide her pregnancy, mostly so that we'd still be relevant when the story came out after she'd given birth.

Jessica, meanwhile, would still be pregnant, and just about to give birth, when the issue hit stands. For the cover, Carter Smith—yes, my old roomie!—photographed Jessica wearing an orange knit Narciso Rodriguez dress. "You look amazing," I told Jessica. "But dare I say it? Should we try this naked?" And Jessica agreed. She trusted our vision and she agreed. Her fiancé, Eric, was even on set and gave his total approval; he was glowing as

"And yet:

# NAKED WAS BEST.

It just was."

much as she was. That's when I decided that no, this wasn't exploitative. It was capturing a really amazing moment in time.

And so with Jessica, it *was* a Demi thing, an unabashed homage to that original naked pregnant lady. Carter photographed her naked, except for a hulking yellow diamond with earrings to match, staring directly at the camera. She looked great and told us she felt great, and it was one of the most positive shoots I'd done in my life. *People need to see as much of this* glow *as they possibly can*, I thought as Carter snapped away. By then, it had been twenty years since Demi's *Vanity Fair* cover. Jessica would be appealing to a whole new generation of people—the Demi Moore for the millennial generation. Unlike Demi, or Cindy, or Heidi, Jessica was pregnant in a thoroughly digital, tabloid-crazed age. And readers were clamoring for a shoot like this; I just knew they were.

Jessica was also a more modern cover mom-to-be because she was a more realistic role model. She didn't look totally amazing throughout her pregnancy—at least not Cindy or Heidi or even Demi amazing—but she never once apologized for it. She talked about being "constantly hungry" and how she "vegged out and laid around" and "let loose." Of all my pregnant celebrity cover girls, Jessica was probably the most relatable. And I knew that would resonate with people.

## " ... WHAT A TESTAMENT

to just how different and individual an experience pregnancy is for every woman who experiences it."

{ OPPOSITE }

Jessica Simpson on the cover of *Elle*, 2012. Up to my old tricks.

(Copyright © Carter Smith)

When our April 2012 cover hit the newsstand, on it a beautifully real Jessica Simpson cradling her belly, I didn't regret the decision to shoot her naked. We also released a version of her fully clothed, but when I saw the two side by side, there was, for me, no comparison. In fact, when I look at the three covers together—Cindy, Heidi, and Jessica—I think, what a testament to just how different and individual an experience pregnancy is for every woman who experiences it. That's what I wanted to celebrate, maybe without knowing it at first.

The response to the story—and the photos—was global. You could say it was the naked pregnant lady seen 'round the world. In the end, we got a billion press impressions from Jessica's cover.

In hindsight, of course, I realized: Though I might have thought, at the time, that I was shocked by the Demi Moore cover, I realized now, I wasn't shocked. I was actually inspired by it. And I certainly talked about it, and thought about it, for many years to come. And that was something, and something very important.

# HOW TO

# DRESS LIKE A MODEL

I PROBABLY SHOULDN'T ADMIT this, but I have a love/hate relationship with meeting new models, or what people in fashion refer to as "go-sees." It's an important part of my job as an editor, but for me it just feels so, I don't know, Simon Cowell on *The X Factor*. Flipping through a girl's portfolio and then dismissing her with a curt "thanks" is awkward; I hate confrontation and letting people down, and I just don't do these brush-offs very well. I can't stand to be even close to mean.

So I usually end up drilling a girl about her life: where she's from, how long she's lived in New York, what she loves about modeling (ask this one enough and you'll learn that most girls, in fact, don't love much about modeling at all). I justify this type of interaction because I truly believe that a great personality can make a girl with a so-so face light up on camera. I've seen it happen.

But what I look forward to most, and really the only reason I still do these go-sees as opposed to handing them off to my assistant or the magazine's model booker, is seeing what the models are wearing. I'm not the only one. The off-duty style of models is so influential that designers are often inspired by their models' senses of style, frequently taking a girl's personal quirks and transforming them into looks that land on the runway.

Back in 1998, when I was at *W*, a model agent at Elite called and asked me to please see one of his new girls, a young Brazilian import named Gisele Bündchen. "Yes, yes, I know it's all about the skinny Belgian girls right now," he said, "but I think you'll really like her." One look at her and I didn't even bother flipping through her pictures. I was mesmerized by this bombshell dressed like a tomboy in jeans, a battered old T-shirt, and Converse—and not a hint of makeup—who talked the entire time, charming me with stories of her life in New York. She left, and I booked her immediately. I had a similar experience years later with a girl who I knew nothing about—other than that she'd recently married tennis star Andy Roddick. And what was Ms. Brooklyn Decker wearing? Cutoff jean shorts and a simple sweater.

Which brings me to my point: It's actually pretty easy to dress like a supermodel in the making. It's all about adhering to my style philosophy—never, ever try too hard—and a few basic wardrobe staples:

### ✓ THE LOOSE WHITE TEE

Or the loose gray tee, for that matter. V-neck is typically the most universally flattering. Brands of choice include Kain, Citizens of Humanity, and J.Crew.

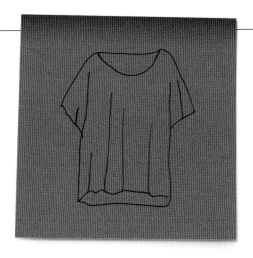

### ✓ MOTORCYCLE BOOTS

Biker boots are timeless, seasonless, and work for pretty much any girl, from the more feminine, who'll pair them with a floral dress, to the actual biker chick, who might wear hers with cutoffs and a T-shirt. Belstaff, Marni, and Rag & Bone always come out with great versions.

### ✓ THE PRINTED DRESS

A "new" basic—whether the season's showing florals or stripes or something totally different—that can be dressed up or down and is inherently more interesting than the ho-hum LBD. Pair it with a denim or leather jacket or a chunky cardigan.

### ✓ CUTOFF SHORTS

Now, I wouldn't recommend wearing these to a professional meeting, unless you're actually a model on a go-see (and even then, while it can obviously work for some girls, I typically prefer a more polished look from those looking to get a job). But for summer weekends, a great pair of cutoffs can take you from day to night and will last forever.

### ✓ THE BLAZER

The cut will change slightly from season to season—from cropped to boyfriend to fitted to loose—but the blazer itself will always be a wardrobe staple. For extra credit, roll up the sleeves.

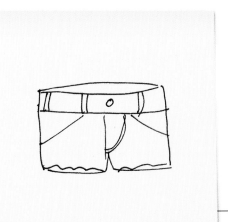

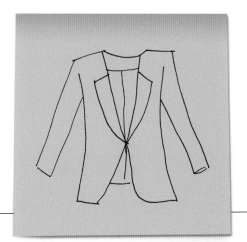

# MY SLASHIE LIFE

**Y**EARS AFTER MY VERY FIRST ENCOUNTER with Richard Avedon, he called me again. I was at *W* by this time, and he was shooting an ad campaign for the plus-size line Avenue, starring model Kate Dillon. Kate was the first plus-size model Avedon had ever photographed, and he wondered if I might be interested in styling her for the campaign.

I've always had more than one job at a time. In my younger years, that meant freelance styling gigs, helping friends of friends figure out what to wear to a big event, or dressing the occasional B-list celebrity. Now it includes styling ad campaigns, dressing and wardrobe consulting for major movie and pop stars, and all kinds of TV. In 2014, I launched a fashion line for QVC called Styled by Joe Zee, I was a spokesperson for Old Navy on their fall campaign, and then I landed a daytime talk show on ABC, in addition to my position at Yahoo. I constantly remind myself it's a good thing I don't require much sleep.

But the truth is, we are officially living in a slash generation. I'm not the only slashie in town, of course—the person with multiple job titles and projects going on at once. A few years back, Tina Brown coined the phrase "gig economy" to describe the project-based careers of so many postrecession

Americans, especially ones who earn a living in creative fields. In the fashion world, my good friend Rachel Zoe is one of the most high profile in the new breed of slashies, but you've also got blogger/designer/author Leandra Medine of Man Repeller and stylist/author/entrepreneur Sophia Amoruso of Nasty Gal. Everyone's got a side gig or four. When the customs official asks me what I do for a living, I say I'm an editor, but I really am no one thing. I *am* an editor, but I'm also a stylist, an author, and a TV producer; a red carpet commentator, a speaker, a host, and a designer. And when I

joined Yahoo, I also became a dot-commer! I never thought I'd be able to say that.

Part of the reason I do so many different things is that I get excited by what's new, so it's just been pretty impossible for me to say no to most offers. Not because I'm a pushover, but because I'm grateful for every opportunity that's presented itself to me, and they've all had some learning value whether the project was exciting or interesting or wacky or even just potential fodder for a great story to tell at a cocktail party. While I take every job I do seriously, I can't pretend that some don't really intimidate me. For those particular moments, I psych myself up by telling myself something I learned from a famous colleague: You have to give everything a try, and in the end, it will be a good time or a good story.

My inability to say no has in fact led to some of the best professional experiences of my life. For instance, about fifteen years ago, I got a call from a party promoter wondering if I'd be interested in deejaying a fashion party at a trendy downtown Manhattan hotel. Now, what did I know about deejaying? I was inclined to say no or respond with some ambivalent "maybe," a promise to "think about it," then never follow up. Except I was strangely drawn to the invitation. I've always loved music, after all. So I agreed, like I often did, and do: without having a single clue what the whole thing entailed.

The night before my DJ debut, I spent the evening casually burning CDs of my favorite dance songs: some Paula Abdul, a little Notorious B.I.G., and Madonna's "Vogue." When I arrived at the Soho Grand Hotel and the seasoned DJ handed over his headphones and quickly ran through how all the equipment worked, using terms like "bpms" and "cross-fade," I realized this was going to require a lot more than some burned CDs. *Whatever*, I thought, *I'll just get through this and never talk about it again.*

And that's when I saw a bunch of bigwig fashion editors in the crowd. One of them waved to me.

# "I'M GRATEFUL FOR EVERY OPPORTUNITY

## that's presented itself to me, and they've all had some learning value."

*Why, why, why do I get myself into these things?* I said to myself, letting the sonic stylings of soul group MFSB drown out my own self-loathing.

And then something miraculous happened: Whatever was happening on that deejay board before me just clicked, like I could suddenly read a foreign language. In that sink-or-swim moment, I swam, and I was good enough that I was even asked back. I ended up with that weekly DJ gig for a while. Until I realized I was probably better off as a fashion editor.

But back to the Kate Dillon shoot. So I arrived at Avedon's Upper East Side headquarters, a former carriage house that contained his photo studio on the bottom floor. This was maybe five years before he died; he was in his late seventies, then, and still working every day. In fact, he worked right up until the day he died. He was a man with much enthusiasm and love of life, and I think that's why we got along so well.

"Come upstairs," he said to me. "I want to show you what I'm thinking."

I hadn't realized that Avedon and his wife actually lived upstairs—though I think she was at their house in Montauk at the time—so I was expecting to be led into his office. Instead, "upstairs" was a sprawling, open loft space filled with all the trimmings of high society: ornate furniture, Persian rugs, lots of leopard, and, smack in the center, a four-poster, carved wood bed worthy of Henry VIII. Or at least that's how I remember it all.

"Sit down," he said, pointing to the mustard-colored velvet bedspread, and I did as I was told.

From a shelf nearby, Dick pulled out some big yellow boxes full of old contact sheets; this was his filing system. There were some strewn on the bed as well. There must have been thousands of boxes shelved throughout the room, I thought. And yet he'd found the one he was looking for. "I'm thinking a playful mood like this," he said, handing me some contact sheets of an old Marilyn Monroe shoot. The edges were yellowed with age, and the grease pencil marks that had been used on certain photos—his original edits—were crumbling toward disintegration. "But I also want some intensity, like this," he continued, passing me another stack of contact sheets, this time some black-and-white shots of Judy Garland. "I know they're different," he said. "Judy and Marilyn. Judy has that sort of very strong, solemn intensity about her, a darkness and sadness and vacancy in her eyes, even when she's smiling." Marilyn, meanwhile, was all fun and color.

He kept talking, explaining his concept for the Avenue shoot, passing me original outtakes of historic photo sessions with these now dead legends, contact sheets that probably belonged in a museum somewhere and not there in my hands, but I was busy having an out-of-body experience. All I could hear was Charlie Brown's teacher talking, *"Woh-woh, woh-woh-woh."* This was not me fulfilling some childhood dream. My wildest dreams had never even been this ambitious.

Toward the end, I snapped back to the present day to play catch-up. I didn't want him to think I wasn't paying attention, but I really wasn't. My thoughts were somewhere else: back in Toronto, maybe, as a kid who knew he was different but never could have quite imagined this. They tell you to follow your dreams, but sometimes your dreams take you places you'd never thought possible—you just have to let them.

* * *

**I** **TRY TO APPROACH STYLING FOR AD CAMPAIGNS** in essentially the same way I do magazine shoots. The main difference is that when I style for magazines, *I'm* the client. When I style an ad campaign, I'm working *for* a client, so my job is to please them. I try not to forget this. When I style a magazine shoot, I can tell a visual story over several pages. With ads, I have to do it in one, so the message has to be more concise.

At the same time, though, my basic styling philosophy doesn't change. Even though I prepare in advance, I arrive willing, expecting, to be flexible. I think mapping out exactly how any photo shoot is going to go is impossible, even when you're working in the confines of advertising (and especially when you're working with celebrities in those advertising campaigns). There are just too many factors.

In 2003, I got a call to style a fall campaign for the Gap called "A New Groove, a New Jean" starring Madonna and Missy Elliott. The Gap was a dream client because they were open to anything and ready to be surprised (hence the fairly unlikely pairing of Madonna and Missy Elliott). I was hired to style Madonna, all the backup dancers, and all the extras. Missy had brought her own styling team.

We shot on the Paramount Studios lot, and the concept was to create a movie lot feel. We cast extras as grips and cameramen, with two little people cast as Martians at the very last minute. I had a hundred other people to get ready, so I sent out an assistant to get something that might approximate Martian costumes, and in smaller sizes. She came back with two silver children's snowsuits and some headgear from a local costume shop. It was perfect—perfectly insane, but perfect nonetheless.

"Now all we need is something to cover their hands," I told my assistant. After scouring the city, she returned with two pairs of nylon children's mittens that she was going to spray-paint silver to match the snowsuits. It was the craziest outfit we'd ever dreamed up on the fly, and it was a tough job for these two actors to be wearing snowsuits in July in LA for ten hours, but they ended up right at the beginning of the commercial, parading casually across the set in their silver Martian snowsuits as Madonna launched into song. It was one of those days when I could not believe this was a job.

The Gap had given me the direction for the commercial. It was about corduroy pants. Now it was up to me to meet with Madonna to discuss what direction we wanted to go in and how she would wear them. I remember going to Madonna's house and meeting with her to discuss the look for these cords. She said, "Why don't we do something different? Why don't we find a way to customize these cords so they feel very personal?" Inspired by my designer jeans when I was teenager back in school, I remembered how important the design on a back pocket was for a pair of status pants, so immediately I suggested to Madonna, "Why don't we do an initial on the back pocket that could resemble a tattoo? Let's use a gothic font so it has that street toughness about it." She loved it. And to top it all off, I had a young designer back in New York silkscreen "Lady M" down one side of her leg, which I knew at the time would be the cherry on the sundae. We paired the cords with an alligator belt, a newsboy hat, a plain white tank, and, of course, five million dollars' worth of Neil Lane diamonds, because you can't do bling without going all the way. Missy, inspired by Madonna, wore bedazzled cords while she rapped the hook in the Madonna song.

The campaign was a huge success, and in the end, everybody shopping for those cords was also inspired by Madonna, and the Gap ended up doing customized back pockets for their shoppers.

Afterward, I ended up working with Madonna on a few personal projects, styling her for some events and doing a bit of personal shopping. With all of the world's best clothes in her closet and a crazy busy schedule, of course Madonna needed an extra set of hands to help her with store, keep, or toss.

In fact, I've been inside some of the best closets in Hollywood. When I was at *Elle*, we did a book for the twenty-fifth anniversary where I shot inside the closets of a lot of Hollywood personalities, among them Anjelica

{ OPPOSITE }

Sarah Jessica Parker trying
on the Oscar de la Renta
dress that he designed
for her lovely fragrance
campaign.

Huston, Lea Michele, and Dita von Teese. Of course there were all the wonderful women I've styled as well, where inevitably you always start dressing them *in* their closets. A closet says so much about a woman; it's like her handbag on steroids. One glance inside and I know right away what she's going to respond to. For example, you might expect Sarah Jessica Parker to be Carrie Bradshaw, with everything jammed in her closet. I know I did. But when I saw it, it was incredibly organized, polished, and edited, much like her own personal style. What's great about going into any woman's closet is that it reminds me of passing through into another world, like in *The Lion, the Witch, and the Wardrobe*. What child doesn't imagine opening those double doors and being transported to a fantasy land? When I grew up, I got to walk through those double doors for real as my job.

\* \* \*

WHEN YOU TALK ABOUT THE QUEEN OF the Closets, I would have to say that's Mariah Carey. I spent many hours and days in her closets (think rooms!) when I started working with her in the nineties. I first worked with the pop diva when I styled a portrait of her for a profile story in *W* in 1999. I put her in a sparkly Marc Jacobs dress and we fell in love—she was so fun and girlie and larger than life. Not long after, she hired Michael Thompson, who'd shot that *W* piece, to photograph the cover of her album, *Butterfly*, and me to style it. After that, I would go on to style the music video for "Honey," her first single off that album. It would be my first music video, and I was psyched.

I was, and am, obsessed with music. I have so much of it that my music library claims it would take forty days to play every song in it. As for videos

# CLOSET ENCOUNTERS OF THE WORST KIND

THERE'S THAT OLD famous saying that "the cobbler's children go unshod." So while my job may be to organize other people's closets, my own closets are candidates for an episode of *Hoarders*. For years, I kept everything I'd ever bought, borrowed, or been gifted, whether it fit or not, whether it was ugly or not. It was hard for me to part with things. Friends who had never been to my apartment always assumed I had this giant walk-in fashion wonderland of a closet featuring a *Clueless*-esque conveyor belt of clothes and shoes or maybe a little closet elf, but really, it was a giant mess. I had so much stuff that jackets and pants were overflowing from drawers and creeping out from beneath my closet doors. Shoeboxes were piled high in every corner. And I didn't wear any of it. Truthfully, I'm always in some version of the same outfit: jeans, a T-shirt, a jacket, and good sneakers. Swap a button-down and tie for the office, actual pants and shoes for an evening event. On weekends, the jacket becomes a hoodie. There was absolutely no need for me to be operating a showroom out of my apartment. Give me some good denim and a sweatshirt and I'm a happy guy.

So instead of spending the cash on having someone install fancy closets—a brief consideration—I resolved one weekend to clean up my act (and by resolved, I mean that my boyfriend, a real Virgo, made me do it). And toss it—like, all of it—off to Goodwill or friends or, in the case of some really special pieces, to consignment. And I devised some rules to ensure it never gets that bad again, which I'm going to share with you here. Take 'em or leave 'em.

✕ **TOSS:**
## MULTIPLES.

At one time or another, we all fall victim to buying things in triplicate. We worry that we so love the original that we'll be left sad and naked when it wears out or gets a stain. Except it doesn't wear out—or, by the time it does, the style has changed. Which means: There's no reason you need two of the same Dolce & Gabbana striped dress. Or four of the same black Vince hoodie, for that matter. Plaid shirts? Unless you're working the ranch, and I bet you aren't, I don't want to see more than four in there.

✓ **KEEP:**
## IRREPLACEABLE VINTAGE.

And no, I'm not talking about those ripped-beyond-wearability jeans from tenth grade that once belonged to your best friend Jamie. Or were they Kari's? It doesn't matter. If you're really attached to them, put them in storage, but keep in mind that sentimentality shouldn't be the reason for saving more than three items. High school was fun and all, but that velvet tie-dye swing dress won't be coming back, not anytime soon, or ever.

✕ **TOSS:**
## THAT THING YOU FORGOT YOU EVEN HAD.

Even if you're happy to see your long-lost floral cropped cardigan, let's be honest: Just like that fling from the summer of '98, you had no idea it even existed anymore. Move on.

✓ **KEEP:**
## BASICS IN SOLID COLORS AND TIMELESS SHAPES.

What tends to happen is that people keep the "special" pieces featuring interesting prints and even more interesting cuts. But then you run the risk of having a closet full of mix-and-match separates that don't actually mix and match. You might be bored with the simple black blazer you wore to death last season, but that's the sort of thing that'll come back around. Put it in the back corner. You'll be glad later.

✕ **TOSS:**
## STAINED AND FALLING-APART ITEMS.

On that note, if you've actually worn something to death—a knit that no longer keeps its shape or has moth holes or a stain, no matter how small, or a jersey dress with pills up the side—dump it. Even if you love it. Don't save it, thinking (as I have done), *Maybe someday I'll have someone make a replica,* because you will never, ever get around to doing that.

themselves, I was endlessly curious about how it all worked technically. Do the singers lip-sync? Or do they really sing nonstop? Does the song play in the background, or is it just added in later, in postproduction?

Let me tell you: The song does play—over and over and over. In fact, for "Honey," the song was playing all the time, booming from giant speakers in whatever location we were shooting at, as Mariah ran through take after take. After the first eight hours of hearing the same song over and over again, I thought: *I am going to end up hating this song, and soon.* And yet I didn't. Somehow, to this day, it's one of my favorite songs, perhaps because it fully and irreversibly worked its way into my DNA for life.

To understand what it was like to shoot a video at that time, you have to remember that this was the late '90s, when people still watched MTV and VH1 for the music videos, and pop stars spent millions and millions on them accordingly. What was supposed to be a three-day shoot kept going and going. It became the *Ben-Hur* of music videos. Mariah taught me that musicians, more than any other type of celebrity, march to the beat of their own drummers. Celebrity shoots hardly ever conform to "normal" hours. Most days we didn't wrap until way after midnight. Often, we'd *start* shooting in the middle of the night. My first day on the set of "Honey" I remember I took the latest flight out of New York and got to Puerto Rico around 1:30 a.m. When I checked in, the front desk gave me my call sheet: I'd be needed on set in an hour and a half. That's right. We'd be starting the day at 3 a.m., and I didn't end that work day until 1 a.m. the next day.

After those first few exhausting days, I realized that this was life on a music video, and I'd better adjust to it. It was like being in a completely different time zone, somewhere on the other side of the world, except we were just on some private island off Puerto Rico, which was rented out for the sole purpose of shooting this one music video.

The making of the video for "Honey" was nothing less than feature-length-production-quality work. It opened in a sprawling marble mansion with Mariah, as "Agent M," tied to a chair (while wearing a black strapless Dolce & Gabbana dress and Gucci heels, her hair blown out to perfection), a hostage to three outlaws played by the Jerky Boys (remember them?) in some insane James Bond–esque setup. She then went on to dodge assassins

# HOW TO

# DO YOU

## JOE ZEE

Over the last few years, I've noticed a real difference in the sorts of questions people ask me about how to launch a career. It used to be that I'd get questions about how to get into magazines or how to become a stylist. Now, people from the next generation ask me: How do I become my own boss? Look around: Your twelve-year-old neighbor is making a mint off a YouTube video and your doctor just launched a new line of products. It's important to know how to present and market yourself well, no matter what industry you're in.

The best advice I have for this is to try out as many different jobs as possible, starting as early as you can. These days, people want to work for themselves. The best way to know how to make that happen is to figure out, by trial and error, what you're best at, where your talents lie. Are you better writing or speaking? Do you look good on camera? (Not everyone is telegenic. You could be drop-dead gorgeous but look awkward on camera.) Once you figure out what you're good at, think about why people would want to buy what you're selling, whether you're selling advice or thoughts or words or entertainment. And then go out and <u>sell</u> it.

# JOE FOR HIRE

**W**HEN NEW PEOPLE I meet at parties or wherever else find out what I do for a living, they instantly step back, take a moment to compose themselves, look down, and ask in a hushed, conspiratorial tone: "Is what I'm wearing okay?" Which inevitably leads to: "I have these motorcycle boots/lace gloves/my great-aunt's mink stole at home. What should I wear them with?" That's when I slip into character, dishing out free style prescriptions. I don't mind doing this, but I don't have all the answers, either. Which is why my best advice usually comes down to this: Forget the fashion rules—at least the ones you think you know. As my mentor Polly Mellen liked to tell me, in so many words, "Style is an art. Living by the rules is for people who have nothing to say." Fashion is rarely black-and-white; that's what's so great about it. Here are some rules that are made to be broken. I hate fashion rules, because who made them?

## MYTH #1

### NO WHITE AFTER LABOR DAY

We shouldn't even be having this conversation anymore. White isn't the problem; it's the style that matters. White boots, white pumps, winter white coats, even white denim—perfectly chic for fall and beyond. Even strappy white sandals can work for an indoor evening affair when paired with a long, elegant gown.

## MYTH #2

### POLISHED IS PERFECTION

Again, this comes down to what you *think* you should be doing, namely looking photo-worthy all the time. But what is "put together," really? Instead of thinking what fashion should be, think about what it *could* be. I always say if a look is slightly "off," it's so much more interesting.

## MYTH #3

### CERTAIN COLORS CLASH

Some of my favorite color combos in recent years have been the ones Mom might have told you are never to meet: pink and red, black and navy, white and off-white. If it looks and feels a little wrong, sometimes that's when it's truly right. (One exception: red and green. Too Christmas. Another: orange and brown. Too Burger King.)

## MYTH #4

### NO BLACK AT WEDDINGS

Every summer, I'm asked no fewer than a dozen times by girlfriends and strangers, "What can I wear to so-and-so's wedding? I only have black dresses." Black is completely and totally wedding-appropriate, so long as it's done mindfully. Make sure dresses have structure, elegance, and an upscale fabrication. A sundress isn't appropriate wedding wear, whether it's black or any other color.

on a watercraft (that never went to sea), host a dance party with some sailors, and, of course, frolic on the beach with a male model. There was a sexy dive-and-rescue scene, where I was tasked with re-creating the classic Bond Girl moment where Ursula Andress, from *Dr. No*, emerges from the water wearing a low-waisted, belted, cream-colored bikini, a dagger strapped to her hip. I had that exact swimsuit copied by a young independent swimsuit designer for Mariah to wear. I had purchased three Betsey Johnson dresses that I cut down the middle and sewed Velcro for her to wear over the bathing suit so when Mariah's body double jumped off a balcony in that scene, she could rip the dress off to reveal the suit. When we came in to film the close-up of Mariah emerging from the water, she had to be wearing the exact same dress, which is why I made three—one for the body double, one for Mariah, and one as backup.

There must have been a hundred people in that video, including backup dancers and the aforementioned sailors, and I dressed every single one of them—armies and armies of people, all of whom required outfits that not only looked great but also wouldn't rip up the back at the hint of a pop-and-lock.

Mariah's "Honey" shoot was supposed to last for three days. I stayed for six, after which I had to tell Mariah's producers that unfortunately I had to go back to New York for my full-time job at *W*. I left my assistants in charge, and they came back three days later. In the end, you know why Mariah was such a major success: She knows what she wants, and she goes after it—and people are willing to work hard for her. I was, too, and I did, but I just didn't know I needed to block off weeks for a three-day job.

I went on to style many album covers after that, album covers that would end up debuting at number one on the Billboard charts, like Celine Dion's *Let's Talk About Love*, Justin Timberlake's *FutureSex/LoveSounds*, and Jennifer Lopez's *J.Lo*, but "Honey" would end up being my only music video. Of course I wanted to style others, but over the years, timing was never on my side. Whenever I'd be asked, I was always busy doing something else, which made me wonder, if filming a music video was so crazy, what would doing a feature film be like?

I had a tiny taste of that when I was asked to work on *Zoolander*, creating "supermalemodel" fashion looks for Ben Stiller's and Owen Wilson's characters, Derek Zoolander and Hansel. My friend Gabe Doppelt was heading up the VH1 Fashion Awards, where Derek Zoolander first made his debut, and was acting as a consultant on the film. She hired me to ensure that Zoolander and Hansel's fashion was accurate, if extreme (I pulled a lot of Gucci). In the film, Zoolander appeared on the covers of magazines like *GQ* and *Details*, for which we created actual magazine covers. I styled those shoots and generally helped the costume director dress Zoolander and

| | | | | | |
|---|---|---|---|---|---|
| **DELAWARE BLUE STEEL INC.** "**ZOOLANDER**" 5455 WILSHIRE BLVD., SUITE 700 LOS ANGELES, CA 90036 | | **VENDOR** | **CHECK DATE** | **CHECK NUMBER** | |
| | | 000000000703 JOE ZEE | 01/03/01 | **572187** | |

| INVOICE DATE | INVOICE NUMBER | DESCRIPTION | GROSS | DISCOUNT | NET |
|---|---|---|---|---|---|
| 01/03/01 | 010103 | REIMB EXPENSES | 748.51 | .00 | 748.51 |
| | | | | Total | 748.51 |

Hi Joe —

hope you're well — we miss you!

love,

Celia + Monica

Amount Subject To Tax .00 *DETACH STATEMENT BEFORE DEPOSITING*

Hansel as slaves to fashion, a few months of work crammed into one August. I read eleven versions of the script, and that was my first taste of Hollywood. I was even given a cameo, in the opening scene. I played a stylist (me!), of course, and I'm shown quite seriously fussing over Derek Zoolander as he fields questions from a reporter. I even had some lines, but they were all cut out because I wasn't in the Screen Actors Guild.

Still, I must have made some sort of impression, since Ben Stiller calls me out in the director's commentary on the DVD, and a year later, I got a call to audition for another movie. A casting director working on *Sweet Home Alabama* called to ask if I might be interested in reading for the part of Reese Witherspoon's assistant. "I'm a fashion editor," I told her. "I'm not an actor."

"Oh, I know exactly who you are," he said. Evidently, a *Zoolander* producer had recommended me. I guess I'd done an excellent job faux-styling Ben Stiller's look in that opening clip. "Can I fax you the sides?" he asked—the term, I'd later learn, for the portions of scripts used for auditions. "Sure," I said. "Why not?" If nothing else, I figured, as always, this would make for a great time or a great story.

When I got the script, the lines were written in broken English, which is how they expected my prospective character, a recent immigrant, I guess, to say them. I showed up to the audition nervous as hell, and even did a shot of tequila downstairs at a bar near the Disney building in New York City before I went in. I didn't get the part, but not because I wasn't any good. In the end, they rewrote the assistant role for a woman. I wasn't heartbroken, even though I had been practicing my best fashion victim phrases (lots of "Oh my Gods" and "No waaaayyyys!") and had been looking forward to taking instead of giving orders for a change. When I watch the movie, I think, *Should that have been me?* No. Everything happens for a reason. And the experience of the audition was enough for me.

# MY FLIGHT OF SHAME

**W**HEN I FIRST STARTED working in fashion, every photo shoot was like the *Vanity Fair* Hollywood portfolio: a major production and insanely expensive. Like, insanely, twice-as-much-as-my-annual-salary—for one shoot—expensive. We'd travel to exotic locations and our crew of twenty would stay at five-star resorts. We'd spend thousands of dollars to ship trunks of clothes and shoes ahead of time, just so we wouldn't have to haul all our overstuffed suitcases through the airports and through customs, where the uniformed, humorless (why is that, anyway?) officers inevitably wanted to know what business I had, exactly, transporting $78,000 worth of sandals across the Atlantic. "I know it's crazy; it's fashion," I'd say with a sigh, rolling my eyes for effect, then smiling big. They'd look at my passport, then back at me, and then resignedly wave me through. I either looked harmless enough or they just didn't want to deal with me and my shoe obsession. I couldn't really blame them.

Some of the exorbitance was justified. Fashion shoots, even the "simple" ones, take a great deal of planning to execute, and there can be as much setup required for a picture that will run at half a page in the magazine as there is for a ten-page fashion story. If you're photographing a person—a model or celebrity or some other live subject as opposed to, say, taking still lifes of shoes or clothes—you need, in addition to the subject and photographer, a hairstylist and makeup artist, otherwise known as HMU in our industry, their assistants, several lighting techs, a digital tech crew, and the stylist, plus multiple assistants. And that's just the beginning. Usually, someone from the magazine's art department will come, the art director or a photo editor, to assist the photographer with direction—or "feel"—or other visual

"You shot my
# SWEET SIXTEEN DRESS
## ON KATE MOSS
for the cover of *W!*"

logistics. There may be a story editor or a writer on hand to liaise with a celebrity's publicist or conduct an interview. Sometimes, we might also have a videographer on hand to shoot footage to run on the website, or "B-roll" to be used for promotional purposes. And, of course, the subject—especially if he or she is famous—will also bring a publicist, an assistant, or a full-on entourage. Interestingly, though, the more famous the subject, the fewer people he or she brings along. A CW network ingenue might have, like, six to eight people in her crew, but Robert De Niro shows up alone.

If we're conducting a shoot on location, as opposed to in a studio, we might also need a producer, a location scout, and a prop stylist. All of these people will travel with their assistants, too. Assistants are *very* important. These are the people who keep the trains running smoothly, leaving their bosses room for the creative work that's so necessary in these jobs.

One of my more major shoots was for the thirtieth anniversary of *W*, the August 2002 issue. I knew we had to make a major fashion statement: Thirty years is a milestone. My idea was to cast the ten biggest supermodels of the previous three decades and dress them in thirty different key looks that defined important fashion moments past and present. I wanted something from Donna Karan's first collection, something from the Marc Jacobs grunge collection, something from Tom Ford's first Gucci collection, and so on.

Once we figured out what these exact desired "moments" were, we had to find all those clothes. Some designers had archives that we could borrow from, but a lot of the rest of it was a treasure hunt. I spent months seeking out vintage shops and dealers around the world, and even went to unexpected resources. I found a Stephen Sprouse dress owned by my friend Sasha Charnin Morrison, who is now the fashion director at *Us Weekly* but who was at *Allure* at the time. Her parents had bought her the dress for her sweet-sixteen party at Studio 54, and I'd remembered her telling me all about it. I called her up and asked if I could borrow her dress for my *W* cover. She thought I was joking but messengered over the dress anyway. When the issue came out, she called me up. "You weren't kidding," she said. "You shot my sweet-sixteen dress on Kate Moss for the cover of *W*!" Years later, she would lend it to the Costume Institute at the Met for an exhibition because a curator had seen it on the cover of *W*.

Each cover, featuring three models, was a gatefold, which meant it opened out into three panels. On top of that, we shot three different gatefold versions. Coordinating this shoot—getting the right looks for the right girls on the right days—was an exercise in tactical precision. But in the end, the cover was a big fashion moment, and it was a big personal one for me, too. It looked effortless and easy, but it wasn't. Did it matter that I didn't sleep much through the process? No. And was it worth it? Absolutely.

One of the industry's most famously ambitious photographers is Bruce Weber. Bruce conducts fashion shoots as if they were movies—and large-scale, big-budget movies at that. Outside of editorial work, he may be most famous for his preppy/sexy Abercrombie & Fitch campaigns, which pretty much brought that brand into the mainstream. Those ads, and the thick catalogs, contain hundreds and hundreds of people, plus dogs and horses. Bruce

# WING WOMAN

A S I'VE MENTIONED, I've had many assistants over my career—probably more than twenty by this point. Sarah Schussheim, an assistant fashion editor at *Elle* and the woman who saw me through much of the writing of this book, saw a good amount of insanity over her four-plus years working alongside me. What was it like to be my assistant? I asked Sarah to fill us in.

*I wasn't fresh out of college when I started working for Joe—I'd worked at* Jane *and done a fair amount of freelance styling for magazines and other clients—but when I arrived at* Elle, *everything exploded. That's because Joe wants the whole world. But that was the best part about him. He had so many things going on that it forced me to figure out how to balance everything, from the magazine responsibilities to his television obligations and freelance jobs. I mean, my very first shoot for the magazine was filmed for an episode of* The City.

*What I loved most about my time with Joe is that it always felt like working with Joe, and not for Joe. There was a great give-and-take. I felt comfortable giving my opinion, and knowing that he'd listen to it and really consider it, even if he didn't end up agreeing with me. He taught me so many things, but I think the most important of them all was the value of never*

{ ABOVE } Me and my former assistant Sarah Schussheim in London.

*taking no for an answer. There is always, always a way to get what you want, whether it's a look or a certain shot. Having good people skills—or developing them, fast—is crucial. Joe has the most insane magic touch with people. He is diplomatic and figures out the way to achieve both what the magazine needs and what the celebrity wants. Styling, after all, is about far more than getting people dressed, or knowing what looks good on film. It's about the big picture.*

*It's also about being insanely organized. On an average shoot, I have at least three other people with me. I'm an assistant, and I have three of my own. The goal for me is to create a beautiful, organized setup. There are hundreds of looks on any given set, hundreds of pairs of shoes, hundreds of pieces of jewelry. I've learned that being successful—at this job or any other—is about having the proper support, so that it looks like everything I do is done with ease.*

*The hardest shoot I ever worked on was in 2013, in Palm Springs. Joe and I had been traveling for weeks, so the team back at the magazine just sent everything—all the clothes, all the accessories—right to set, without our having seen any of it. "Everything" turned out to be forty trunks. There we were, basically on the side of the road at some remote location, in the darkness of the desert at 4 in the morning, pawing through forty trunks of looks for a shoot that was to start in three hours. You'd be surprised how physically demanding being a stylist can be, and I've developed a great respect for professional movers. I own my own pair of batting gloves to open dirty, sharp trunks, and otherwise survive a day on set. That's something I didn't imagine when I got my first job in fashion, I'll tell you that.*

*—S.S.*

loves people and animals. He loves having them around, and he loves bringing unlikely groups of them together. If you were to visit one of Bruce's sets and see, say, a cellist, some grade school ballerinas, an eighteen-year-old male beefcake in tighty whities, a golden retriever, and Christy Turlington—and this is entirely within the realm of possibility—you might think, what do all these characters have in common? It may seem to make no sense. But when you see Bruce's photos, it makes perfect sense. He is a master story-teller, and somehow, those ensemble casts come together, through his lens,

## "I've always wondered if he finds his CREATIVITY IN CHAOS."

to create the most intimate-feeling, soulful portraits. I've always wondered if he finds his creativity in chaos.

Of course, such "extras" will generally add to the total cost of a shoot, too. Many of Bruce's extraneous cast members may agree to participate for the fun—and the prestige of being photographed by Bruce Weber—or to get a great image for their portfolios. But "professional extras" are paid. That includes animals, some of which earn a healthy living as commercial models. One of my friends worked as a senior-level editor at a teen fashion magazine that once photographed an actress snuggling with a beautiful white-and-gray Persian cat. My friend will never forget the day not long after that she happened upon a fax that had come in—the invoice for the cat. That pretty little cat earned more in a day than my friend did in a month.

One of my first shoots with Bruce was also among my most memorable. It was the mid-2000s, for *W* magazine. For a fourteen-page story, I was

{ OPPOSITE }

None of *these* cats were paid!

called on to dress a total of sixty-five people, among them Olympic medal-ists, supermodels, actresses, editors, writers, musicians, artists, and politi-cians. Who even knows what the story was about—for me it was just a whir, a conveyor belt of people. There was always someone standing before me waiting to be dressed. One minute I'd have a big-time editor from a compet-ing magazine stripping down to her bra and underwear as some male mod-els casually shot the breeze on a nearby couch, unconcerned that they were stark naked; the next—literally, the next minute, since I put these people in and out of clothes in an instant, like Katy Perry live in concert—I'd have some Olympic athlete in front of me complaining that her outfit made her shoulders look broad. It was a total crash course in working with Bruce, and in staying sane under pressure besides. Through that shoot and others, Bruce taught me the value of keeping your cool and not getting over-whelmed. You may feel stressed out now, he'd tell me; it may seem like too much to handle, but you can. You can handle it. And it will always work out in the end. And it did.

\* \* \*

WHEN I WAS TEN YEARS OLD, I told my parents I wanted to be a flight attendant when I grew up. I thought that was the way I was going to see the world. I was obsessed with traveling, with get-ting on an airplane, with seeing new cul-tures, eating new food, trying new things, and I thought, well, what better way to guarantee I see as much as I possibly can? I used to practice giving the flight preamble, directing my sib-lings and their stuffed animals on the proper way to buckle their seat belts and pull down the oxygen masks in event of emergency. Nothing to do with safety or preparedness; this was the ham in me, all the way.

So many times as I've found myself packing for yet another big trip, or string of trips, I've thought, *Be careful what you wish for, Joe.*

Not that I haven't loved seeing so much of the world. I've been to doz-ens of places I would never have even thought to go on my own, like the

{ ABOVE }

On location for
*W* in Thailand.

castle in the English countryside where they filmed many of the Harry Pot-
ter films, Saint Petersburg, Sicily, and Capri. And yet on so many of these
shoots, I didn't actually get to see much of anything. Once, believe it or not,
I flew to Germany from New York City for a two-hour meeting. It was a
Monday and I was in Manhattan shooting Christy Turlington with Michael
Thompson, and when we finished that day at 5 p.m., everyone went home.
But not me. Instead, I got into a car and headed for JFK airport. I boarded
an overnight flight to Munich and landed the following morning, European
time, got picked up, driven to my meeting, had it, and was back in the car
two hours later, heading back to the airport. I flew out of Germany and connected in London on one of their last ever Concorde flights back to New
York City, letting me land back in New York City at 7:45 a.m. Tuesday morning. I zipped back to the studio by 9 to continue my shoot as if, like everyone
else, I had simply gone home to a lovely evening of dinner and family time.
Except, of course, I was wearing the exact same outfit as the day before. It
was a total flight of shame.

# CASE CLOSED

I LIKE TO SAY there are two types of travelers: smart packers and overpackers.

I am, wholly and unapologetically, the latter.

I wish I could say differently. I make my living as an *editor*, after all. But while I can whittle thousands of runway looks down to just the best of the season, my suitcase is a disaster of epic proportions. I like to be able to decide what I want to wear based on how I feel when I wake up. My approach to getting dressed, even if it's always based around the same basic jeans-and-T-shirt uniform, is all instinct. I know many women feel the same. Of course, that gets more difficult now that designers are mixing up what were previously hard-and-fast rules for the seasons: Spring collections are littered with leather and fur, while swimwear and sheer seem newly appropriate for fall.

That said, though I may not be able to control my own overpacking instincts, I'm a great packing coach. A few of my favorite tips:

### ✓ THE RUSSIAN DOLL

Tuck smaller bags into larger bags, lingerie and socks into shoes, and jewelry into clothing pockets. I'm not a big proponent of rolling clothes to ward off wrinkles or save space; instead, I like to avoid wrinkles by laying things flat as much as I can.

### ✓ FEDEX DEFUZZ

I was so proud of myself when I figured out that the sticky adhesive used to seal up a flat FedEx or UPS envelope can double as a lint roller. You can also use this trick with a few pieces of packing tape.

### ✓ COLOR MIND

If you pack in a color theme, you can cut down on unnecessary extras (like those orange pants and purple pumps you insist on bringing . . . just in case). I tend to dress in shades of black, navy, gray, and green anyway, but I find that making a conscious effort to pack according to a predetermined color palette enhances mix-and-match-ability and cuts down on the things you'll never end up wearing anyway.

# MISTAKES ON THE PLANE!

I DON'T SUBSCRIBE TO flying in a suit—I'm probably just envious of those Tom Ford types who can pull it off so effortlessly—but I also don't believe that air travel is an excuse to wear your pajamas and bunny slippers outside the house. Even though I might travel up to 180 days in a given year, I'm a firm believer in adhering to at least a modicum of decorum. Luckily, it's not so hard to do.

### ✕ SKIP THE HEELS.

Flats, flat boots, or sneakers (preferably not the ones you wear to pound the treadmill) are airport musts. As the master of the last-minute plane catch, I know how important it is to have the option of sprinting toward your gate. Also, there are just too many fashionable flat options (my own footwear of choice are brogues by Church's or tennis shoes by Superga). You want to be able to run around. Sofia Vergara might travel in her five-inch Louboutins, but we can't all be Sofia Vergara (unfortunately).

### ✕ DON'T SKIP THE SOCKS.

This is more about comfort, and courtesy, than fashion. If you even think you *may* want to remove your shoes after takeoff, you absolutely need some socks, preferably cute ones. Pack an extra pair in your carry-on so they're not the same ones you stuffed into your shoes just an hour earlier.

### ✓ WELL-FITTING JEANS.

(Or even stylish sweats.) If I had to pick one outfit to take with me to a desert island, it would be a T-shirt and jeans.

Denim is both comfortable and quite easy to make look polished. At the same time, many designers are doing sweat-style trousers in sport jersey and French terry. Your college sweats? No. Alexander Wang's version? Totally fine.

### ✓ LAYER UP.

However you choose to do it: T-shirt, long sleeve, hoodie or cardigan, scarf in cottons, jersey, knits. Wear pieces you can easily take off and put back on. I love to wear a vest over a hoodie over a long-sleeve tee over a short-sleeve tee, and in most cases I'll spend the duration of the flight with the hood up, which keeps me warm and the small talk with my neighbor to a minimum.

### ✓ TUNES.

A must, at least for me. Despite my many miles logged, I am an anxious flyer. I once made my entire row—and the row behind us—stand up and search their laps and beneath their seats for my missing iPhone. (It was in my pocket.) I can't take off without a catchy tune to distract me.

# FASHION'S FAVORITE DESTINATIONS

### TRASIERRA
*Seville, Spain*
*trasierra.eu*
Tucked into the mountains above Seville, this homey resort specializes in simple luxury and has fans like Bruce Weber, designer Anya Hindmarch, and Net-a-porter founder Natalie Massenet.

### SAN YSIDRO RANCH
*Montecito, California*
*sanysidroranch.com*
Founded by multibillionaire Ty Warner yet not at all flashy, San Ysidro attracts creative and boldface types who like to come here for hiking, great food, and lots of wine. (Audrey Hepburn and Winston Churchill loved it here, but my favorite historic guest to name-check is Bing Crosby!)

### LE SIRENUSE
*Positano, Italy*
*sirenuse.it*
Perched above Positano's harbor but in the middle of town, the historic hotel is at once part of the action and away from it all. Reese Witherspoon honeymooned here.

### THE WINVIAN
*Litchfield, Connecticut*
*winvian.com*
When the New York fashion set want a weekend getaway they can drive to—without risk of running into anyone else they know—it's this quietly luxurious countryside hotel and (five-thousand-square-foot) spa.

### TORTUGA BAY HOTEL
*Punta Cana, Dominican Republic*
*puntacana.com*
Designed by Oscar de la Renta, a Dominican Republic native, this hotel is the best in the DR, fashion's preferred island escape (at least right now).

{ OPPOSITE } My Russian visa.
{ FOLLOWING SPREAD } On location for *Elle* at the Kremlin in Moscow.

For many years, this was normal. Dennis Freedman, then creative director of *W* and my boss for many years, loved shooting on location and bringing different parts of the world to readers through our fashion stories. One fall, I packed a bag and traveled from New York to LA, then right from LA to Milan Fashion Week. From there I flew to Bangkok for a shoot with supermodel Nadja Auermann, then back to Paris to cover Paris Fashion Week, then off to São Paulo, and then to Stockholm, for another shoot. Sounds fun and exciting, right? Let me tell you: By the time Stockholm came around, all I could think about was how much I hated all my clothes since I'd been wearing and rewearing the same things—cleaned by way of various hotel laundry services—for the last two months.

My Stockholm experience was pretty much three days spent in a black room—black walls, black floorboards. Black. Dennis was an art obsessive, and so I worked with a lot of art photographers at the time, some of them fairly obscure. One was Jean-Pierre Khazem, a French artist known for taking photos of resin plaster cast heads atop human bodies. Khazem was having an exhibition in Stockholm, as you do, so that's where we went to shoot the story. I saw nothing of Sweden other than the airport and this room, because we spent the entire five-day shoot inside.

The concept was swimwear. I brought over trunkloads of it. We flew in an American model. We also flew in a hairdresser to style the wig that was attached to the a thick resin molding to be fitted to the model's head, as well as a makeup artist to do the makeup on her resin face, even though the resin heads, somehow, already had makeup. Does it sound ridiculous? It was.

On the second day, as the hairstylist was flat-ironing the hair of this resin head—the model was not in it at the time, thankfully—he pulled too hard. The head fell off the table and we all panicked; for one thing, as an original piece of art, this head was one pricey prop. "Quick!" I yelled as it rolled across the uneven wooden floor like a soccer ball. "That's our entire photo shoot there! Catch it!" Once inside the head, the model started to get claustrophobic, which I realized when she began pointing to the head and maneuvering her arms like she was raising the roof on some '90s dance floor.

The whole thing was so over the top and ridiculous, and exactly what people assume the fashion industry is all about. This, I thought, is how

{ OPPOSITE TOP }

Carter Smith and me on location for *W* at the Great Wall of China.

{ OPPOSITE BOTTOM }

On location for *W* at the Forbidden City in Beijing, China.

people imagine I spend my days, as if my life were a movie. In the end, the final resulting shoot was loved by some readers and left others confused (a resin head on a live body after all!), but I still look back to those days and think that despite the artistic concept, flying me, an assistant, a model, a hairdresser, a makeup artist, a custom-made resin head, and two trunkfuls of bathing suits to Sweden to shoot in a dark room might have just been a silly exercise or episode of *Fashion Punk'd*. Of course, it would have been. . . .

{ RIGHT }

The famous rolling head of Stockholm.

## "The whole thing was so OVER THE TOP AND RIDICULOUS, and exactly what people assume the fashion industry is all about."

But at least this crazy shoot made it into my magazine. For a while, in a different era, many big magazines would spend tens of thousands of dollars on photo shoots that would never even see the light of day, overproducing to have the luxury of deciding the best mix of stories every single month. A stylist friend of mine once worked on a photo shoot with the male and female costars of a big-budget remake. The pair had been dating when the cover was booked; by the time the shoot happened, however—a $100,000 affair that had a twenty-plus-member team of editors, stylists, writers, hair and makeup, and the various assistants, plus the requisite big-name photographer on location for a week in sunny Rio de Janeiro—they'd broken up, she'd gained fifteen pounds, and they hated each other. The chemistry was, not surprisingly, disastrous. The shoot, which had been planned as a cover and a major inside feature, was "killed." A single image ran a year later at maybe half a page, at most.

Today, some magazines may still overassign in this way, though most don't anymore. At *Elle*, we would assign every story—photos and text—with the idea that it would absolutely run. At *Vitals*, a scrappy new magazine with a very low budget, a fashion shoot still might have cost fifteen to twenty thousand dollars, while at bigger magazines, it could cost four of five times that.

\* \* \*

AS THE NEWLY MINTED FASHION DIRECTOR at *W*, my first assignment abroad had me traveling to Cuba. It was December 1999, and we were collaborating with the American art photographer Philip-Lorca diCorcia, one of the most influential photographers working today. He's known for work that bridges documentary and theater, reality and fantasy. *W* was all about artists like that. The entire crew was incredible, in fact: Our model was Guinevere Van Seenus, and we had Dick Page on makeup and Serge Normant on hair.

Perhaps expectedly, the most difficult part was getting there. We applied for journalist visas months in advance, and the flight was through Canada on some crazy chartered airline that was only allowed to fly into and out of Havana. My seat was literally duct-taped together. I'm not kidding. This, I thought, was fashion glamour.

In the last few years, I've had many friends visit Cuba, some more than once, and they have returned with stories about how very beautiful it is, how warm the people are, how dynamic the landscape. But we landed in

Cuba at a particularly difficult time in their history with the United States. The shoot had been planned for months, and it happened only weeks after Elián González had been found clinging to an inner tube in the Atlantic waters north of Miami. The United States had placed him with family in Florida. His Cuban father wanted him returned to his custody there. The two countries were fighting over him, big time, which was not entirely surprising given the history of discord between the two.

There literally could not have been a worse time to be an American fashion editor in Cuba. I couldn't walk on the street without being stopped by Cuban police demanding to see my ID. The electricity and plumbing at the locations where we were shooting only worked between 7 and 9 in the morning and 5 and 7 at night. I remember not wanting to drink a lot of water because I didn't want to have to go to the bathroom since the toilets wouldn't flush. On the third day, we were in the middle of shooting at a private residence in Havana when we got word that we needed to shut everything down. The government was sending buses to collect all locals to take them downtown for a mandatory anti-American rally in the name of getting Elián González back.

We had a local Cuban woman helping us out as a producer and location scout. She'd advise on locations that suited our needs and then do whatever needed to be done to get us permission to shoot there. She got us inside many people's homes. But she couldn't come into our hotel. At that time—maybe even still—locals weren't allowed in Cuban hotels, only foreigners. That first day, she spotted a *People* magazine in my tote. "Can I have that?" she asked, her eyes wide. American magazines were, of course, embargoed. She took all of our magazines and read them cover to cover, over and over again until she'd memorized actual lines in them. For the rest of the week all she wanted to talk about was celebrity news: Hugh Grant, *The Matrix*, whether I'd ever met Enrique Iglesias. At one point, she suggested pizza for lunch, which sounded great to all us Americans, especially the more homesick among us. We pulled up to a crumbling stucco house, its windows boarded over and the front door padlocked. "Ah, shit," she said. "They closed it." I asked why they had to board up the windows like that if it was just closed. Also, wasn't this someone's house? "No, I mean shut down," she

said. "All of the restaurants are in people's homes, but if the government realizes that something is too popular, they shut it down."

She hopped out to make a call from a pay phone on a nearby corner, and an hour later, a friend of hers appeared holding a giant black trash bag: lunch. At the bottom of the garbage bag were slices of pizza, individually wrapped in toilet paper.

I'm not a snob. I love adventure. But that was it for me. Presentation matters at least a little, and it didn't matter how desperate I was for pizza; the toilet paper wrap was a deal breaker. Though the Cuban landscape was beautiful, and our resulting photos were very arresting, I can't deny that shooting in a country where even simple things were often difficult made a photo shoot with so many moving parts all the more trying. But to this day, I still love that photo shoot more than anything, and some of those photos have been shown in contemporary art exhibits around the world.

{ ABOVE }

On location for *W* in the Dominican Republic.

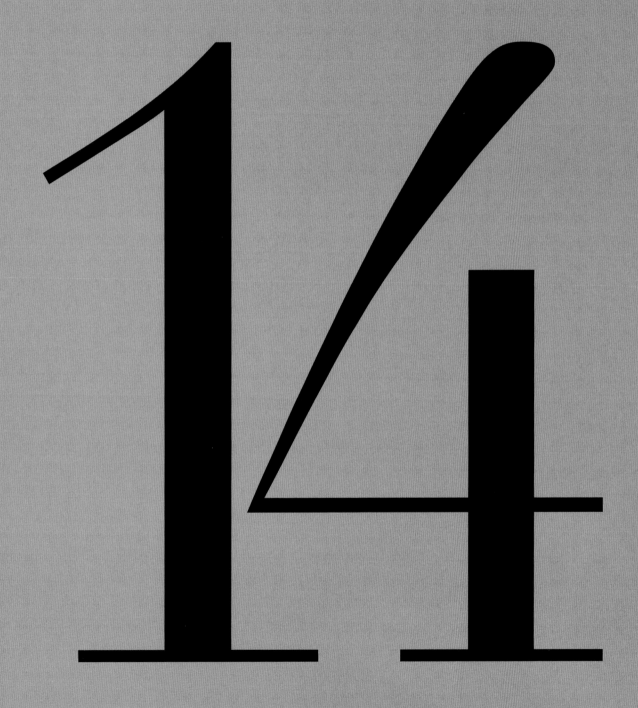

# THE

# ROAD TO REALITY

I N 2007, I HAD BEEN AT *ELLE* ONLY A FEW
months when a reality show producer working with the CW
network pitched the idea of a *Devil Wears Prada*–type competition series called *Stylista*. The premise: A motley (and
yet carefully curated) bunch of aspiring fashion editors
would compete against one another for an editorial job at *Elle*. The magazine's partnership with *Project Runway* over the previous years had been
very successful, and *Elle* was eager to continue growing its readership
through the exposure television provided. "Reality" was still something of a
dirty word, and *Stylista* had been pitched to many other magazines, all of
which had turned the producers down. Reality just seemed too low-rent.
But *Elle* went for it, and I think we were really visionary in doing so. Five
years later, every magazine would want to be part of a reality show. *Elle* was
at the forefront, and overnight became a household name among people
who just hadn't ever been interested in fashion magazines before.

Coincidentally or not, reality shows featuring magazines started to spring
up around the time that people thought magazines were going away for good.
(Meanwhile, people have been saying that for ten years, and magazines are
still around.) Still, these TV projects have given people a behind-the-scenes
look at a very private industry few ever really knew about and, some people

Hosting the red carpet for the Style Awards on CNN and plugging *Elle*, clearly!

say, have done wonders for the publishing world. Whether or not that's true, the curtain has certainly been pulled back, and I think to its benefit. More people come up to me because they've seen me on TV than anywhere else.

That said, *Stylista*, back then, was itself probably not the most accurate depiction of the fashion publishing world. It wasn't a time when anyone was hiring a lot of new employees, and yet here was a game show version of How to Launch a Career.

It may have felt a little ridiculous—but I think it was pretty genius. And very fun.

My then colleague Anne Slowey, *Elle*'s fashion news director, was the main personality of *Stylista*. I'd known Anne for a good decade before arriv-

# "REALITY TV
## —IT JUST ISN'T REAL
… What your're seeing is really there but
… a little enhanced."

ing at *Elle*, but once I got to spend significant time with her, I realized that this was a woman destined for her own TV show. She'd long been known in industry circles for her big personality and fabulous wardrobe, which was a mix of Lanvin and Second Avenue flea market. I have never met anyone more willing to try new things than Anne, and whatever situation she found herself in, she always knew how to wrap it up with that perfect quip.

Though the junior editor contestants would primarily answer to Anne, I was asked to appear as a judge for their various competitions, which ranged from creating a magazine cover to doing Anne's shopping to interviewing with editor in chief Robbie Myers. TV was instantly appealing to me, not because I loved the spotlight (in fact, it was a full year before I could bring myself to watch an episode I was featured in; I don't know how anyone can get used to the sound of his own voice) or even because I was such a TV fanatic, though that certainly helped. Mostly, I loved doing TV because it was another vehicle through which I could tell a story. How you tell a story on TV, I learned, can be similar in many ways to how you tell a story in a magazine. It can also be very different.

The first thing to know, and hopefully I'm not the one breaking this to you: Reality TV—it just isn't real. It might be real-ish, or "based in reality"—those *are* actual human beings you see on screen—but just as a fashion story or celebrity profile in a magazine needs to have an "angle" and an "approach" in order to both make sense and be compelling, so, too, does reality TV. So there is editing. And there is angling. Think of it as akin to airbrushing: What you're seeing is really there but, perhaps, has been a little enhanced. Everyone is made to feel as if he or she was cast to play a part, which they all sort of were, and so they do, without much deviation: the spoiled brat, the wide-eyed fashion ignoramus, the full-figured girl. Filming was insanely labor intensive, the most time-consuming job I'd ever had. Because so many of the show's storylines came together in editing, producers liked to get as much footage as they possibly could so that they had plenty to work with later on.

Now, I am not a person who needs much sleep—four or five hours a night is my average. But I don't want to actually sleep at the office, and sometimes we'd finish shooting at 4 in the morning and I'd be expected back at work at 10. Later, I'd learn that this was not entirely normal, even in the world of reality TV.

When all was said and done, a perfect *Elle* employee was pulled from the glorious wreckage of that oh-so-random cast: Johanna Cox, a twenty-seven-year-old former Chinese linguist (as I said: random). And she really did

*Be careful what you say when you're mic'ed.*

{ LEFT }

Early-morning coffee with *Good Morning America*.

# THE REALITY OF THE SAMPLE SIZE

FASHION, I'LL ADMIT, tends to exclude women who don't fit its rarefied ideals. As a magazine editor, I shoulder some of the responsibility. At fashion magazines, we all feature ultrathin models who fit into the sample sizes designers provide at the start of each season, often the same actual pieces of clothing that have paraded down the runway. Our mission is always to show readers the newest and latest, but "newest and latest" is available only in those smaller sizes—until the clothes hit stores. Meanwhile, everyone gets many letters from readers who complain that some designers don't cut sizes above a 12, despite the fact that the average American woman is a size 14. So whose fault is it? It's no one's—and it's everyone's. One thing I did learn in my career is to aim to feature models and actresses who don't conform to the "industry standard." It's not a complete solution, but it's a beginning. I know at *Yahoo Style*, I now feature plus size fashion on a regular basis.

come to work at *Elle*. You might have read in the gossip pages that she dated Alec Baldwin while working at *Elle*: also true. For a year, her salary was paid for by the show—she also got a paid lease on a Manhattan apartment and a clothing allowance—but even after the year was up, the magazine elected to keep her on, at least for a while. That's because she earned it. Turns out, Johanna was a good writer. She proved herself.

The craziness of *Stylista*, however, had nothing on *The City*. How *Elle* got involved in *that* show was something of an accident. A friend of mine was the head of public relations for Diane von Furstenberg, where stars Whitney Port and Olivia Palermo were "working" in the show's first season. Whitney was a reality TV vet, having gotten her accidental start in television as Lauren Conrad's fellow *Teen Vogue* intern on *The Hills*. Whitney was an actual intern, having applied for and gotten the job; Lauren, of course, was the former star of reality series *Laguna Beach* (it must be said, one of my all-time favorite reality shows). My friend at DVF (as the brand is referred to among those in the industry) asked if I might be interested in making an on-camera cameo appearance as myself during a filmed party scene for *The City*.

That day I learned something new about reality TV. Even after all I'd seen on *Stylista*, I somehow still expected *The City* to be somewhat real. But in an instant, the curtain was pulled back.

I showed up to the party they were filming expecting it to be like any other fashion party I'd ever been to: the same people, passed flutes of champagne, zero to eat. But when I got there, I was told that I couldn't just walk in. Instead, I was shown to a place off camera where I would get miked up and wait. No one brought me any champagne. I was given a cue for when to walk in, and then and only then could I make my "casual party entrance."

The industry drama for reality dramas is "scripted/nonscripted," and I liken it to how a Woody Allen movie comes together, when the actors are given a general sense of what's supposed to go down in the scene but the actual dialogue—how they get there—is often ad libbed. On reality TV, there's a storyline that's largely created by the show's writers and producers (which should be your first tell: reality shows employ writers). The difference, of course, is that Woody Allen has Alec Baldwin and Cate Blanchett.

Reality show directors and producers have people like me who likely never planned to get into acting in the first place, and so their jobs are that much harder. The director of that scene worked as hard as I did to make my entrance to the party natural. This happens throughout an entire episode.

But I guess I did okay because MTV producer extraordinaire Adam DiVello came calling, and in season two of *The City*, Olivia Palermo came to work at *Elle*. She was technically assigned to the accessories department, but found herself working under then PR director Erin Kaplan, though the storylines had her involved in everything from styling to on-camera commentating to covering parties. But while the characters were real and the events that provided the backdrop were mostly real (Fashion Week, for example), the plot points were sometimes fudged. Scripted/nonscripted meant that our director would say, okay, today we're shooting a scene in which you're upset with Olivia for *x*, *y*, and *z*. (Fans of *The City* will know that I, or someone on staff, was pretty much always upset at Olivia.) Though at the beginning we tried to film in sequence—like, you know, as life would happen—as time went on we'd often film out of order, for expediency. Sometimes I'd have to critique an event one of the girls had worked on when the event hadn't actually even happened yet. Or I'd be asked to praise someone for hard work she hadn't actually done (nor would she ever). When *Elle* first joined the show, I got tons of letters from viewers who thought hiring Olivia was the worst decision the magazine had ever made, or that I was often a pushover as a boss. The irony, of course, is that Olivia didn't really "work" at *Elle*—at all. She was given a call time, and she showed up, filmed, changed outfits a few times, filmed again, and left, at which point the intern who in real life sat at "Olivia's desk" could come back from whatever corner she'd been dispatched to while the cameras were around. Did Olivia do stuff for *Elle* occasionally? Yes, but not full-time.

That said, there was much truth in what you saw on TV. The fights Olivia had with Erin were very real. There was a genuine staff-wide skepticism about her, probably mostly because she did come in and play the part so well, throwing around her real opinions about how people with real experience did their jobs. I found myself encouraging Olivia a lot in real life, to be more of a team player, take her work more seriously, be nicer.

I loved the soap opera quality of it all. Adam DiVello is truly a genius. He was the first person to create a scripted/nonscripted show in which every scene tells a story that leads into the next scene without using interviews with cast members, so it seems like a real show and not like a documentary, as shows like *The Real World* and the *Real Housewives* franchise can. Those shows use interviews to bridge the scenes, explain why something happened or how someone feels, and move the story along. Adam didn't rely on interviews, instead working hard to find the transitions within the actual scene, like a true movie director. No one does it this way but Adam because it's far more difficult. But his shows are so much better for it.

To be fair, Olivia was pushed into the sort of villain role by producers and editors, and excelled at it, and in the end, people loved her, because she represented what people thought fashion girls were like. For me, I think the producers at first thought I was going to play a *Devil Wears Prada* role, and be much more "super snobby fashion editor" than I really am, or could ever be. Before I started *Stylista*, my good friend Marcy gave me some great advice I still adhere to. "Just be authentic," she said. "Be yourself. Do not ever be anything that is not you." At the time, it seemed like a really innocuous, not to mention obvious, piece of advice. But producers have a way of convincing you that you should be a little more this, or a little more that, until finally you've become the character they always had in mind for you.

It became clear pretty quickly, though, that I was more encouraging than discouraging by nature, even when provoked. Not every fashion editor is Miranda Priestly. And once the producers saw that viewers were okay with that, they didn't need me to be a devil after all.

That said, my own portrayal wasn't always without exaggeration. My life was often made to seem much more glamorous than it really is. Since the show, I've met many people who think all I do is run around to fashion shows or movie premieres, then have dinner with an Oscar winner. TV might make the life of a fashion editor look paved in gold and Louboutins, but it's certainly not all that. It's a lot of long hours and grunt work and paying your dues.

And I got my fair share of criticism as a boss figure. Not everyone wanted to see me be Mr. Nice Guy. People said I was too nice to Olivia, that I sided with her too often, that I fell for her tricks. I learned pretty quickly

to never read things about myself, and it was hard not to care too much about how people thought I handled my staff when, number one (and a pretty important number one at that), she wasn't even my staff. At the end of the scene, she went home! There were times when producers insisted that I freak out, for story purposes, but it was rare that I actually screamed directly to anyone's face. Instead, there were some times that I'd freak out to an empty chair, berating the air in front of me like some Acting 101 exercise, just so that they could still get in the sense that "Joe is angry! She's done it this time!" No one had to listen to it, and more important for me, I didn't have to act that way to another person. It was hard enough shouting at thin air—believe me. Of course, with editing magic, when the scene aired, it looked like I was really yelling at somebody else.

\* \* \*

S A TELEVISION JUNKIE, OF COURSE I got a huge kick out of seeing how everything worked on the set of a television show. Before I was on a reality TV show, I thought reality happened with cameras installed everywhere running twenty-four hours a day. That's not the case at all. Filming was very scheduled and strategic—Thursday from 1 to 4, for example—and you usually knew the storyline in advance. Reality producers are skilled at coaxing real-seeming reactions out of nonactors and call on many different tricks and manipulations in order to solicit specific sound bites or emotions or facial expressions. Whatever is needed to move the story line along.

Maybe I'm unusual, but I never once watched a complete episode of *The City,* but not because it wasn't good. It was just difficult watching myself, and especially difficult watching myself edited. During filming, I learned the term "frankenbite." A frankenbite is a quote, or sound bite, made possible with the help of advanced technology splicing. Producers can, and will, piece together your words from different conversations to assemble a quote that suits their needs. What you say onscreen, then, can actually be nothing close to what you said in real life. You said the words at some point, of course, and that's your voice, but you didn't say them in that order or that context.

Here's an example: For the season two finale, I was being filmed as a guest on *Today*, where I was booked (in real life) to talk about fashion trends. For purposes of *The City*, Olivia was tasked with pulling together

# "FRANKENBITE

## ...A QUOTE, OR SOUND BITE,

made possible with the help of
advanced technology splicing."

some things for the appearance. In reality, my assistants and I had prepped the appearance back at the office without Olivia's help. I went on the show and did the segment with Kathie Lee and Hoda, and it went fabulously.

But "went fabulously" does not a season finale cliff-hanger make. So when the event was replayed a few months later as an episode of *The City*, the episode arc was that I was going on live TV, Olivia hadn't prepped me adequately, and I was freaking out. In the episode, you see me calling out Olivia for totally failing at her job—and Olivia, in return, being defensive and making her various excuses. In the reality version of my appearance on *Today*, postproduction editing made it seem like I'm stuttering and don't know the answer to something Kathie Lee asks—because Olivia hasn't prepared me well enough.

{ BELOW }

Going on live at
*New York Live.*

# DRESSED TO FLATTER

T HE MOST COMMON questions I field from women—the case twenty years ago, when I started, and still the case today—have to do with dressing to look thinner.

**FAQ #1**
Will horizontal stripes make me look wider?

**FAQ #2**
Will wearing all black make me look thinner?

**FAQ #3**
Will heels make me look skinnier?

The answer to this one is yes. Stripes are big business lately, with designers of all, ahem, stripes working them into their collections. But while very chic, horizontal stripes will absolutely make you look wider by drawing the eye to the outer edges of your body. To combat that, you might try pairing your favorite horizontal top with a solid-colored blazer, to accentuate your waist, or belt a striped dress.

Again, yep. Wearing all black has withstood the test of time for a reason. A solid black outfit will create the illusion of slenderness by sending the eye up and down the body. But you can also typically get the same effect from navy, charcoal, or deep green.

This one seems obvious. Yes, heels will make you look taller and thinner, and probably make you walk with more confidence, too. That's just what they do. Heels make every woman look longer and leaner, whether you're wearing jeans or a dress. Take the time to find a style you feel comfortable in, and learn to walk in them, too.

This, of course, never happened. But for story purposes, it gave producers a reason to have me get "upset" at Olivia for not doing her job.

"But," I remember saying to one producer, "anybody can look up the actual clip on NBC's website, or YouTube, and see that I didn't stutter. I answered the question."

"They can," the producer replied. "But nobody will."

He was right, of course, and that's part of what makes reality TV so enduring. Most viewers know that not everything they're seeing is real, but they don't care. Because it's entertainment. Audiences like getting caught up in the story, the drama, and the idea that some parts might not be real but other parts are. The part where Anne Slowey comes to work at 8 a.m. wearing a cocktail dress—that's real. But a lot of it is "creative reality." I don't think people watched *The City*, or continue to watch shows like it, for truth. They like the glamour, the insideriness, and the access to a whole new world. So if everything wasn't exactly true to life, who cares? It was fun to watch and fun to make.

\* \* \*

I N 2011, I GOT A CALL FROM THE SUNDANCE Channel to get my thoughts on hosting my own reality show, one that gave viewers a real look at what it takes to become a working fashion designer. That show, *All on the Line*, is about as real as you can get, though I like to say that anytime there's a camera present, it can only be real up to 80 percent. Because even when you're playing "you," you never really forget the cameras are there, which means you might edit yourself a bit, hold back (or overemphasize) when expressing emotion, or unconsciously show only a certain side. That's just human nature.

Though there is certainly drama, the premise of *All on the Line* is to provide real advice to actual, struggling fashion designers whose businesses really are on the line. Usually there's a common theme: too much passion and not enough revenue. This is a dilemma many creative types face when aiming to turn their art into profit. I advise on their process and their look, help connect them with buyers, get them meetings, and help them network.

# YOU DON'T
# KNOW JOE

?

H ERE ARE TEN things you may not know about Joe, from the man who knows him best—his boyfriend, Rob!

{ ABOVE } On set in Madison Square Park for *Revealing*, my Sundance Channel special in 2013.

1.
Even though he dresses up for work, Joe's favorite outfit is not
a suit. He loves a particular Roots sweatshirt and black, very
worn-in jeans (both are falling apart and I always threaten to
throw them out).

2.
Joe is an incredible hip-hop dancer. His entire body language
changes the minute he enters the dance class, and you wouldn't recognize
him as the guy you see on TV.

3.
His favorite food is white rice. He hates leftovers unless they
are something he can throw over white rice.

4.
Joe is not a "sweets" person, but loves Black Forest Cake. If he
does eat cake, he only eats the cake and leaves all the icing.

5.
Joe hates cheese, but suffered through his first visit home with
me when every dish my mom cooked had some cheesy element!

6.
Joe is the busiest person I have ever known. He frequently falls asleep
while reading texts, phone mid-air in his hand, or with his fingers on
the keyboard of his computer in bed.

7.
Joe and I actually met on his Sundance show *All on the Line*.

8.
On our first date, I dressed up. Joe had only seen me in jeans
and a tee, so I wore nice pants and a blazer. He had always been
in suits, so he wore jeans and a blue polo shirt. We laughed
when we saw each other.

9.
Joe's favorite cocktail is an Old-Fashioned, but when it comes
to wine, he likes dry reds. Most people send champagne as a gift,
but our basement is full of it because he doesn't drink it!

10.
Joe's favorite airplane activity is listening to the *Titanic* soundtrack.
*Titanic* is his favorite film and he's seen it countless times, but he
he still cries when Jack dies.

My job is to figure out a way for these designers to remain viable, and that might mean being a therapist, a voice of reason, a marriage counselor, a referee, a teacher, a fashion editor, or all of the above. I spend about three weeks working with each business, and we film episodes chronologically. Though scenes are of course edited, it's not produced, like, say, *The City*. Nothing is skewed, no characters are "created"; these people are who they are, their problems are real, and my advice is the best I can offer. So when Layla L'obatti, a lingerie designer who brought her label, Between the Sheets, on the show in its first season, came across to viewers as uninterested in my advice—and blows a big meeting with a department store after refusing to take that advice—that's all real.

Of course, given that these are people who are in some sort of dire financial straits, or at a crossroads—and therefore at least a little anxious—there is inherent drama. These are real people. In one episode with designer Gemma Kahng, I had questioned the work of one of her employees, and Gemma eventually decided that it was best to let him go. After that, the employee started obsessively emailing me as well as my producers and it all felt threatening enough that I filed a police report. Consequently, the network hired security to follow me around for a few days, which was embarrassing but necessary. They even slept outside my apartment door.

One of my favorite episodes featured *Project Runway* alum Kara Janx. Thanks to that show, she found success early on in her career. But she struggled to maintain it. I suggested she design a line to be shown on a size-8 woman rather than on the now industry standard 0. She resisted, but I really believed it would work and I pushed back. Ultimately, it came together, though not without a few tears, some choice words, and some very real hard feelings, on both our parts.

Again, it's important to keep in mind that the forty-four minutes you see have been edited down from three weeks of shooting. And when you're with somebody for three weeks, there are going to be ups and downs. Sometimes I think *All on the Line* producers pull out the most extreme moments of me, and that's okay. But the ultimate goal of the show for me is real and genuine. I always wanted the designers to succeed. A few times these designers have thought it was just a television show. And I've had to tell them no: We're

{ OPPOSITE }

This is the police report I filed on a stalker who was harassing me when I was filming my show *All on the Line*.

really doing this. I'm trying to help, albeit through the show, but I'm still trying to help. I give my absolute best advice, but it's up to them to take it or not. You know what they say: You can lead a horse to water, etc.

I try not to get too attached. If people don't take my advice, I hope that they're right in not taking it. At the same time, I know that the conflict of them not taking it makes for good TV. And at the end of the day: I love good TV.

---

**INCIDENT INFORMATION SLIP**
PD 301-164 (Rev. 3-98)-Pent (RMU)

Date: 1/2

Welcome to <u>10th Precinct 230 W. 20th Street, Bet. 7 & 8 Avenue, NY, NY 10011 (212) 741-8.</u>
(Command)        (Address)                                                    (Telephone No.)

We hope that your business with us was handled satisfactorily. Your particular matter has been assigned the following number(s):

Complaint Report No.: _____  Accident Report No.: _____  Aided Report No.: _____

Reported to: _SPAA Blakely_____  Date of Occurrence: 1/9/11  Time: 0400
(Rank) (Name)         (Shield No.)

Location of Occurrence: 1/5/0 300 W 23 ST NY, NY

Crime: Agg Harassment

Please keep this report should you have to refer to this matter in the future. If you need any further assistance feel free to contact us at telephone number **(212) 741-8231** (124 Rm.) . Please let us know if you have any suggestions on how we can better serve you. As you may already know, we will provide you with a crime prevention survey of your residence or business.

Please ask for more information on this and other crime prevention initiatives. Our goal is to make you and your property safe.

**COURTESY — PROFESSIONALISM — RESPECT**

**REMEMBER: CALL "911" FOR EMERGENCIES ONLY!!!!**

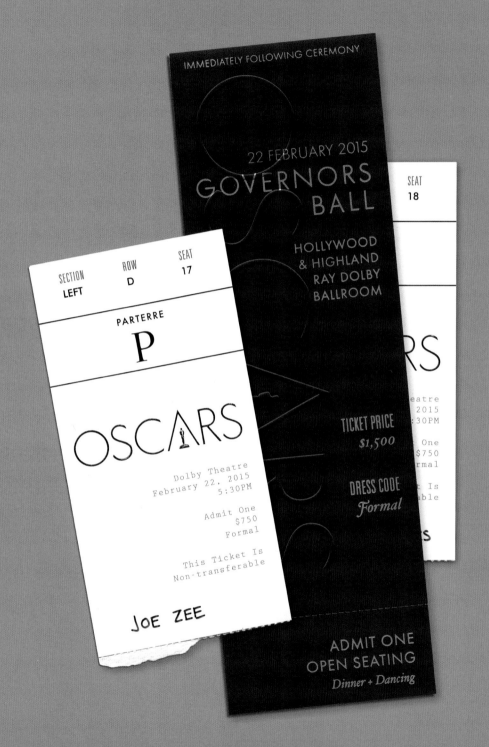

# LIFE ON THE
# RED CARPET

**I**WAS TWELVE IN 1981 WHEN DIANA MARRIED
Prince Charles. The night before, being five hours behind in
Toronto, I set the alarm for 3 a.m. so that I could catch the
live broadcast. When the buzzer went off, I literally jumped
out of bed. I went to the living room to unroll my sleeping
bag so that I could watch from the floor, then woke my grandmother and
insisted she come join me.

The experience of watching that wedding was entirely worth the
abbreviated sleep: from Diana's sequin-and-pearl dress with the twenty-
five-foot train to the pomp and circumstance to that royal couple's first kiss!
It was a real-life rom com that lasted for hours—and, best of all, it was live.
The idea that I was seeing something as it was actually happening, right
that minute, was what blew my mind the most. She was so young, and so
beautiful, and she was living a literal fairy tale. But it was the feeling of
being invited that I loved the most: witnessing such an intimate and special
moment between two people whom I felt I knew personally.

Back then, of course, the coverage of the royal wedding was more about
world news than the gossipy, fashion-police spectator sport we all wit-
nessed when Kate Middleton married Prince William. Now that red carpet
commentary is an actual thing, it's impossible to find *any* event where there

isn't *someone* critiquing the clothes. And you know what? I love that. Tucked into my sleeping bag on the floor of my childhood home, I only wanted to observe the wedding. I didn't really care what anybody else but Diana wore. For the more recent royal nuptials, though, I was primed to see any *royal* fashion mishaps. Just like when I was a kid, I set my alarm early, getting up at 3, making coffee, and settling into my couch (minus the sleeping bag this time and, sadly, my grandmother). While I still paid attention to the romance of it all—and, of course, what the princess-to-be was wearing—I was even more enthralled by the fashion choices made by the arriving guests and what the rest of the world thought about them, too. While I watched, I was also feverishly writing a fashion grading column of all the guests' outfits for elle.com.

Posh and Becks entered looking immaculate, per usual, the very pregnant former Spice showing off in six-inch heels and a flawless ponytail. Princess Beatrice was properly dazzling in a prim Valentino dress and attention-getting Philip Treacy hat. But the best part was the not-so-unimpeachable choices. Socialite Tara Palmer-Tomkinson (I had never even heard of some of these people before) wore a gloriously bad five-piece ensemble all in the same Smurfy royal blue. And, with much respect, I must question the person who put Queen Elizabeth in that canary-yellow suit. Talk about risk-taking fashion: There is no more universally difficult color to pull off than yellow. And the little handbag was beyond superfluous. What does the queen need to carry? House keys? Lip gloss? Her AmEx? *What could possibly be in there?* I wondered. But you know what? The wondering—which I did out loud in my living room but also with millions of others via all these Twitter conversations I was engaged in—was what made it so fun. I love fashion and pop culture, but I *really* love talking about it with others. It's just so not a solo endeavor to me.

\* \* \*

**VEN THOUGH I SHOWED ONLY** moderate artistry when it came to red carpet dressing, a few years back I was enlisted as a Special Fashion Correspondent for *Extra*, tasked with covering the Emmys. Turns out I might not be able to dress a celebrity for the red carpet, at least to my own satisfaction, but I could critique others who dared to do so! Ironic, yes, but that's fashion for you.

Although I am quick to point out the good and not-so-good about regular folks' outfits while walking down any given street, red carpet commentary has been one of the greatest challenges of my career. It's not because of the pressure of performing on live TV. It's because being mean just doesn't come naturally to me, and I hate thinking I might hurt someone's feelings. Though I can unabashedly critique the queen in the privacy of my own living room or even call her an Easter Peep on elle.com, I could never publicly embarrass the person behind the getup. I know exactly what goes into red carpet dressing, so I also know that it's not just the celebrity you're critiquing but his or her stylist, too. Someone's job could potentially be on the line, never mind his or her feelings. Besides, who am I to say something is bad fashion?

My general unwillingness to be dictatorial in terms of fashion has affected me throughout my career and, I think, in a good way. As a boss, if I'm not happy with something, or if I question a decision someone on my staff makes, I don't berate or overrule or lay down any laws. I always start from a place of discussion instead. Before I make any sort of judgment call, I want to learn the thinking behind it. And then I want to have a conversation. In fact, I don't even use the word "boss." It just feels so . . . bossy. I've taken the best parts of every boss I've worked with, and these are my rules for being one. (1) Don't micromanage; let your staff do the best thing they can do. (2) Encourage, don't discourage. You want your staff to work out of inspiration and not fear. (3) Set them free when it's time. As sad as it is to lose them, always be proud of their new opportunity.

While I was working at *W*, I was given the chance to, more or less, do my own thing, learn as I go, and not be micromanaged. And I figured out who I was as a stylist because of it. So that's what I try to do now, whether we're talking about people on my staff or people I work with on a photo shoot. If I come into a project with a checklist of things I want or think I *must* have, if I'm too busy checking off the laundry list or adhering to The Plan, I run the risk of missing out on something beautiful that comes out of spontaneity. For this reason, I never fight with people on set—whether it's a photographer or another stylist. If you feel very strongly about something specific, there's a reason you feel that way, so I'm willing to see that through. The best way to work with creative people, I've found, is to let them be creative, and I also don't like confrontation.

## "Telling people how they should do things, or WHAT THEY SHOULD WEAR, takes all the fun out of fashion."

Similarly, I'm also not a fashion dictator, which makes me sort of an unnatural red carpet commentator. To me, telling people how they should do things, or what they should wear, takes all the fun out of fashion. This point of view isn't especially common in my line of work; people around here—"here" being the New York fashion world—take things very, very seriously. But fashion is not a fascist industry, and as far as I'm concerned, there are far too many rules. For example: Why can't you wear Uggs if you feel comfortable in them (and let's admit, they're damn comfortable)? Why can't you wear boot-cut jeans if that's the most flattering cut for you? Because *fashion people* say these things are out? I obviously believe in the importance of looking good and presenting yourself well. I think what you wear says a whole lot about you. But getting dressed is also supposed to be

about having fun. If you're not having fun with it, if it's not your thing, then you shouldn't be made to feel inferior. And sometimes the fashion industry tries to do that—with help, of course, from retailers whose livelihood depends on you thinking that you need something new; that last year's boots are just, well, you aren't going to wear those out of the house, are you?

And so in my various platforms—my old *Elle* column, my TV commentary, any of my fashion shoots, and now Yahoo—I like to make suggestions and expose people to possibilities, but I try to never say something is in while something else is out. In the end, I very much feel the decision about how to present yourself is yours to make. And mine to respect.

{ ABOVE }

Rocsi Diaz formerly of
*Entertainment Tonight*
and me on the red carpet
at the Oscars (2014).

{ OPPOSITE }

The evidence of all my red
carpet and backstage work
over the years. One of my
favorites is still the 2013
presidential inauguration.

This point of view can be at odds with what I'm being asked to do on the red carpet, which is provide some insight into what someone was thinking when he or she got dressed that afternoon, and whether that thought process was entirely sound. How can I be a critic when I so celebrate being yourself? But then I realized: Who says you need to be a critic? Not everyone needs to be the Fashion Police.

For years, Erin Kaplan, *Elle*'s incredible PR person who rose to fame with *The City*, had been lobbying for me to do fashion commentary for awards shows, back before anyone besides newscasters or professional hosts were doing that sort of thing, and she'd finally managed to book me as a guest host for entertainment magazine show *Extra*, covering that year's Emmy Awards. I was already proficient in TV appearances, having dissected awards show fashion the mornings after big events like the Oscars and Emmys for programs like *Today* and *Good Morning America*. Now, though, I'd have to actually talk to the celebrities wearing the outfits, not just to Kathie Lee and Hoda.

Even though I had experience talking on camera, I was nervous. That late August afternoon, I showed up to LA's Nokia Theatre at 11. The preshow didn't start until 2 p.m. (5 p.m. East Coast time), but show producers wanted

to be very, very sure we all knew where we were supposed to be, and when. I got that, but if you think three hours' prep time is quite a lot for a show that, by nature, cannot be rehearsed—it is. Especially considering it was blazing hot and I was dressed in a very chic, but very slim, Burberry Prorsum tuxedo. I felt like Jon Hamm in *Mad Men*. I wasn't sure how I was going to make it a half hour, never mind all the way to arrival time, without sweating through my jacket. "Jesus," I remember saying to a producer in a headset and a gown. "How come you never see anyone with sweat stains on the red carpet?"

Very quickly, though, I got caught up in the moment and forgot all about my own discomfort. Being a nearly lifelong cynical New Yorker, I hadn't been awestruck in a long while. But that's how I felt as I saw the scene that was unfolding: hundreds of reporters setting up, literally thousands of cameramen, dozens and dozens of clipboard-wielding, headset-wearing producers running around in floor-length gowns and full tuxedos. The giant Emmy statue loomed over all of us.

And then the carpet opened (that's what they call it—the carpet "opens," like something out of *Aladdin*). For a while, it was my familiar crowd: just me and my cohosts, Mario Lopez and Lauren Sanchez, on our ten-by-ten platform, along with the hosts and guest hosts from all the other networks on their own platforms, plus everyone's harried producers. Slowly, a few people started to trickle in. I craned my neck to look and spotted . . . Was that Eva Longoria? Then, *boom*. Everyone, and I mean *everyone*, arrived all at once, and it was—there's no better way to describe it—a total shit show, a tsunami of celebrities.

That night was a total whirlwind; I barely remember a thing. But I got called back, so I must have done okay. I worked with *Extra* twice more, and then I got called by *Entertainment Tonight*. As part of the red carpet team for *ET* at the time, which is the most-watched syndicated entertainment news program, we have the biggest platform at the start of the carpet. We talk to the biggest stars. Stars cannot avoid us. That first year with *ET*, I thought: *Holy shit, am I really doing this?* It was such a big deal.

What you don't see from your vantage point on the couch: It might look seamless and casual on TV, but stars don't just wander up to us, or anyone else, on the red carpet. There are production assistants—those tiny girls in headsets—giving me and hosts like me about three seconds' notice before literally shoving a celebrity to be interviewed our way. "Incoming, Sofia Vergara!" I'd hear through my earpiece, as I was midconversation with Emily Blunt and nowhere close to ready to move on. It's sheer mania, and I love it. It's like all the energy of New York City crammed into a short red carpet.

I'm such a pop culture junkie—with a focused addiction in television—that from the start I didn't have any problem figuring out what to talk about. I know the last three and next three projects of pretty much any woman or man who walks that carpet, so I am never at a loss. I get in the requisite dress/shoe/jewelry questions, of course, but then I go on to chitchat away about when they are going to make a movie or what's going to happen on the upcoming season of *The Good Wife*. Sure, I want to hear about the Louboutins and the Harry Winston. But what I really want to know is some dirt about what's going to happen on my favorite TV shows. On occasion, some star will elude the production assistants or cut in line, and I might be called on to talk to someone whom I know I've seen before but whose name I can't quite remember. Thankfully, I'm a highly practiced small talker. It's just like running into people you've met before in real life: There's no letting on. "Who are you excited to see here tonight?" and "How long did it take for you to pick out that dress?" are my go-tos. "Sooo great to see you!" I call out after them as they stride away.

I also spend lots of time asking celebrities about the whole getting-ready process, which fascinates me. I think many people at home watch the red carpet arrivals and assume Anne Hathaway woke up, had some lunch, got her hair and makeup done, and put on a nice dress that someone had picked out for her. They don't realize that one look can take months to prepare, endless fittings, probably lots of calorie restriction, and not a little fretting and fussing. And as someone who had been criticized for his red-carpet styling in the past, I try to err on the side of kindness. Every star picks out what they're wearing for a reason. And does it always work? No. But you don't have to bring them down for it, and I certainly choose not to.

# LA MY WAY

**M**OST NEW YORKERS have a love/hate relationship with Los Angeles—that is, they love to hate it. The traffic! The fake boobs! And what's with all the yoga pants? But I happen to love LA. The weather is amazing, the people are far friendlier than in New York, and there's plenty of style thanks to a rise in major LA-based labels (Band of Outsiders, Rodarte, and Tom Binns, to name a few). Also, the nights end earlier, which, as I get older, I appreciate. But what I love most about LA is that it's a place where anything goes. There are no rules, and that's refreshing. You can be a grungy rocker in a ripped T-shirt and studded bracelets lunching at the Ivy, or you can be a network exec biking down Venice Beach. Either way, no one bats an eye. How great is that?

Which is one reason I find myself there so often, both for business and for pleasure. I still love New York, of course, but like children—or pets—I can't rank one above the other. Some of my favorite LA hangouts:

### SUNSET MARQUIS
1200 Alta Loma Road,
sunsetmarquis.com
My favorite West Coast hotel, just off the Sunset Strip in West Hollywood. I stay here so often that the valets know me by name.

### SILVERLAKE JUICE & TEA
2813 West Sunset Boulevard,
silverlakejuice.com
Worth the drive for a very LA fresh-pressed beet-apple-carrot-ginger juice. (Afterward, I head to Intelligentsia down the street for my caffeine fix. Hey, I'm only human.)

### ARCLIGHT CINEMAS
6360 West Sunset Boulevard,
arclightcinemas.com
*The* movie theater, this place is where you'll run into every starlet, network exec, and casting agent in town. Reserved seating is a must.

### CAFÉ GRATITUDE
639 North Larchmont Boulevard,
cafegratitudela.com
My team and I often hit this spot for healthy vegetarian and vegan working lunches. When in LA . . .

{ OPPOSITE } Rob and me on my birthday at Disneyland,
the happiest place on earth (2014).

### EDGE

6300 Romaine Street,
edgepac.com
I'm a hip-hop fanatic. It's my favorite form of exercise, mainly because it's so much fun (and, of course, because I'm obsessed with dance competition shows—call me, *Dancing with the Stars*!).

### MILK STUDIOS

855 North Cahuenga Boulevard,
milkstudios.com
This photo studio isn't open to the public, but it's where I spend most of my time when I'm in LA shooting our latest cover girl or celebrity fashion story. Hang out in front for a while and you've got a pretty good chance of seeing at least one famous person. That said, while a drive-by or two is perfectly okay, don't be a total stalker.

### DISNEYLAND

1313 Disneyland Drive, Anaheim,
disneyland.com
Sorry! But it has to be said: Whenever I need a quick hit of fun—or have a birthday to celebrate—this is where I go. I hope I never become too fashionable for a pair of Mickey Mouse slippers—or ears.

# EPILOGUE

## FROM CHIC TO GEEK
### *or, the Accidental Techie*

**I**N APRIL OF 2014, I SHOCKED THE FASHION world—maybe even myself, a bit—by announcing that I would be leaving *Elle* and print publishing and going digital. I had decided to take a job as the editor in chief and chief creative officer of *Yahoo Style*.

As you know by now, I've never been one to turn down an opportunity just because it scares me. In fact, I run toward them. I know those are, in fact, the best sorts of opportunities. Still, leaving *Elle*—where I had been for so many years—for Yahoo, which is one of the web's most respected and exciting brands, was not easy. This was going to be a big change, and I knew there would be a lot I would have to learn.

I have become obsessed with social media over the last few years, and I was thrilled to dive headfirst into this new frontier of digital magazines, which really excited me, even though it was a head-scratching move for a lot of my traditional peers. And plus, I'd only had three major job changes in my whole life. I knew it was time to take a risk.

How I got the job is an interesting story. I hadn't intended to leave *Elle*. I wasn't looking. But I really believe that the best jobs aren't the ones you go looking for but the ones that come looking for you.

Being a goofball at the Yahoo headquarters in Sunnyvale, California, in 2014.

I got the best advice of my life right after I didn't get that very first job at *WWD*—remember, the one where I bombed the test shoot?—and went back to Toronto, brokenhearted and depressed. An art director friend who was ten years older and wiser than me offered this advice: Have a very clear path and plan for exactly what you want in life—and then throw it out. I didn't really understand at that time exactly what he was talking about, but I grew to understand it as the years passed. You need the path to start your journey, but it's the detours that are going to make your life.

For my entire career, this outlook has helped me get through the rough patches—not landing a job I thought I wanted, getting my heart broken, losing opportunities or friends or pets. It's cliché, I know, but I believe that if you work hard and act with integrity, everything turns out as it should. You can never go wrong by staying true to yourself, while also realizing that in this life, you can't control everything. So don't even try.

Right before I got the call from Yahoo, a different job opportunity presented itself, and as incredible as it sounded, it wasn't for me. But it did spark a conversation with my friend Andrea over dinner one night. "Is there *anything* about it that's interesting to you?" Andrea asked me. I admitted that I liked companies in the middle of major rebranding, and coincidentally I used Yahoo as an example because I had been reading a lot of profiles of Marissa Mayer, who sounded like a fascinating woman.

This is when it gets interesting. Two days later, I got a call on my cell. A woman with a British accent left a message telling me that she was calling from Yahoo and wanted "to talk about something." Obviously, I thought it was a joke, so I never called her back. Four days later, she tried again. This time, I picked up.

A few days later, I was meeting with some people at Yahoo, and a week after that, I was meeting some more. When I got to Silicon Valley and sat down with Marissa Mayer and Kathy Savitt, the chief marketing officer, they both explained to me what they wanted to do with launching a digital fashion magazine, and I got intrigued. The best part: They had no clear picture of how the magazines should look or read—that was entirely up to me. "Consider this your playground," they said. "What would *you* want?" And I knew the answer. I was already consuming content in a very digital way. For years, I'd been following the same routine: wake up at 4 or 5, read the day's news on Twitter, Facebook, BuzzFeed. The media these days is all about reacting, and fast. And I knew, sitting in that office in Silicon Valley, that this would be my next detour.

Marissa and Kathy offered me the job, and I accepted, excited for this new opportunity.

As bittersweet as it was to leave *Elle*, I was immediately rejuvenated by the newness of the tech world, and I added one more slash to my résumé. I hired a small staff, and we embarked on what seemed like the impossible task of creating a new digital concept from scratch. Yahoo is a giant tech company, and yet it felt like we were in the basement making stuff happen, and that feeling, to me, is so gratifying. I love the scrappiness. We launched *Yahoo Style* on September 3, 2014, which was the Wednesday after Labor Day and the beginning of Fashion Week. The night before, our merry little band was still gathered at 4:30 a.m., banging away, getting stuff done. But I am being totally honest when I say no one was complaining. I finally left the office at 5 a.m. to go home to get an hour of sleep so that I could be back up and over to Rock Center by 7 a.m. to be a guest on the *Today* show. This was the world of digital, all right. I loved it.

From the start, we knew that *Yahoo Style* would not be just another website. That was the whole point. I still loved print magazines, and I wanted to incorporate some of what I thought still worked for print into the digital realm. Magazines, for me, were never just about the printed page, but about how the rich storytelling and beautiful photography can make you feel—or emotion, as I call it—and there was no reason we couldn't replicate that online. Even though you wouldn't be flipping pages in your hands, you could still be swept away by compelling stories and beautiful imagery. The first thing I decided was that we needed to do a cover for two reasons. One, because it allowed us to showcase the newest fashions on a pop culture, newsy celebrity, but two, also allowed us to create pictures that people could share with their friends. When I was fourteen, I ripped pages out of a magazine and taped it to my wall. Today's fourteen-year-old shares pictures on his friend's Tumblr or Facebook wall. The idea is different, but the impulse to share what you love with other people is the same.

I knew exactly who to call to help me launch this concept: my friend, who was also my first cover at *Elle,* Jessica Biel. She would be my lucky number one cover again.

That first day, we got almost twenty million page views. I was in awe that so many people could (and did) read the site and react to it with feedback in real time. I was hooked. The Internet moves at lightning speed, all the time. And you know what? I also move at lightning speed, all the time! At *Yahoo Style*, we can do things in such a quick and immediate way, a way we can't do in print. We can react, and have real-time conversations. That entirely suits me, because I talk fast, I walk fast, I think fast. Here, I get to be magazine editor, blogger, stylist, and techie—all at once. I can literally have an idea while traveling in London, write it on my phone, post it within the hour, and hear back almost instantly from any number of our millions of readers. You don't get that anywhere else.

So, are print magazines dead? I've gotten this question for years. I don't have any definitive answers, but I have to say I'd be surprised to see the true end of print anytime soon. Radio didn't die once TV came along. It struggled, sure, but then it figured out how to redefine itself and where it still fit within pop culture. You have to have a unique personality, and a specialty. I think print will figure it out, and that once the growing pains settle, print and online will be nice companions.

In the meantime, to the people who say that online isn't the same as print—let me tell you, it's true. It isn't, and that's what I love about it. When I left print to go work in the tech world, everyone warned me that it was a very nimble industry and to be prepared for it constantly changing. I think, ultimately, that is a better description of our world in general. We're already living it, this new world. Everyone is consuming everything online and on their phone, in snack-sized increments and on the go. Everything is changing, and change is great. Change is what brought me into the world of fashion, change brought me to New York City, and now change is making me an accidental techie. Is change scary? Absolutely, but you close your eyes and dive. The best decisions I've made in my life are the big ones and the ones that scared the hell out of me. But at the same time, those big risks are the ones that pay off in a big way, whether as a lesson learned or mission accomplished. My good friend Marcy recently asked me how I could just move on to the next big project without ever looking back and make the break so black-and-white. She found it to be such an admirable trait. I don't think it's so much a conscious decision but more the fact that I love new, I love next, I love what's to come. I can remember and respect the past, but the future excites me. And without the new, you can't have that next big idea.

# AND THAT'S WHAT FASHION IS.

# ACKNOWLEDGMENTS

THERE ARE SO MANY AMAZING PEOPLE I HAVE to acknowledge who have played a huge part in the publishing of this book and the inspiration and support in my career.

To Kat Brzozowski, my incredible editor, who throughout this entire writing and editing process never lost patience with me or this project, despite its many delays (thanks to me). Thanks for spending time with me on the phone, late into the night, so I could practice my old-school dictation skills with you as we went through the manuscript. It makes me so grateful.

To Thomas Dunne, who believed in me so much that he wore a very sharp tie to our first meeting.

To Alyssa Giacobbe, for being as awesome as everyone told me you were.

To Giau Nguyen for helping me put the pieces of this book together.

To Paul Kepple from Headcase Design, who designed this book for me from deciphering my words and boxes of old pictures and doodles and thank-you notes. Only an artistic person would understand that mind-set. Thanks for being a visual genius.

To Max Stubblefield, Allison Wallach, Ennis Kamcili, Stacy O'Neil, Missy Malkin, Howard Fishman, Ryan Nord, J. L. Stermer, and Jennifer Abel, the smartest group of individuals and friends a guy could ask for. I thank you all for always guiding me right.

To Jed Root, who has been behind me and supporting me for almost twenty years. Thanks for keeping me in line.

To Rob, for being you. Always.

To all my amazing mentors, Polly Mellen, Linda Wells, Patrick McCarthy, Mary Berner, Dennis Freedman, Bridget Foley, Ed Nardoza, Etta Froio, Dan Peres, David Carey, Michael Clinton, and Robbie Myers, who, during my two-decade-plus career, taught me the best things about being a magazine editor.

To Marissa Mayer, Kathy Savitt, Lisa, Becky, Rob, Susan, Lori, Jen, Sandy, Kat, Anne, and everyone at Yahoo for believing in this print guy and letting me do my thing.

To my editors and writers at *Yahoo Style*: Britt, Sarah, Bifen, Dora, Stephanie, Maura, Nick, Lauren, Erika, Chris, Sarah K., Ash, Laia, and Sam (of course). Thank you for being smart, excited, tireless, and awesome people who teach me new things every single day.

To my new ABC Daytime family, Ben, Lisa, Sheila, Tomii, Patrick, Mark, Tyra, and of course my FABulous girls, Chrissy, Lauren, and Leah, thanks for letting me talk.

To Lisa, Doug, Rachel, Rhema, Anita, Elaine, and everyone at QVC and Lai Apparel, for taking a chance on me.

To Nicole Defusco, who got me from the start.

To Marcy and Julia, who gave me the best advice when I first started and it's always stayed with me.

To Carter Smith, who I am glad I met that day at school because I have loved every collaboration we have ever done together, and we've both surpassed those dreams behind that ice cream sundae.

To all the incredible photographers, hair stylists, makeup artists, models, assistants, set designers, prop stylists, and everyone involved in pulling all my photo shoots together. It all came together because of our team effort and I am inspired every day by all of you.

To all the designers who made fabulous clothes for me to style and shoot all these years.

To Michael Thompson, whose collaboration I am so grateful for after all these years.

To all the amazing TV producers, network executives, showrunners, writers, directors, thank you for thinking I had anything good to say.

To all my current and former assistants, Sarah, Annie, Jen, Meenal, Sam, among many others, I couldn't thank you guys enough for keeping that train on the tracks, even through my crazy schedule.

To my staff then and now, you guys kill it every day.

To my dance family, you guys keep me sane.

To Porkchop and Cornelius, two nuggets I can't live without.

And last but not least, all my amazing friends and supporters and allies in my life. You are all my family. Andrea, Keith, Thomas, John, Sandey, Esther, Keli, Juliet, Ty, Abby, D, Stacey, Laurie, Roxanne, Laya, and many others whose names would take another book to fill.